The Governance of Online Expression in a Networked World

In recent years, we have witnessed the mushrooming of pro- democracy and protest movements not only in the Arab world, but also within Europe and the Americas. Such movements have ranged from popular upheavals, like in Tunisia and Egypt, to the organization of large-scale demonstrations against unpopular policies, as in Spain, Greece and Poland. What connects these different events are not only their democratic aspirations, but also their innovative forms of communication and organization through online means, which are sometimes considered to be outside of the State's control. At the same time, however, it has become more and more apparent that countries are attempting to increase their understanding of, and control over, their citizens' actions in the digital sphere. This involves striving to develop surveillance instruments, control mechanisms and processes engineered to dominate the digital public sphere, which necessitates the assistance and support of private actors such as Internet intermediaries. Examples include the growing use of Internet surveillance technology with which online data traffic is analysed, and the extensive monitoring of social networks. Despite increased media attention, academic debate on the ambivalence of these technologies, mechanisms and techniques remains relatively limited, as is discussion of the involvement of corporate actors. The purpose of this edited volume is to reflect on how Internet-related technologies, mechanisms and techniques may be used as a means to enable expression, but also to restrict speech, manipulate public debate and govern global populaces.

This book was published as a special issue of the *Journal of Information Technology & Politics*.

Helena Carrapico is Lecturer in Politics and International Relations at Aston University. Her research focuses on European Security, in particular cyber security and cyber crime.

Benjamin Farrand is Lecturer in Intellectual Property Law and Policy at the University of Strathclyde Law School. His research focuses on the interaction between law and politics in technology regulation.

The Governance of Online Expression in a Networked World

Edited by
Helena Carrapico and Benjamin Farrand

LONDON AND NEW YORK

First published 2016
by Routledge
2 Park Square, Milton Park, Abingdon, Oxon, OX14 4RN, UK

and by Routledge
711 Third Avenue, New York, NY 10017, USA

Routledge is an imprint of the Taylor & Francis Group, an informa business

British Library Cataloguing in Publication Data
A catalogue record for this book is available from the British Library

ISBN 13: 978-1-138-92707-0

Typeset in Times New Roman
by RefineCatch Limited, Bungay, Suffolk

Publisher's Note
The publisher accepts responsibility for any inconsistencies that may have
arisen during the conversion of this book from journal articles to book chapters,
namely the possible inclusion of journal terminology.

Disclaimer
Every effort has been made to contact copyright holders for their permission to
reprint material in this book. The publishers would be grateful to hear from any
copyright holder who is not here acknowledged and will undertake to rectify
any errors or omissions in future editions of this book.

Contents

Citation information   vii

1. Networked Governance and the Regulation of Expression on the Internet: The Blurring of the
   Role of Public and Private Actors as Content Regulators   1
   Benjamin Farrand and Helena Carrapico

2. Internet Content Regulation in France and Germany: Regulatory Paths, Actor Constellations,
   and Policies   13
   Yana Breindl and Bjoern Kuellmer

3. Governing Internet Expression: How Public and Private Regulation Shape Expression
   Governance   33
   Ben Wagner

4. Regulatory Capitalism, Decentered Enforcement, and its Legal Consequences for Digital
   Expression: The Use of Copyright Law to Restrict Freedom of Speech Online   48
   Benjamin Farrand

5. Speaking for Freedom, Normalizing the Net?   67
   Peter Jay Smith

6. Occupy Wall Street: A New Political Form of Movement and Community?   88
   Michael J. Jensen and Henrik P. Bang

7. A Policymaking Process "Tug-of-War": National Information Security Policies in Comparative
   Perspective   106
   Kenneth Rogerson and Daniel Milton

Index   121

Citation Information

The chapters in this book were originally published in the *Journal of Information Technology and Politics*, volume 10, issue 4 (2013). When citing this material, please use the original page numbering for each article, as follows:

Chapter 1
Networked Governance and the Regulation of Expression on the Internet: The Blurring of the Role of Public and Private Actors as Content Regulators
Benjamin Farrand and Helena Carrapico
Journal of Information Technology and Politics, volume 10, issue 4 (2013) pp. 357–368

Chapter 2
Internet Content Regulation in France and Germany: Regulatory Paths, Actor Constellations, and Policies
Yana Breindl and Bjoern Kuellmer
Journal of Information Technology and Politics, volume 10, issue 4 (2013) pp. 369–388

Chapter 4
Governing Internet Expression: How Public and Private Regulation Shape Expression Governance
Ben Wagner
Journal of Information Technology and Politics, volume 10, issue 4 (2013) pp. 389–403

Chapter 5
Regulatory Capitalism, Decentered Enforcement, and its Legal Consequences for Digital Expression: The Use of Copyright Law to Restrict Freedom of Speech Online
Benjamin Farrand
Journal of Information Technology and Politics, volume 10, issue 4 (2013) pp. 404–422

Chapter 6
Speaking for Freedom, Normalizing the Net?
Peter Jay Smith
Journal of Information Technology and Politics, volume 10, issue 4 (2013) pp. 423–443

Chapter 7
Occupy Wall Street: A New Political Form of Movement and Community?
Michael J. Jensen and Henrik P. Bang
Journal of Information Technology and Politics, volume 10, issue 4 (2013) pp. 444–461

Chapter 8
A Policymaking Process "Tug-of-War": National Information Security Policies in Comparative Perspective
Kenneth Rogerson and Daniel Milton
Journal of Information Technology and Politics, volume 10, issue 4 (2013) pp. 462–476

For any permission-related enquiries please visit: http://www.tandfonline.com/page/help/permissions

Networked Governance and the Regulation of Expression on the Internet: The Blurring of the Role of Public and Private Actors as Content Regulators

Benjamin Farrand
Helena Carrapico

ABSTRACT. This editorial provides an overview of the themes of network governance and content regulation that are expanded upon in the subsequent articles, identifying key issues and concerns that are prevalent in the literature in this field. In particular, this text considers governance not as an Internet-specific phenomenon, but as a global phenomenon, identifying and discussing literature pertaining to governance both online and offline, and providing examples of theories that seek to explain these forms of governance. Focusing on the interaction between public and private actors in content regulation, this editorial highlights that content regulation is a complex and contested issue that cannot be separated from its social and cultural contexts, and provides an overview of the articles contained.

Benjamin Farrand is Lecturer in Intellectual Property Law and Policy at the University of Strathclyde in Glasgow, Scotland. He holds a Ph.D. in law from the European University Institute in Florence, Italy, on the cross-border regulation of digital copyright. His current research focuses on lobbying processes in the field of intellectual property law, in addition to the law, philosophy, and governance of human enhancement technologies.

Helena Carrapico is a Newton International Fellow at the University of Dundee in Dundee, Scotland. Prior to her current position, she was a researcher at the Center for Social Studies of the University of Coimbra, Portugal. She holds a doctoral degree in social and political sciences from the European University Institute (Florence), where she developed her thesis on EU policies on organized crime. Her current research focuses on the United Kingdom opt-in and opt-out strategies in the area of justice and home affairs, and on the reasoning behind the United Kingdom's model of selective participation in the area of freedom, security, and justice. Other areas of research include the external dimension of Justice and Home Affairs and European Union organized crime policies. Her broader interests comprise critical security studies.

This special issue of the *Journal of Information Technology & Politics* began as the result of a discussion panel at the 2012 International Studies Association International Convention in San Diego, California, an event significantly influenced by events in Tunisia and Egypt now known as the "Arab Spring." One theme that developed as a result of these discussions was that liberal democracies such as those in Europe and the United States are not averse to repressing forms of expression viewed as undesirable; where there were differences appeared to be in the form and structure of the regulatory models that were used. Discussions centered on the role of agreements between public and private actors, and the importance of the Internet as both a means of facilitating expression and a means of repressing it. One point commonly made was that scholarship and discussions concerning the social impacts of the Internet should avoid characterizations that could be considered purely "cyber-utopian" or "cyber-dystopian."

This editorial begins by considering the concept of "network," not as it pertains to the infrastructure of the Internet, but as a form of governance model that highlights the importance of both public and private actors as regulators. Taking into account both general governance literature and Internet-specific literature, the first section of this text expands upon theorizations of this model, and also the justifications for its existence that concern the perception of expertise possessed by private actors and the comparative inability of public actors to regulate the Internet without private support. The second section of this article expands on the concept of content regulation, demonstrating that the Internet has the technical potential to both facilitate and suppress expression, leading to a divergence in literature between that which views the emancipatory potential of digital communications technology optimistically, and that which views it pessimistically. This editorial seeks to present a more nuanced view, demonstrating the "dual-use" function of the Internet, and that conceptualizations of what content should be regulated, and how, are dependent upon social, political, and cultural contexts, which are often transitory and malleable, allowing for both increased

control and resistance. Finally, this text provides an overview of the key themes and issues identified in the remaining six articles comprising this special issue.

THE REGULATION OF THE INTERNET: FROM LEVIATHAN TO THE NETWORK

One central theme that links the articles in this special issue, and indeed, scholarship on contemporary forms of regulation and governance more generally, is that of the networked nature of regulation. Traditionally, "political philosophy is too often inclined to reduce power solely to the central authority, Leviathan," Veyne has argued (2010, p. 94), with the result that complex relationships that guide legislative and policy processes are not made apparent. However, academic thought is diverging from such conceptualizations of regulation, not only in political science and communications, but also disciplines perceived as being somewhat more conservative, such as law. Scholarship that is influenced by a range of different theoretical and methodological approaches has nevertheless come to similar conclusions concerning policy-making, namely that the state is not the sole regulatory body of society, but one of many interlinked actors. From a Foucauldian perspective, this is framed in terms of the relationships between actors, whether state and non-state, or individuals within society. It is wrong, Foucault argues, to think of the power to regulate as being one possessed by the powerful and exerted hierarchically onto the "powerless." Instead he says, "power must . . . be analyzed as something that circulates. . . . Power functions. Power is exercised through networks" (Foucault, 2004, p. 29). Power is relational, and as a result, the power to influence how the Internet is regulated is also relational. Governments do not develop these policies purely through the exercise of sovereign power, but through the relations that both influence and are influenced by governments through the production of knowledge (Dean, 2010, Chapter 1; Downing, 2008, p. 18; see, for example, Kelly, 2012, p. 33–34; Kiersey, 2011, p. 17). At a less conceptually abstract level, others have considered the networked nature of governance in terms of the relationships between state or public actors and private actors. This approach considers that political decision-making is not restricted to formal governmental institutions, but is the result of the creation, construction, and establishment of policy networks (Koimann, 2000; Marcussen & Torfing, 2003; Marsh & Rhodes, 1992). For Mueller (2010), these policy networks are typified by corporate actors forming strong and stable network relations, being "drawn into regularized interaction around a set of laws and regulations in a specific sector" (p. 38). Castells (2011) also uses the term "network" to explain contemporary forms of governance. Each interdependent actor constitutes a node in the governance network, be it a state institution, corporate actor or individual, the importance of which varies depending on the particular activity being undertaken, and the level of competence and information possessed by that particular node (Castells, 2011, pp. 18–19). The increasingly networked nature of governance has been conceptualized as being the result of "neoliberal" reforms in the late 1980s and a discourse of the inefficiency, ineffectiveness, and undesirability of state regulation (Harvey, 2007), the proliferation of independent regulatory agencies, "public–private partnerships," and the delegation of state competences (Black, 2001; Braithwaite, 2008; Levi-Faur, 2005; Wright, 2011), or the perception of the need for external knowledge or expertise not possessed by governmental institutions (Baumgartner, 2009; Culpepper, 2011). In other words, it is not only governance of the Internet that is defined by networked relations, but also governance as a general phenomenon.

This transformation of conceptualizations of regulation is evident in discussions concerning the Internet as a specific phenomenon. John Perry Barlow's (in)famous Declaration of the Independence of Cyberspace in 1996 showed a preoccupation with the state as an oppressive actor, and the Internet as being free from that oppression through both technological and legal limitation: "You have no sovereignty where we gather." In this "cyber-libertarian" conceptualization of the Internet, "cyberspace" was a place that should be free from governmental or state interference, with decision-making regarding the regulation of the Internet viewed as being best approached through the consensus of users, or ensuring compliance with technical standards (Friedland, 1996; see for example Johnson & Post, 1996). However, the view of the Internet as the "Wild West" or unregulated frontier of communications was quickly replaced by one that acknowledged the networked nature of governance on the Internet, and the interaction between state actors and corporate/private actors such as Internet Service Providers and ICANN (Deibert, 2009; Goldsmith & Wu, 2006; see, for example, Lessig, 2004; Mueller, 2010; Wu, 2010). The speedy drafting and implementation of legislation pertaining to the regulation of content on the Internet, such as the Digital Millennium Copyright Act (1998) in the U.S., and E-Commerce (2000/31/EC) and Information Society Directives (2001/29/EC) in the EU and cross-jurisdictional cases concerning content removal such as *Licra v. Yahoo!* (2000), demonstrated that the conceptualization of the Internet as unregulated and unregulable was somewhat mistaken. Instead, state and non-state actors have demonstrated both the willingness and ability to actively regulate Internet-based activities, through coordinated action. Furthermore, other writers have considered that the Internet has the potential to widen participation in political processes, allowing looser coalitions of citizens to become involved in the framing of regulatory issues through combinations of on- and offline activism (Bimber, Stohl, & Flanagin, 2009; MacKinnon, 2012; Ward & Gibson, 2009). Dutton and Peltu (2009) refer not to networked governance but to "multi-stakeholder" processes, in which governments, infrastructure providers, and corporations are joined by nongovernmental organizations, civil society groups, and individuals in discussions concerning governance on the Internet (pp. 390–393). While the model for the governance of the Internet may not be Leviathan, the single overarching sovereign power centrally regulating all conduct, neither is it a model free from regulation, or regulation solely by technical bodies or corporations. Instead, the regulation of the Internet is the result of complex relationships between both public and private actors who act both in coordination and competition with each other in order to ensure preferred regulatory outcomes.

The relationship between public and private actors in the digital environment appears to be one that mirrors general approaches to governance in the offline environment, in which "rule-making displaces public ownership and centralized administration" (Wright, 2011, p. 31). Within this framework, governments or legislative institutions pass laws or regulations that dictate how a particular sector should be regulated, leaving the actual act of regulation to the private sector. These private actors take on the role of "self-regulated regulators" (see also Brown, 2010; Parker, 2002; Price & Verhulst, 2005), performing regulatory activities perceived as lying within the competence of the state (as shall be expanded upon in the next section). Again, this is a phenomenon that is not limited to Internet governance, but is reflected by partnerships between governments and industry in, for example, environmental regulation (Héretier & Eckert, 2008) or the regulation of finance, telecommunications, and broadcasting (Coen & Thatcher, 2008, p. 58). The oft-cited explanation for private, nongovernmental actors choosing to act as "self-regulated regulators" is the implied threat of increased legislative regulation of their business sectors (Bartle & Vass, 2007, p. 895; Héretier & Eckert, 2008, p. 116). The "safe harbor" provisions of legislation, such as under Articles 14–16 of the E-Commerce Directive, work on such an understanding; should an Internet service provider quickly respond to notification of illegal content (whether in the form of copyright infringements, child abuse images, or other materials), then the service provider has no liability for the hosting of that material. In terms of regulation, this may be framed in terms of "self-regulating regulation." While governments (or in this case, the EU) provide a legislative framework for regulation, the act of regulation is performed by the service provider. In doing so, the service provider regulates its own conduct, namely the speedy response to notification of the existence of illegal content. The service provider then removes the content. Should a service provider fail to do so, action may be taken against that service provider in national courts. One example of the implied threat of regulation comes in the form of "encouragement" of voluntary arrangements between service providers and copyright holders by institutions such as the European Commission. In order to better facilitate speedy cooperation, the Commission has identified voluntary agreements as being the preferred approach; however, should service providers fail to come to such arrangements, the Commission stated that it was "ready to consider alternative approaches" (European Commission, 2009, sec. 4.2). It is for this reason that Héretier and Eckert (2008) have described self-regulated regulators in network governance as operating "within the shadow of hierarchy" (p. 113). Nevertheless, corporate actors are not passive in the development of such forms of regulation, as they often take an active role in shaping that regulation through the participation of legal experts and corporate leaders (see also Amable, 2003, pp. 10–12; Culpepper, 2011, pp. 7–10; Lütz, Eberle, & Lauter, 2011, p. 331). If regulation is the result of networks, so too is the framing of that regulation. This is not to suggest that corporate or private actors are always completely willing participants in these regulatory deliberations, or that these arrangements will be particularly successful. In the EU context, Internet service providers have resisted attempts to impose upon them an active duty to monitor the use of their services in the context of alleged intellectual property infringements. In the cases of *Scarlet Extended* (2011) and *SABAM v. Netlog* (2012), Internet service providers argued that such an imposed duty would be in breach of the E-Commerce Directive accepted by the Court of Justice of the European Union. As the E-Commerce Directive does not allow for a responsibility on the part of service providers to specifically and actively monitor the use of their services by users, the legal imposition of such a duty by a national court was considered to be in breach of EU law. However, the prevention of the imposition of a *legal* duty does not preclude the possibility of a *voluntary* duty that an intermediary agrees to under the implied threat of subsequent legislation. If, for example, the E-Commerce Directive would be reformed to include an active duty to monitor, then such resistance by intermediaries would not be effective. Nor does it mean that policy actors will be unified over the most suitable form of regulation, or indeed the nature of the content to be regulated. For example, information security in the digital environment would appear to be a particularly contested area of policy-making, especially where it concerns the balance between the perceived need for secrecy and a desire for transparency and information dissemination (Rogerson & Milton, this issue

On the part of governments and legislative bodies, two key themes recur in discussions as to *why* the involvement of private actors in regulation is considered desirable. The first is that of expertise. Governments rely on the perceived expertise of corporate actors in their particular fields of activity, considering that those actors understand their businesses, their needs, and their abilities better than state actors (Bernhagen & Bräuninger, 2005; see for example Esterling, 2004). At the level of rapidly developing digital technologies such as the Internet, the perceived need for technical experts to be involved in regulation is magnified (Christou & Simpson, 2006; Yu, 2010). Due to the perceived high technical complexity of the functioning of the Internet, governmental and legislative bodies defer to the expertise of actors such as Internet service providers concerning the most suitable means of regulating content; in this respect, policy-making competence is shared, with the public actor stating "this is the problem" or "this is the proscribed conduct," and the private actor proposing a technical, often code-based solution (Lessig, 2006). Related to this point on expertise is that of capacity. Given the transnational character of Internet access, national attempts to regulate the Internet by traditional public authorities such as the police or administrative bodies are substantially limited if there is no support from the private providers of these services. Whereas Goldsmith and Wu (2006) have stated that the conceptualization of the Internet as borderless is ultimately an "illusion," and that nation states quickly legislated jurisdictional issues concerning offences committed over the Internet, this system of regulation still requires the involvement of intermediary Internet service providers in order

to be effective. In the above mentioned *Licra v. Yahoo!* (2000) case, the jurisdiction of French courts over the access by French citizens to illegal sales of Nazi memorabilia (under French law) was quickly established. While the advertisements were made in the U.S., where such sales were legal, the French courts nevertheless required that this information was to be made inaccessible in France—a technical requirement that could only be performed by the Internet service provider, rather than state regulators. Effective regulation of this content then requires the involvement of and interaction between public and private actors. As Mueller states (2010), "Most of the real world governance of the Internet is decentralized and emergent: it comes from the interactions of tens of thousands of network operators and service providers" (p. 9). The Internet by design is a system of distributed control, dispersing "participation in and authority over networking" (Mueller, 2010, p. 4). This, combined with the high volume of Internet traffic to be processed, requires the involvement and intervention of well-placed intermediary organizations that have the technical capacity to regulate, as well as the expertise.

THE ANSWER TO THE MACHINE IS NOT ONLY IN THE MACHINE: CULTURAL AND SOCIAL IMPACTS ON THE REGULATION OF CONTENT ONLINE

Scholarship concerning the role of the Internet in society can be undertaken from a "cyber-utopian" perspective, in which the Internet is the facilitator of expression, an emancipatory tool, and a means of encouraging citizen participation in democratic processes, so long as the Internet is not unduly interfered with or restricted by states or corporations (see for example Benkler, 2006; Shirky, 2011), or from a "cyber-pessimist" or "cyber-dystopian" perspective, considering the role of the Internet in state and/or corporate repression, the "balkanization" of opinion, and the appeal to "lowest common dominator" entertainment and politics (Lanier, 2013; see for example Morozov, 2011; Zittrain, 2008). Indeed, the Internet has the potential for both. While there is, without doubt, the urge to perceive new technologies in light of all the potential they may have for increasing the quality of life, or in light of all the potential they may have for decreasing the quality of life, such black and white assessments provide little more than best-case or worst-case scenarios. The Internet has the potential to be both a tool of facilitation, allowing for mobilization, activism, and the sharing of information, or a tool of repression, allowing for surveillance, the dissemination of propaganda, and the control or blocking of information. For example, the Internet has been used by civil society groups and activists to politically organize and rally behind a presidential candidate (Gil de Zúñiga, Veenstra, Vraga, & Shah, 2010). Irrespective of the views of the legitimacy of such action, the Internet has been used to release information perceived by leakers to be in the public interest, such as the infamous leaking of U.S. diplomatic cables by WikiLeaks and Chelsea Manning (see for example McGreal, 2010). Regardless of the subsequent successes or failures of the "Arab Spring" movement, the Internet has been argued to have played an important role in the mobilization and coordination of protesters in Egypt (MacKinnon, 2012), and has also assisted in the coordination of activists and resistance movements, such as the "Occupy" movement (see Jensen & Bang, this issue) and ACTA protestors (Farrand, 2014; Smith, this issue). It can also be used for the facilitation of more violent forms of participation, such as those of alleged protestors/rioters in London in 2011 (Bright, 2011; Halliday, 2011). Yet digital technologies have also been used to monitor and suppress, the most recent example being the leaking of information concerning widespread surveillance by the NSA as part of the PRISM project (see The Guardian, 2013, for comprehensive coverage of the information leaked). These technologies have been used by more repressive regimes such as China and Saudi Arabia to limit access to information through the use of centralized firewall systems (Deibert, Palfrey, Rohozinski, & Zittrain, 2008, 2010, 2012), but also through the use of specific filtering systems used to prevent access to content considered illegal, such as child abuse material or materials deemed to

infringe copyright in "Western liberal" democracies (Deibert et al., 2010; Goldsmith & Wu, 2006; McIntyre, 2012). States typified by more authoritarian approaches to governance may have overt systems of control, in which the existence of filtering mechanisms is explicitly recognized and attempts to access proscribed materials result in a specific message that warns users that they have attempted to access illegal content. States typified by less authoritarian approaches to governance may have more subvert systems of control, in which the filtering of content deemed illegal results in an error or "page not found" message, rather than specific mention made of the attempt (intentional or otherwise) to access that content. Alternatively, rather than the use of filtering or other forms of blocking of content, Western liberal democracies or private actors may use other means of suppressing or removing content through the use of other means, such as copyright infringement notices (see Farrand, this issue; Smith, this issue). These alternate means may be used through the combination of human assessment and technology to block access or remove material, or alternatively may be an automated computer process. Internet technologies therefore allow for both facilitation and repression, for emancipation and for control.

This, however, is not to suggest that technology in itself is neutral. While the answer to the machine may be in the machine, to use a common expression, the answer is not provided by the machine alone. While, as Lessig states "code is law" (Lessig, 2006, p. 1), neither code nor law constitute neutral, or politically or socially disconnected phenomena. Code, whether as a form of governance or as a set of written instructions to achieve a particular technological result (such as blocking certain kinds of content), is influenced by social, political, and cultural mores. It is difficult, if not impossible, to disassociate forms of content regulation and what content is deemed to be illegal, unethical, or otherwise undesirable from the sociopolitical and cultural context in which that regulation operates (see for example Zeno-Zencovich, 2008). For example, in China, a country considered Communist or (more recently) Authoritarian Capitalist, material deemed to challenge or condemn the ruling party is forbidden. Access to pornography, which is deemed contrary to public morality, is also severely restricted. In comparison, in countries such as the U.S. or UK, where challenging the decisions of governmental actors is ostensibly perceived as a vital part of a healthy participative democracy, such content will not normally (or overtly) be restricted. Pornography, or other socially contentious material, may be less restricted or regulated than in countries such as China, save where the content in question is deemed to be illegal and/or obscene (such as child abuse images) or where it is subject to a "moral panic" (Breindl & Kuellmer, this issue; Jenkins, 2001; Wagner, this issue). One example is that of the UK's "section 63" of the Criminal Justice and Immigration Act 2008, which concerns "extreme pornographic images" that are deemed illegal, such as acts likely to result in injury to sexual organs, regardless of whether that act was both performed with consent and not illegal in itself to perform. This controversial section (Johnson, 2010; Murray, 2009) was drafted as the result of a citizen campaign following a highly mediatized criminal case in which an individual with a history of viewing extreme pornography online was convicted of murdering a woman (Murray, 2009). In a more recent example, the UK's current Conservative-Liberal Democrat coalition government has announced successful negotiation with several Internet service providers for the establishment by January 2014 of an "opt-in" system that limits access to pornography and other forms of "extreme content" until a user specifically requests access to such content (Shubber, 2013). This is not to say that such laws or regulations are not subject to criticism or challenge, or that all members of a society wholly accept them. Instead, the purpose is to demonstrate that content regulation is ultimately determined by notions of acceptability, levels of social permissibility, and other cultural factors that are fluid and malleable.

The use of digital technologies, and the role of private actors in this form of content regulation, is not without its controversies. Brown (2010) refers to these processes as lacking procedural fairness and not having due regard for fundamental rights, with few

schemes including "any substantive protection for individuals' rights to freedom of expression, association, or privacy" (p. 99). Frequently, the regulation of content on the Internet is the result of secretive negotiation processes rather than overt law making, which results in questions being raised over the lack of transparency and the legitimacy of online content regulation (Koumartzis & Veglis, 2011; Marsden, 2011, p. 12). This is particularly the case when dealing with information deemed to be highly confidential, such as that pertaining to national security (Rogerson & Milton, this issue). However, concerns over legitimacy and accountability can also be raised when "public" acts of regulation are performed by private entities without governmental oversight (or where such governmental oversight is limited and accountability mechanisms lacking), such as monitoring performed by bodies such as the Internet Watch Foundation in the UK (Wagner, this issue) or Freiwillige Selbstkontrolle Multimedia-Dienstanbieter in Germany (Breindl & Kuellmer, this issue). It is also possible for Internet-based systems of "regulated self-regulation" to be open to abuse, such as the use of copyright "notice and takedown" procedures as a way of suppressing embarrassing or damaging information, or silencing dissent. This is not to suggest that the potential for use of certain laws such as copyright laws for as a means of suppressing content is limited to notice and takedown on the Internet (see for example Patterson, 1987), but only that the use of the regulated self-regulation model and decision-making by private actors makes such actions easier on the Internet, and more difficult to challenge in the courts (Farrand, this issue). Nevertheless, the Internet can serve as a means of resisting these forms of content regulation, and indeed regulation both online and offline, through providing the means to more widely disseminate informational content and coordinate action between activists (Castells, 2011; see also Jensen, this issue; Smith, this issue). The same technologies that are used to remove or block access to Web sites can also be used as a means of protesting or raising awareness of issues, such as Wikipedia and other sites going "black" (thereby becoming inaccessible) to protest against the Stop Online

Piracy Act in the U.S. (see for example Smith, this issue). Furthermore, services such as the TOR onion browser can be used to allow near-anonymous use of the Internet and access to restricted content (Roberts, Zuckerman, York, Faris, & Palfrey, 2011)—although such services are neither immune from infiltration nor from their use for illegal content distribution, as was confirmed by the recent insertion of a security exploit by the FBI into Web sites hosted by Freedom Hosting, which identified users of the TOR browser as part of an investigation into the hosting and distribution of child abuse images (Poulsen, 2013). As has been discussed in this editorial, the Internet provides the means to both facilitate and suppress; to both allow and prevent activities deemed desirable in certain contexts, such as the provision of information detrimental to autocratic regimes; and to allow and prevent activities deemed undesirable, such as to distribute materials that are considered illegal or obscene. The purpose of this special issue of the *Journal of Information Technology & Politics* is to delve further into these issues, considering in greater detail the ways in which expression is governed in the digital environment, taking into account the ways the Internet can be used to facilitate and repress, and the regulatory structures that allow the Internet to be used in these ways. The next section of this editorial will provide an overview of these articles.

OVERVIEW OF THE ARTICLES IN THIS SPECIAL ISSUE

As evidenced by the previous sections of this editorial, the key theme of this special issue is that of networked governance and the role of public–private partnerships, coalitions, and agreements in the regulation of expression on the Internet. The six articles comprising this special issue consider content regulation as it pertains to materials generally accepted as illegal and harmful, such as sexual abuse images, to more contentious forms of content regulation, such as that of online copyright enforcement and the withholding of information deemed to be in the national security interest. In particular, this special issue considers the role of the Internet

as both facilitator and suppressor of expression, as well as the facilitator and repressor of means of resisting that control. For this reason, articles focus both on the ways that the Internet is used as a means of regulating through multi-stakeholder processes, but also the way in which multi-stakeholder processes challenge contemporary modes of regulation.

The article by Yana Breindl and Bjoern Kuellmer on "Internet Content Regulation in France and Germany: Regulatory Paths, Actor Constellations, and Policies" focuses on how and why Internet content is regulated in liberal democracies, in particular considering how institutions are influencing such regulation. Based on actor-centered institutionalism and informed by technology-aware policy research, the article proposes two case studies that analyze online content regulation in France and Germany through technical filtering mechanisms. In order to answer how free speech is being regulated for each case study, the influence of institutional variables and actor constellation is analyzed, with a particular focus on private actors and self-regulation. As the article clearly demonstrates, France and Germany have chosen different regulatory paths. France has opted for a much more legislative control, whereas Germany has chosen self-regulation with limited public oversight. The divergence in paths between France and Germany is related to the different institutional settings and actor constellations that influence the governance of this field, resulting in different political debates. This text also highlights that filtering and blocking have become usual procedures, which are implemented by democratic and authoritarian governments alike. These processes are often outsourced to third parties, leading to problems of transparency and legitimacy. Finally, this article concludes by reiterating specified concerns with technical content regulation, in particular with regard to the protection of freedom of expression, privacy, rule of law, and due process.

Continuing with this theme of the private regulation of digital content, Ben Wagner's article on "Governing Internet Expression: How Public and Private Regulation Shape Expression Governance" explores how freedom of expression is governed online. The emergence of the Internet has led to a redistribution of the governance capacity away from states towards private actors. Given that liberal democracies cannot directly intervene to regulate the actions of private actors in the area of media and communication technologies, this article explores what tools are left at the disposal of states to govern this specific area. Furthermore, the rapid expansion of the Internet and the limited capacity of public actors alone to regulate it have also led to the creation of a "space of expression," where different forms of speech do not always co-exist peacefully. The article looks at two case studies, one concerning a public actor and one concerning a private one: the U.S., which was the first state to consider strategies for online content regulation, and Facebook, a private actor that has achieved a de facto monopoly on social networking. The article analyzes how the freedom of expression is regulated, but also how the boundaries of free speech are established, considering the role of power as constitutive in defining such boundaries. More specifically, the article explores practices used in the creation of acceptable bounds for freedom of expression and their discursive framing, as well as the practices used for the implementation of such boundaries.

Whereas the previous two articles focus on the way in which content is regulated through agreements between private and public actors, and focusing on the relationships that foster this kind of regulation, Benjamin Farrand's article, "Regulatory Capitalism, Decentered Enforcement and its Legal Consequences for Digital Expression: The Use of Copyright Law to Restrict Freedom of Speech Online", considers the way in which copyright law can be misused as a means of suppressing embarrassing or politically sensitive information in the digital environment. In comparison to the previous articles, the predominant focus of this text is on the alleged abuse of such systems of regulation. Beginning with the consideration of contemporary governance as being an example of "regulatory capitalism," in which powers and activities that are traditionally considered the prerogative of the state are delegated to private, non-state actors in a form of "regulated self-regulation," this article argues that choice of governance

structure impacts the way in which content is regulated. Whereas attempts to limit access to information considered sensitive through the use of copyright infringement allegations have been used in the offline environment, these attempts have been criticized by U.S. courts as a misuse of a law that was intended to ensure protection of information as a means of ensuring the dissemination of that content. However, as this article continues, the creation of a system of self-regulating "notice and takedown," where administrative decisions are made by private actors such as Internet intermediaries, makes the challenging of such decisions much more difficult, raising concerns over accountability and transparency. It also allows for the suppression of information by both state and non-state actors, indicating that the arguments in favor of limiting the application of the First Amendment (concerning freedom of speech) to the actions of public actors are less convincing within a system where private rather than state actors take an active role in the regulation of content.

Peter Jay Smith's article, "Speaking for Freedom, Normalizing the Net?", continues the analysis of how freedom of expression online can be limited through indirect ways through the usage of copyright legislation, and means by which it can be resisted. Departing from the idea that scholarly attention has increasingly been focusing on the control of online expression through censorship, in countries such as Iran and China, to the detriment of more concealed forms of control in liberal democracies, the author looks at U.S. attempts to curtail Internet freedoms through the adoption and enforcement of restrictive intellectual property legislation, such as the Anti-Counterfeiting Trade Agreement. Basing itself on the risk and security literature, the article focuses in particular on how the U.S. has, throughout the years, shifted the forum it uses to export copyright norms in an attempt to identify the most efficient venue. It also argues that such attempts have led to the emergence of widespread global resistance on the side of civil society, which is demanding the disappearance of online controls. The article concludes by pointing out that such resistance has diminished the capacity of the U.S. to impose its intellectual property norms through multilateral negotiations, leading it to have recourse to bilateral agreements, which have, however, not been particularly efficient.

Continuing with themes of activism, resistance, and mobilization, Michael J. Jensen and Henrik P. Bang's article, "Occupy Wall Street: A New Form of Movement and Community?", discusses the means by which the Internet is providing the communication infrastructure necessary for the development and expansion of social movements, resulting in more innovative forms of collaboration and mobilization. Specifically, the online environment provides tools to shape meanings, knowledge, and identities. Within this context, the article compares old and new forms of social political movements. In order to study how the Occupy movement operates between the old and new forms of political participation, the authors develop an analytical framework that is based on four typologies. Focusing on the Twitter profiles of 50,000 participants, the article addresses how their conceptualization of the movement interacts with configurations of old and new forms of political participation involving both traditional associations concerned with voting and political parties, and the establishment of issue and cause-related politics. The article indicates that the variety of identities constructed and mobilized online during Occupy Wall Street (OWS) demonstrations do not coincide with the analyzed Twitter profiles, which are actually much more diverse than the image projected by the OWS movement. In particular, the authors find that the movement incorporated not only "leftist" or "liberal" actors, but also traditionally conservative and religious ones. This study shows, however, that common identities and interests are not automatically necessary for collective action to develop. Instead, the OWS movement appears to be one where participants develop and coordinate common action despite their social, cultural, moral, religious, and political differences, through mutual acceptance and recognition of difference.

In the final article, Kenneth Rogerson and Daniel Milton's "A Policymaking Process 'Tug of War': National Information Security Policies in Comparative Perspective" analyzes how states develop policies on information security. In comparison to other articles in this special issue, which highlight aspects of cooperation and cohesion between the interests of state and private actors in these forms of regulation, this text instead focuses on divisions in opinion between actors, and the inherent competition involved in establishing their preferred approaches as the commonly accepted one. Departing from the question of whether a greater flow of online information automatically leads to more democracy, the authors focus on how the flow of information is controlled and what arguments are used to justify such control. More specifically, the article explores ways in which we can understand competing policy makers' interests and the factors influencing the type of information security policy countries have. The authors propose that outcomes in information policy vary according to the type of information governments are attempting to control, that democracies often limit information when faced with external threats in order to protect their population, and that some countries attribute greater importance to privacy than others. As a result of such insights, the article concludes that the development of models to understand policy-making on information security must include elements as varied as the interests of the different actors involved in the field, the arguments they are presenting and the contexts in which they are proposing these arguments.

This special issue of the *Journal of Information Technology & Politics* constitutes a contribution to the development of the literature concerning governance on the Internet. It provides a range of different theoretical and methodological approaches, indicating that irrespective of approach taken, key themes such as the interaction between state and private actors become readily apparent. In particular, these articles indicate that certain concerns exist due to these forms of cooperation, including over transparency, legitimacy and accountability. For this reason, it is submitted that further research needs to be conducted in this field, going beyond the traditional Internet studies literature to take into account literature and theoretical conceptualizations that seek to consider the role of governance by private actors in a more holistic way. While this special issue focuses on the Internet as a form of "case study," and seeking to reveal issues that arise as a result of this type of governance, the editors propose that this online content regulation is representative of a more general approach to governance that applies to both online and offline environments.

REFERENCES

Amable, B. (2003). *The diversity of modern capitalism.* Oxford, England: Oxford University Press.

Bartle, I., & Vass, P. (2007). Self-regulation within the regulatory state: Towards a new regulatory paradigm? *Public Administration, 85*(4), 885–905.

Baumgartner, F. R. (2009). *Lobbying and policy change: Who wins, who loses, and why.* Chicago: University of Chicago Press.

Benkler, Y. (2006). *The wealth of networks: How social production transforms markets and freedom.* New Haven, CT: Yale University Press.

Berkman Center for Internet and Society. (2011). *International bloggers and Internet control.* Cambridge, MA: Roberts, H., Zuckerman, E., York, J., Faris, R., & Palfrey, J. G.

Bernhagen, P., & Bräuninger, T. (2005). Structural power and public policy: A Signaling Model of Business Lobbying in Democratic Capitalism. *Political Studies, 53*(1), 43–64.

Bimber, B., Stohl, C., & Flanagin, A. J. (2009). Technological change and the shifting nature of political organization. In A. Chadwick & P. N. Howard (Eds.), *Routledge handbook of Internet politics* (pp. 72–85). London: Routledge.

Black, J. (2001). Decentering regulation: Understanding the role of regulation and self regulation in a "post-regulatory" world. *Current Legal Problems, 54*(1), 103–146.

Braithwaite, J. (2008). *Regulatory capitalism: How it works, ideas for making it work better.* Cheltenham, England: Edward Elgar.

Bright, P. (2011, August 10). How the London riots showed us two sides of social networking. *Ars Technica.* Retrieved from http://arstechnica.com/tech-policy/news/2011/08/the-two-sides-of-social-networking-on-display-in-the-london-riots

Brown, I. (2010). Internet self-regulation and fundamental rights. *Index on Censorship, 1*, 98–106.

Castells, M. (2011). *Communication power.* Oxford, England: Oxford University Press.

Christou, G., & Simpson, S. (2006). The Internet and public-private governance in the European Union. *Journal of Public Policy, 26*(1), 43–61.

Coen, D., & Thatcher, M. (2008). Network governance and multi-level delegation: European networks of regulatory agencies. *Journal of Public Policy, 28*(1), 49–71.

Culpepper, D. (2011). *Quiet politics and business power: Corporate control in Europe and Japan.* Cambridge, England: Cambridge University Press.

Dean, M. (2010). *Governmentality: Power and rule in modern society* (2nd ed.). London: SAGE.

Deibert, R., Palfrey, J. G., Rohozinski, R., & Zittrain, J. (2008). *Access denied: The practice and policy of global Internet filtering.* Cambridge, MA: MIT Press.

Deibert, R., Palfrey, J. G., Rohozinski, R., & Zittrain, J. (2010). *Access controlled: The shaping of power, rights, and rule in cyberspace.* Cambridge, MA: MIT Press.

Deibert, R., Palfrey, J. G., Rohozinski, R., & Zittrain, J. (2012). *Access contested: Security, identity, and resistance in Asian cyberspace information revolution and global politics.* Cambridge, MA: MIT Press.

Deibert, R. J. (2009). The geopolitics of Internet control: Censorship, sovereignty, and cyberspace. In A. Chadwick & P. N. Howard (Eds.), *Routledge handbook of Internet politics* (pp. 323–336). London: Routledge.

Downing, L. (2008). *The Cambridge introduction to Michel Foucault.* Cambridge, England: Cambridge University Press.

Dutton, W. H., & Peltu, M. (2009). The new politics of the Internet: Multi-stakeholder policy-making and the Internet technocracy. In A. Chadwick & P. N. Howard (Eds.), *Routledge handbook of Internet politics* (pp. 384–400). London: Routledge.

Esterling, K. M. (2004). *The political economy of expertise: Information and efficiency in American national politics.* Ann Arbor: University of Michigan Press.

European Commission. (2009). *Communication from the Commission to the Council, the European Parliament and the European Economic and Social Committee: Enhancing the enforcement of intellectual property rights in the internal market* (No. COM(2009) 467 final). Brussels: European Commission.

Farrand, B. (2014). *Networks of Power in Digital Copyright Law and Policy: Political Salience, Expertise, and the Legislative Process.* London: Routledge.

Foucault, M. (2004). *Society must be defended: Lectures at the Collège de France, 1975–76.* (D. Macey, Trans.). London: Penguin.

Friedland, L. A. (1996). Electronic democracy and the new citizenship. *Media, Culture and Society, 18*, 185–212.

Gil de Zúñiga, H., Veenstra, A., Vraga, E., & Shah, D. (2010). Digital democracy: Reimagining pathways to political participation. *Journal of Information Technology & Politics, 7*(1), 36–51.

Goldsmith, J. L., & Wu, T. (2006). *Who controls the Internet? Illusions of a borderless world.* Oxford, England: Oxford University Press.

Halliday, J. (2011, August 8). London riots: How BlackBerry Messenger played a key role. *The Guardian.* Retrieved from http://www.theguardian.com/media/2011/aug/08/london-riots-facebook-twitter-blackberry

Harvey, D. (2007). Neoliberalism as creative destruction. *The ANNALS of the American Academy of Political and Social Science, 610*(1), 21–44.

Héretier, A., & Eckert, S. (2008). New modes of governance in the shadow of hierarchy: Self-regulation by industry in Europe. *Journal of Public Policy, 28*(1), 113–138.

Jenkins, P. (2001). *Beyond Tolerance: Child Pornogaphy on the Internet.* New York: New York University Press.

Johnson, D., & Post, D. G. (1996). Law and borders: The rise of law in cyberspace. *Stanford Law Review, 48,* 1367.

Johnson, P. (2010). Law, morality and disgust: The regulation of "extreme pornography' in England and Wales. *Social & Legal Studies, 19*(2), 147–163.

Kelly, M. G. E. (2012). *The political philosophy of Michel Foucault.* London: Routledge.

Kiersey, N. J. (2011). Neoliberal political economy and the subjectivity of crisis: Why governmentality is not hollow. In N. J. Kiersey & D. Stokes (Eds.), *Foucault and international relations: New critical engagements* (pp. 1–24). New York: Routledge.

Koimann, J. (2000). Societal governance: Levels, modes, and orders of social-political interaction. In J. Pierre (Ed.), *Debating governance: Authority, steering, and democracy* (pp. 138–166). Oxford, England: Clarendon.

Koumartzis, N., & Veglis, A. (2011). Internet regulation: The need for more transparent Internet filtering systems and improved measurement of public opinion on Internet filtering. *First Monday, 16*(10). Retrieved from http://firstmonday.org/ojs/index.php/fm/article/view/3266/3071

Lanier, J. (2013). *Who owns the future?* London: Allen Lane.

Lessig, L. (2004). *Free culture: The nature and future of creativity.* New York: Penguin Press.

Lessig, L. (2006). *Code 2.0.* New York: Basic Books.

Levi-Faur, D. (2005). The rise of regulatory capitalism: The global diffusion of a new order. *The ANNALS of the American Academy of Political and Social Science, 598*(1), 12–32.

Lütz, S., Eberle, D., & Lauter, D. (2011). Varieties of private self-regulation in European capitalism: Corporate governance codes in the UK and Germany. *Socio-Economic Review, 9*(2), 315–338.

MacKinnon, R. (2012). *Consent of the networked: The worldwide struggle for Internet freedom.* New York: Basic Books.

Marcussen, M., & Torfing, J. (2003). Grasping governance networks. *Centre for Democratic Network Governance Working Paper Series, 5,* 1–31.

Marsden, C. T. (2011). *Internet co-regulation: European law, regulatory governance and legitimacy in cyberspace.* Cambridge, England: Cambridge University Press.

Marsh, D., & Rhodes, R. A. (1992). *Policy networks in British government.* New York: Oxford University Press.

McGreal, C. (2010, April 5). WikiLeaks reveals video showing US air crew shooting down Iraqi civilians. *The Guardian.* Retrieved from http://www.theguardian.com/world/2010/apr/05/wikileaks-us-army-iraq-attack

McIntyre, T. (2012). Child abuse images and cleanfeeds: Assessing Internet blocking systems. In I. Brown (Ed.), *Research handbook on governance of the Internet* (pp. 277–308). Cheltenham, England: Edward Elgar Publishing.

Morozov, E. (2011). *The net delusion: The dark side of Internet freedom.* New York: PublicAffairs.

Mueller, M. (2010). *Networks and states: The global politics of Internet governance.* Cambridge, MA: MIT Press.

Murray, A. D. (2009). The reclassification of extreme pornographic images. *The Modern Law Review, 72*(1), 73–90.

Parker, C. (2002). *The open corporation: Effective self-regulation and democracy.* New York: Cambridge University Press.

Patterson, L. R. (1987). Free speech, copyright and fair use. *Vanderbilt Law Review, 40,* 1.

Poulsen, K. (2013, August 5). Feds are suspects in new malware that attacks Tor anonymity. *Wired.* Retrieved from http://www.wired.com/threatlevel/2013/08/freedom-hosting/

Price, M. E., & Verhulst, S. G. (2005). *Self-regulation and the Internet.* The Hague: Kluwer Law International

Shirky, C. (2011). *Cognitive surplus: Creativity and generosity in a connected age.* London: Penguin.

Shubber, K. (2013, June 14). ISPs to include porn filters as standard in UK by 2014. *Wired UK.* Retrieved from http://www.wired.co.uk/news/archive/2013-06/14/parental-filtering-industry-standard

The Guardian. (2013, June 8). The NSA files. Retrieved from http://www.theguardian.com/world/the-nsa-files

Veyne, P. (2010). *Foucault: His thought, his character.* Cambridge, England: Polity.

Ward, S., & Gibson, R. (2009). European political organizations and the Internet: Mobilization, participation, and change. In A. Chadwick & P. N. Howard (Eds.), *Routledge handbook of Internet politics* (pp. 25–39). London: Routledge.

Wright, J. S. (2011). Regulatory capitalism and the UK Labour Government's reregulation of commissioning in the English National Health Service. *Law and Policy, 33*(1), 27–59.

Wu, T. (2010). *The master switch: The rise and fall of information empires.* New York: Random House.

Yu, K. (2010). The graduated response. *Florida Law Review, 62,* 1373–1430.

Zeno-Zencovich, V. (2008). *Freedom of expression: A critical and comparative analysis.* Abingdon, Oxon, England: Routledge-Cavendish.

Zittrain, J. (2008). *The future of the Internet: And how to stop it.* London: Allen Lane.

Internet Content Regulation in France and Germany: Regulatory Paths, Actor Constellations, and Policies

Yana Breindl

Bjoern Kuellmer

ABSTRACT. The article focuses on online content regulation in France and Germany. We examine institutional characteristics and actor constellations that led to different policy choices and situate these in the broader discussion on Internet content regulation. While in the early 1990s courts were settling disputes regarding problematic content by applying existing regulation to the digital realm, both countries have since chosen separate regulatory paths. France opted for legislative control, while Germany developed a system of "regulated self-regulation," in which private actors self-regulate with limited state supervision. Both cases provide insights into the possibilities and limits of state intervention on the Internet.

The digitization of content along with the convergence of various transmission canals to the Internet poses new challenges in terms of scale, spread, and control of content considered as problematic by private and public actors. The definition of what is harmful or illegal in liberal democracies is largely shaped by existing policies and varies according to cultural and historical patterns (Zeno-Zencovich, 2009). However, digital content largely ignores existing geographical boundaries. In the early 1990s, the Internet's decentralized structure and the possibilities for every user to offer and gain access to information anonymously and unhindered by territorial and juridical borders challenged governmental authority and sovereignty in particular (Johnston & Post, 1996), especially since private actors own most of the Internet's infrastructure and maintain and develop its protocols.

Filtering and blocking of digital content was first studied in authoritarian states, which already restrict basic civil rights such as freedom of expression or freedom of information (Deibert, Palfrey, Rohozinkinski, & Zittrain, 2008). However, in liberal democracies that are characterized by freedom of expression (Dahl, 1971; Freedom House, 2012), debates arose already in the mid-1990s over the necessity and enforceability of regulation mechanisms on the Internet. "Information wants to be

Yana Breindl is a post-doctoral research fellow at the Institute for Political Science and the Göttingen Centre for Digital Humanities at Georg-August Universität, Göttingen, Germany. Her research focuses on the political implications of Internet technologies, including in particular digital rights activism, discourse networks, and Internet content regulation in liberal democracies.

Bjoern Kuellmer is a Ph.D. candidate in the Department of Comparative Politics and Political Economy at Georg-August Universität, Göttingen, Germany. His research interests are in Internet politics, analysis of the policy process, and comparative institutional change.

free," argued cyberlibertarians who perceived the Internet as the absolute medium of global free expression. For others, "information needs to be regulated," because new technologies (e.g., file-sharing, voice-over-IP) are considered to threaten existing business models, undermine social norms, and challenge public order and security. The actors' perceptions of digital content largely influence their policy orientations, leading to the formation of new and shifting actor constellations.

Filtering and blocking have become global norms as states and corporate actors make use of increasingly sophisticated technologies to deal with problematic content. They have become policy tools much appreciated by democratic governments as well (Deibert, Palfrey, Rohozinski, and Zittrain, 2010; Deibert & Crete-Nishihata, 2012; McIntyre, 2012). Governments increasingly outsource their content enforcement competences to the level of network intermediaries (e.g., Internet service or content providers), which generates issues of legitimacy and transparency (Brown, 2010; DeBeer & Clemmer, 2009). In liberal democracies, automatic content restrictions pose a series of legal, political, and technical questions that are answered differently according to the institutional context, the actors involved, and their modes of interaction. It is thus necessary to explicitly study how and why online content is regulated, in particular in liberal democracies.

This article focuses on two European countries, France and Germany, to examine how regulation of Internet content is implemented by looking at actor interactions in two distinct institutional settings. The objective of the research is to provide an in-depth account of Internet content regulation in two liberal democracies known for their relatively strict content regulations to answer the following questions: How do liberal states deal with digital content? How do actors and institutional settings influence Internet content regulation?

THEORETICAL FRAMEWORK

Our analysis is informed by technology-aware policy research as proposed by Bendrath and Mueller (2011). Building upon actor-centered institutionalism (ACI; Mayntz & Scharpf, 1995; Scharpf, 1997), Bendrath and Mueller argue that technology and technological change needs to be acknowledged in its own right to explain policy change and adaptation. Through their analysis of deep-packet inspection, they show that the specific properties of new technologies contribute to new interest formations and the emergence of different capabilities or power resources. Technological change is considered an input or policy problem for political interactions, in which actors interact in a particular institutional setting to produce new policies: "Political interactions around new technological capabilities will be shaped by existing laws and regulations, by the existence or non-existence of partisan groups promoting specific norms and their degree of organization, and by the properties and legacies of the political system" (Bendrath & Mueller, 2011, p. 9). Our analysis therefore focuses on the type of interactions between actors in two separate institutional settings in response to issues with digital content (see the following section, Internet Content Regulation).

The institutional setting presents opportunities and restraints to actors without fully determining their actions. These opportunities and restraints offer a particular context for interaction, requiring particular behaviors and procedures from actors in particular situations. Institutions can provide actors with financial, legal, technical, or other types of resources. States can create new actors and bestow new tasks and competencies to existing ones. Institutions create occasions and arenas for interaction, providing rules that shape actors' possibilities for action. However, not all interactions are framed by institutions. ACI explicitly acknowledges that norms can be broken and rules disobeyed, and that informal interactions outside of institutional arrangements exist (Mayntz & Scharpf, 1995).

Institutions such as states are not only part of a broader setting that shapes action, but are also actors in their own right. ACI focuses on corporate actors, formally organized, although non-institutional actors or quasigroups can be considered as collective actors when their action is consciously directed toward a common goal. An actor's orientation is influenced by cognitive and motivational factors. In terms of cognitive processes, an actor's orientation can be conflicted by multiple relationships to social entities such as a region, a political party, or a country. The perception of a particular reality or policy problem can be different from actor to actor. A shared assessment of a particular situation is necessary to act collectively, but actors will frequently have to interact in constellations with actors with divergent "cognitive maps" (Axelrod, 1979). Motivational factors include interests, norms, and identities. Corporate actors act to secure their own existence, resources, and autonomy (Schimank, 1991). Normative expectations as well as individual and collective or corporate identities play an equally important role in shaping an actor's orientation. Finally, they are shaped by relational aspects, i.e., interaction orientations, that range from cooperative to hostile behavior (Mayntz & Scharpf, 1995).

Actors act in particular situations. A specific setting can activate different types of interests: for example, survival when a situation is threatening an actor's existence or values and norms in less threatening situations. The situation will also shape an actor's feeling of belonging to a particular group or entity when events affect a broader set of actors or interests. Situations also offer different action possibilities, which are not solely institutionally determined. This is the case of resources available as well as alternative paths of action. A situation is also determined by its degree of complexity, stability, or variability. These aspects can be perceived differently by actors (Mayntz & Scharpf, 1995).

Policy issues generally lead to interactions between constellations of actors with interdependent action possibilities. The coordination between different actors takes the shape of adaption, negotiation, voting, or hierarchical decision-making. An actor can thus adapt his or her behavior to other actors' actions, without seeking to influence the others' actions, yet possibly in the knowledge of the other actors' interests and resources. Actors can negotiate agreements to act collectively. They can vote on a particular outcome or be subject to top-down decision making. How actors interact, because of their particular interests and orientations shaped by their perception of a particular situation, in a given institutional setting determines the outcome of regulation, including on Internet content (an issue discussed in the next section).

INTERNET CONTENT REGULATION

The Internet has fueled a wide variety of social, economic, and political changes that require new policy responses in a diversity of domains (Margetts, 2009). However, governments' attempts at regulating parts of the digital information flows that affect their territory have been challenged by the global, private, and decentralized character of the network of networks (Mueller, 2010). In the 1990s, Internet adoption was still very low in continental Europe, and the market was dominated by U.S. corporations (Marsden, 2011). The general approach of the time was to avoid over-regulation to leave the new medium open for innovation and business ventures. At the time, the predominant cyberlibertarian perspective was that the Internet constituted a realm of self-organization by peers, as had been the case within early Internet communities (Murray, 2007). However, states, their regulatory agencies, and corporations have continually attempted to assert control over the global flow of information for which the Internet is praised (Goldsmith & Wu, 2006).

States have traditionally played a central role in content regulation. Print media and audiovisual transmissions could be more readily confined to particular geographic areas (Akdeniz, 2010). In contrast, digital content poses new challenges in terms of scale, spread, and possibilities for control to policy-makers. The Internet "disrupt[ed] the regulation of media content by nation-states," argues Mueller (2010, p. 185). Previous control mechanisms such as rating or classification systems have generally failed when applied to the digital realm due to the lack of market adoption (Brown & Marsden, 2013; Mueller, 2010).

The definition of what is illegal or harmful is influenced by cultural and historical factors

(Zeno-Zencovich, 2009), resulting in different policy responses as mentioned previously. These differences make a coordinated approach at the global level difficult. While some states, such as China or Iran, have implemented pervasive surveillance and censorship systems, many countries are more selective in the content they censor, depending generally on the degree of freedom of expression in the country (Deibert et al., 2008, 2010, 2011; Freedom House, 2012; Reporters Without Borders, 2012). Liberal democracies have vowed a long-term commitment to freedom of expression, which is enshrined in a series of national, supranational [e.g,. the French and German constitution, the U.S. Constitution's First Amendment, the European Convention on Human Rights (ECHR), etc.], and international legal instruments (in particular the Universal Declaration of Human Rights and the International Covenant on Civil and Political Rights). Because the Internet allows millions of humans to access and share information, communicate, and participate in politics, access to the Internet is increasingly framed as a condition for exercising one's human rights (La Rue, 2011; Marsden, 2011), with some countries considering Internet access to be a right "in and of itself."[1]

However, not all types of content are welcome in liberal democracies. In particular, issues of youth and child protection (e.g., opposing violent or sexually explicit content or material promoting the use of drugs, anorexia, or suicide), security concerns (e.g., terrorism), hate speech, and criminal prosecution, but also the protection of economic interests (e.g., communication services, copyright, gambling state monopolies, etc.) play a central role in the push for more content control (Deibert et al., 2011). Indeed, "[s]tates differ not in their intent to censor material . . . but in the content they target, how precisely they block it, and how involved their citizens are in these choices" (Bambauer, 2009, p. 3). It is thus to be expected that content blocking in liberal democracies is more respectful of democratic principles than in authoritarian regimes. However, legal scholars point to a diversity of issues posed by automatic filtering technologies in relation to the respect of constitutional and legal principles.

The national setting remains the main source for public policies on digital content. Although many Internet-related directives originate from the European Union, they leave room for interpretation when implemented at national levels (Akdeniz, 2010). Problematic content is generally legislated in separate texts, depending on the type of content. However, the technical modalities of filtering, once in place, can be implemented for any type of content, thus leading to possible new actor constellations based on shared interests.

U.S. cyberlawyer Lawrence Lessig argued already in 1999 that the decentralized and anonymous structure of the Internet depends on its manmade architecture built on computer code, and thus could be changed to enable control and surveillance (Lessig, 2006). Whether Internet design choices are regulatory modalities in and of themselves or not, code plays a central role in controlling user behavior, often in support of legal arrangements (DeNardis, 2012; McIntyre & Scott, 2008; Mueller, 2010). Proposals to territorialize the Internet emerged in the mid-1990s (Goldsmith, 1997/1998) and led to "walled gardens" where governmental control could be established, such as through the Chinese "Great Firewall." The same amount of control was impossible to achieve in liberal states without cutting down democratic principles and human rights protections. In the U.S., attempts to introduce mandatory filtering systems were rejected as unconstitutional in terms of free speech protections. The overall regulatory environment of the 1990s was dominated by self-regulation, followed by attempts at re-regulation in the early 2000s and increased co-regulatory mechanisms since 2005, at least in the EU, making the Internet a testing ground for new types of regulatory mechanisms (Froomkin, 2011; Marsden, 2011).

Early attempts to enforce content regulation focused on the endpoints of the network, i.e., the producers and consumers of controversial content (Zittrain, 2003). However, enforcement remains problematic when the endpoint is not situated in the state's territory and traditional legal procedures cannot cope with the exponential amount of digital content (Mueller, 2010). As a result, government and corporate actors' attempts at content control have increasingly focused on making Internet intermediaries such as Internet service providers (ISPs) "cooperate" or "be responsible" regarding the content they carry through their networks. As "gatekeepers" of the Internet, ISPs have the technical capability to monitor their users' activities and are able to block access to particular types of content through ever-more sophisticated blocking techniques (for an overview, see Murdoch & Anderson, 2008). This approach poses not only questions of restrictions to freedom of expression but also to privacy, as some blocking techniques are highly invasive.

In both the U.S. and Europe, ISPs hold no liability for the content hosted, cached, or carried by them if they fulfill a certain number of provisions, as spelled out in the U.S. Communications Decency Act (1996) and the European E-Commerce Directive (2000). They are considered "mere conduits" of information that is generated by third parties, and their liability is thus different than for publishers or authors of Web content. However, ISPs are expected to remove or make inaccessible illegal content when they are notified about its infringing character. Nonetheless, various European courts have issued rulings holding ISPs responsible for illegal content or to preemptively prevent access to such content. In two recent cases, the European Court of Justice reminded member states that, under the E-Commerce directive, ISPs could not be compelled to install general monitoring devices of their users, and restrictions need to balance the protection of intellectual property rights with the "freedom to conduct business, the right to protection of personal data and the freedom to impart information."[2]

Pressure from government or content owners has led to increased forms of "intermediary-based regulations," which allow governments to transfer the technical implementation of their content legislation to those offering access to the Internet. For Marsden (2011), "governments have outsourced constitutionally fundamental regulation to private agents, with little or no regard for the legitimacy claims" (p. 12). In practice, ISPs thus follow a way of self-regulation or co-regulation in association with governmental or independent institutions

(Marsden, 2011; McIntyre, 2012). This way of action tends to become standard in governmental regulation of the Internet, but creates also new problems of effectiveness, transparency, and accountability (Brown, 2010; Deibert et al., 2010). Internet blocking techniques have led to several occasions of "over-blocking," where legitimate content was equally blocked, and are often criticized for being ineffective, as Internet users can choose from a wide-range of tools to circumvent blocking. Furthermore, blocking raises questions as to its proportionality in restricting fundamental rights, such as freedom of expression and privacy, and questions of due process and the rule of law in what regards its implementation (Bambauer, 2009; Brown, 2010). The next section discusses content regulation in two particular settings: France and Germany.

CASE STUDIES

Our analysis focuses on two European continental states, France and Germany, which are both known for their commitment to fundamental rights but also their restrictions of some types of speech. In particular, for obvious historical reasons, the public incitement of hatred against minorities and Holocaust denial (in France, also the denial of the Armenian genocide) are prohibited. While studies of online content restrictions in liberal democracies have overwhelmingly focused on the U.S. or the UK (McIntyre, 2012; Mueller, 2010), it is worthwhile to focus on civil law continental European countries to investigate how liberal democracies regulate online content.

Both France and Germany derive ever-increasing parts of their legislation from the European Union. Both states are, however, very influential in determining EU policy, as they are, respectively, the largest and the most populated European country, as well as being among the initiators of European integration. France and Germany are regarded as the drivers of European integration and have often acted together to defend their interests at the European level. However, in terms of their institutional structure, France and Germany are rather different.

Lijphart (2012) found that, based on their institutional characteristics, liberal democracies can be classified along a continuum between two ideal types of democracy: a majoritarian model, where the majority of the people decide on the general direction of government, and a consensual model, which is aimed at "broad participation in government and broad agreement on the policies that the government should pursue" (p. 2). While no country is absolutely consensual or majoritarian, France certainly holds more characteristics of the majoritarian model, with a strong unitary state, a strong executive, and a rather pluralist interest group structure, while Germany is a good example of consensual government, which is characterized by a federal structure, corporatism, and proportionality rules.

Internet Blocking in France

France is a unitary state where administrative competencies have been transferred to local entities, but the political power remains centralized at the state level (Lijphart, 2012). From 2002 to 2012, France has been ruled by the right-wing *Union pour un Mouvement Populaire* (UMP), which has held a majority in the parliament as well as the presidency under Jacques Chirac (2002–2007) and Nicolas Sarkozy (2007–2012). In 2000, the mandate of the president was shortened from seven to five years to allow for the parliamentary elections to coincide with the presidential elections. The possibility for cohabitation, in which the prime minister is from a different party than the president, which would turn the presidential regime into a parliamentary system in practice (Lijphart, 2012), is since unlikely. The same party is thus in charge of domestic as well as foreign policy, strengthening the executive powers of the president.

Although the dominant discourse in France denies any form of participation of private interests in public policy processes, empirical evidence suggests the contrary. Saurugger and Grossman (2006) assert for instance that, since the 1980s, the French interest group structure has undergone important changes. Under the combined influence of external (e.g., European integration) as well as internal factors (e.g.,

the reform of the French state and the transformation of society), France has witnessed an increase in the number of associative and participative structures that are aimed to engage in the political system and the creation by the state of new forums for public deliberation. In parallel, the action repertoire of interest groups has changed, notably with the adoption of a 1995 bill forbidding legal entities to finance political parties, and thus depriving well-resourced interest groups from this mean of exerting influence. Researchers observe a renewal of action repertoires, in particular for trade unions who complement traditional strikes with long marches and sector-wide collective negotiations, while employers' associations remain distrustful of institutionalized forms of political communication, abandoning participation in joint committees for launching their own public deliberation and communication activities. French interest groups have gained in professionalization, and have recruited public affairs and communication professionals as well as researchers and specialists to substantiate their claims. In sum, however, institutionalized forms of exchanges between interest groups and other political actors, in particular political parties, remain weak, with most exchanges being organized informally as well as on a local basis (Saurugger & Grossman, 2006).

Content regulation in France

France has attempted repeatedly to enforce content regulations online. As argued by Mailland (2010), content control has been historically considered legitimate and necessary in a democracy. Although freedom of expression has been protected since the 1789 Declaration of the Rights of Man and of the Citizen, there are several limitations to this right. Indeed, the 1789 declaration already stated that "[t]he Law has the right to forbid . . . those actions that are injurious to society" (Mailland, 2010, p. 1184). French law restricts some type of content, such as hate speech or defamation, while promoting other types of content, such as the use of the French language. In particular, the 1990 Gayssot law forbids racist, anti-Semite, or xenophobic expressions, or any discrimination based on ethnical, national, racial, or religious grounds. A 2004 bill forbids expressions generating hatred or violence against persons based on their gender, sexual orientation, or a handicap. Young people have been protected since 1949 by a special committee that can sanction editors or prevent the publication of foreign material considered as inappropriate for a young public. Since a 2011 modification of the law, this includes content that presents a danger for youth due to its pornographic character or is likely to induce discrimination, violence, crime, or hatred; harms human dignity; promotes the use of drugs; or contains publicity that might "demoralize childhood or youth."[3] It is furthermore forbidden to present the use of drugs in a favorable light under the public health code. Individuals are also protected against defamation: France's privacy protections, including the right to one's image, are among the most protective in the world (Freedom House, 2012). Particular to France is also that the law explicitly promotes the use of some expressions over others.[4]

Historically, the early introduction of the Minitel in 1982, which has been developed and state-subsidized since the 1980s, allowed the government to gain experience in controlling electronic information networks (Mailland, 2010). The *Conseil supérieur de l'audiovisuel* (CSA, Superior Broadcasting Council) is in charge of monitoring and enforcing content regulation in the broadcasting sector, including the Minitel, which ceased to exist in June 2012. Because of its centralized structure, the Minitel was relatively easy to control, even after the privatization of the main access provider France Télécom in the 1990s. An administrative agency, the *Conseil supérieur de la Télématique* (CST, Superior Council of Telematics) issued deontological recommendations on the contents that are inserted into France Telecom's user contracts, which, if violated, can be terminated. Interestingly, the fight against images of child abuse did not constitute a priority for the French government at the time (Mailland, 2010).

French Internet penetration has been slightly delayed compared to other European states due to the government's attachment to its own electronic information retrieval system, the Minitel. In 1998, only 2% of French

inhabitants were Internet users, leading the state to adopt a program to "prepare the entry of France into the Information Society." Since 2000, France's Internet adoption rates have been growing rapidly, with consumers, businesses, and governments increasingly moving online (Hutchinson & Minton, n.d.).

Contrary to the Minitel, the Internet is highly decentralized and spread across the globe. These characteristics challenge state content regulation, as discussed previously. Electronic communications are regulated by the *Autorité de régulation des communications électroniques et des postes* (ARCEP), although there are current plans of a possible merger with the more content-oriented CSA. While the government pursues an open access policy and recognizes the informational and economic value of the Internet, it continues to enforce content regulations on the Internet.

The pressure on Internet service and content providers to care about the content they carry is thus expectedly high. The *Loi dans la confiance dans l'économie numérique* (LCEN 2004-575), which implements the European E-Commerce Directive (2000), establishes a system of limited liability for ISPs as long as they act rapidly to remove or block access to the content from the moment they are made aware of it. ISPs are expected to notify the hosting Web site when removing or blocking the material (Deibert et al., 2010). Content that is subject to notice-and-takedown procedures includes defamatory material and incitation to hatred based on race, religion, or sexual orientation, as well as the denial of the Holocaust or the Armenian genocide, or the promotion of terrorism. The protection of minors is also a concern. These restrictions to freedom of expression have continually been applied by French courts, including for content generated and hosted abroad but illegal in France[5] or Web sites linking to "unlawful" material.[6]

In this context, industry actors have adopted a series of self-regulatory measures. The *Association des Fournisseurs d'Accès et de Services Internet* (AFA, Association of Internet Access and Service Providers) was constituted in 1997. One year later, it founded a hotline for users to report problematic content, extended to mobile networks in 2009. It also proposes parental control filters and has proposed codes of conduct and has carried out labeling efforts since 2005.[7] The government has welcomed these efforts while proposing its own hotline in parallel.[8] The government and industry associations have also carried out joint education campaigns regarding online content.

Although self-regulatory mechanisms are in place, the French state has continually asserted its territorial sovereignty on the Internet. It has supported a series of advisory bodies, such as the *Forum des droits sur l'Internet* (Forum on Rights on the Internet) launched to reflect on judicial issues regarding the Internet, but which ceased to exist, after the government stopped to subsidize it in December 2010. The government then established the *Conseil national du numérique* (National Council on Digital Matters), in April 2011, to advise the government on digital issues. However, the government is not bound to follow its recommendations, and no civil society groups are represented in the Council. The governments' policies have been shaped by president Sarkozy's repeated calls to "civilize" the Internet—a claim that shifted to making the Internet more "responsible" at the eG8 Summit organized in Deauville, France.

To deal with problematic content, France has turned to technical measures by introducing blocking requirements into legislation. Blocking mechanisms were already considered in the Freedom of Communication Law (2000–79), which has since been replaced by article 4 of the *Loi d'orientation et de programmation pour la performance de la sécurité intérieure* (LOPPSI) bill, that individuals or companies providing access to public online communication services need to "inform their subscribers of the existence of technical means to restrict access to certain services and . . . to propose at least one of these means."[9] Filtering software needs thus to be included in browsers, and ISPs are required to propose optional filtering software to their customers. In 2008, France signed an agreement to block access to child abuse images and sites promoting racial violence and terrorism (Deibert et al., 2010). The NGO Reporters Without Borders stated in its 2012 report that "filtering is becoming commonplace [in France], even without adequate judicial supervision" (Reporters Without Borders, 2012, p. 48). Various types of Internet blocking mechanisms are in place in the domains of online copyright enforcement, online gambling Web sites, and the distribution of sexual images of children on the Internet.

Copyright

France is among the countries with the strictest online copyright enforcement legislation. The pro-entertainment industry stance of the right-wing governments has led to the adoption of a series of copyright bills. To increase their chance of adoption, the bills were all government-sponsored, which was attributed to the cultural affairs committee that is traditionally sensitive to French artists and entertainment companies, and the "emergency" procedure was invoked, limiting the legislative procedure to one reading per chamber (Breindl & Briatte, in press). Furthermore, literary and artistic property law, as copyright law is referred to in France,[10] has long been considered an esoteric and obscure issue that is reserved to specialists. As Lapousterle (2009) argues, the technicality and complexity of intellectual property rights (IPRs) increases the dependency of legislators to organized interest groups. Legislators, who do not hold specialized knowledge, need to rely on the input of technical expertise from stakeholders to draft and implement laws. Furthermore, the relatively recent politicization of the issue at the national, European, and international level has led to increased competition between the powerful, internationally organized rightsholder lobby and other interest groups, in particular civil rights groups and some sectors of the Internet industry (Breindl & Briatte, 2013; Yu, 2004).

The 2006 DADVSI bill,[11] which implements the European 2001 Copyright directive, was the first IPRs law to generate a considerable amount of political controversy and public awareness when it was examined by the French Parliament between December 2005 and June 2006. It opposed the entertainments sector's lobbying for harsher copyright enforcement measures by a grassroots effort of free and open source software promoters, who were advocating for increased interoperability and the noncriminalization of anticircumvention software. After being censored by the Constitutional Council, the bill came into force in August 2006, and applied financial and penal sanctions to the production of copyright infringing and anticircumvention software through unclear and inoperable provisions (Briatte, 2008; Breindl & Briatte, 2013). As Breindl and Briatte (2013) and Lapousterle (2009) have argued, the public authorities were in fact encouraging the engagement of competing interest groups, who extended their lobbying effort to the Constitutional Council (Lapousterle, 2009, p. 55). The result was a law that made concessions to all stakeholders without arbitrating between incompatible interests, being in fact complex, obscure, difficult to apply, and to interpret. By the time the law was adopted, it was clear that the bill would be inoperable to solve online copyright questions and would need to be complemented or replaced by a new bill.

The 2009 HADOPI bill[12] developed into another legislative minefield for the right-wing government of then-president Nicolas Sarkozy, who had declared the fight for the "civilization of the Internet."[13] Inspired by the report of Denis Olivennes (2007), then-director of a French retail chain of cultural and electronic products, the first version of the bill was heavily amended throughout the parliamentary readings. Its "graduated response"[14] mechanism was considered as the solution to "online piracy" by the entertainment industry, with France being the most likely candidate for setting a global example (Yu, 2010). The free software and digital rights activists who had engaged against DADVSI previously launched in May 2008 a collective, *La Quadrature du Net* (Squaring the Net), which became the most vocal opponent to the graduated response measure. Supporters and opponents of the measure heavily lobbied the national assembly, resulting in a first rejection of the bill in April 2009 that represented "an almost unique event under the French Fifth Republic" (Breindl & Briatte, 2013, p. 12). The government reintroduced a new bill, heavily amended, which was finally adopted in May 2009 only to be struck down as unconstitutional

by the Constitutional Court for violating the presumption of innocence by reversing the burden of proof from the prosecution to the defendant.[15]

A separate HADOPI 2 bill was quickly prepared and voted in September 2009, which amended the proposal by introducing a review process. The mechanism continues to be denounced as costly (12 million euros in 2011, paid by the ministry of culture), and its impact on reducing copyright infringement remains contested. Although François Hollande proclaimed during his presidential campaign that he would abolish HADOPI ("La fin de L'Hadopi reportée à mars 2013," 2012), it is yet uncertain whether this will be the case. The new socialist government has already cut the budget of the high authority ("Le budget de la Hadopi passe à 8 millions d'euros," 2012) and a new Commission has been launched to reflect on the French cultural exception in the digital age, including the future of HADOPI ("Exception culturelle," 2012). However, copyright reform groups have already denounced that yet another private actor with interests in the entertainment business and defending stricter copyright enforcement measures heads the mission, including HADOPI. The organizations decided to boycott what they consider a "caricature of democratic debate" ("Pourquoi nous ne participerons," 2012).

In parallel to the HADOPI bills, French and British members of the European Parliament (MEPs) attempted to introduce graduated-response at the European level by adding copyright amendments to the reform of the EU Telecommunications Rules of 2002. The attempt at venue shopping was, however, countered by strong opposition by digital rights activists and telecommunication and network operators, who were unwilling to be involved in the monitoring and criminalization of their customers (Breindl, 2012; Horten, 2011). The result, in terms of content regulation not supposed to be the object of the bill in the first place, and was again a diluted text, leaving it up to member states to settle the matter. The case of online gambling presents another example of French state intervention in online content regulation.

Online gambling

The passing of the Online Gambling Law on May 12, 2010,[16] which introduced the blocking of illegal gambling sites after judicial review, has generated far less controversy than the copyright bills. The bill opened up the national gambling sector, after the French state had come under pressure by a series of EU Commission infringement proceedings against various member states for breaching EU rules on freedom to provide services. Similarly to other member states, France had agreed to partly liberalize the market, however also subjecting foreign gambling sites to acquiring a national license for operating on the French territory. The regulation, which was officially implemented to protect gamblers from addiction and to comply with EU law, also generates new income for the French state in the shape of tax revenues from the licensed Web sites. The French law was passed one month before the World Cup soccer tournament, and generated 83 million euros in tax revenues for the licensed Web sites—the double of what had been earned previously by the state (Pfanner, 2010).[17]

The blocking procedure is similar to HADOPI, with the notable exception that the Web site is blocked, not the Internet access of the alleged infringer, involving a newly created administrative authority and a two-step process. The bill established the *Autorité de Régulation des Jeux en Ligne* (ARJEL, authority for the regulation of online gambling), which can invoke an emergency procedure by a court to require ISPs to block the access to illegal gambling sites if these have not ceased their activities eight days after a first notification. Illegal gambling sites are Web sites that offer games for a fee that have not been officially approved by ARJEL. To obtain a license, a financial fee has to be paid. Similarly to the HADOPI debates, the intervention of a judge before access blocking was the primary object of dispute; this measure was removed and eventually reintroduced into the law to comply with the HADOPI ruling by the Constitutional Court.

During a court hearing against an illegal gambling site in August 2010, ARJEL argued for the blocking of an illegal gambling Web site by invoking public order and security, the protection of minors, and the prevention of money laundering and criminal activities. ISPs countered that the blocking result cannot be guaranteed, that the gambling company was deprived of a right to a fair trial, that the blocking measures should be strictly regulated to prevent collateral damages, and that the blocking costs should be reimbursed. The judge rejected the ISPs' arguments, stating that any type of blocking should be implemented separately or jointly to achieve the desired result. For the costs, the judge refers to the need for a decree that had not been adopted by then (Rees, 2010). The decree was finally introduced on December 30, 2011; it asked ISPs to use DNS tampering and said that ARJEL would provide a certain financial compensation for the costs of this filtering system. Other filtering methods can be used but will not be compensated.

The French procedure is in line with similar approaches across the EU, notably in Italy. Also, the European Commission has explicitly acknowledged the need to "explore the benefits and possible limits of responsive enforcement measures, such as payment blocking and disabling access to Web sites, at the EU level," as well as "provide clarification on the procedures for notifying and acting on unauthorized content hosted in the EU by online intermediaries" (European Commission, 2012, p. 9). Finally, we will turn to "child pornography," the third category of content that was explicitly targeted by a French law introducing access blocking.

"Cyber child pornography"

France's most recent Internet blocking measures were part of the controversial Law on Guidelines and Programming for the Performance of Internal Security (LOPPSI 2).[18] The bill was criticized as a "catch-all" text, as it mixed video-surveillance, computer security, police databases, and the fight against the distribution of child pornographic material (Breindl, 2012). On July 30, 2010, after riots in a Grenoble suburb that followed the killing of a robber by police forces, president Sarkozy held a polemic speech promising new security measures. As a result, the LOPPSI

2 bill was amended with 12 new articles, most of which were censored by the review of the Constitutional Council, who ruled unconstitutional a record number of 13 articles in March 2011.

The bill extended the long list of security laws that has been approved since the terrorist attacks of 9/11 ("Dix-huit lois sur la sécurité depuis 2001," 2009). The law was heavily debated, notably due to the establishment of a complementary punishment of foreign criminals or the forced evacuation of illegal settlements. Next to extending police forces' surveillance powers, implementing generalized video surveillance of public places, the bill also included the blocking of child pornographic material, without judicial review, in its article 4. Contrary to its HADOPI ruling, the Constitutional Court considered that the fight against child abuse justifies measures that the protection of intellectual property rights does not. The Court decided that access blocking was a proportionate measure, and struck the right balance between public order and freedom of expression.[19] In July 2012, a minister delegate of the newly elected socialist government under president François Hollande announced, however, that the controversial blocking without prior judiciary oversight would not been implemented by the government (Lausson, 2012).

Internet Blocking in Germany

After World War II, freedom of expression in Germany was defined with regard to other fundamental duties of the German democratic state to protect the inviolability of personal dignity (Article 1 of the German *Grundgesetz*, or Constitution) and to protect the youth (Article 5). To fulfill these aims, the *Bundesprüfstelle für jugendgefährdende Schriften* (BPjS, Federal Department for Writings Harmful to Young Persons) was established in 1953 and was bestowed with powers to rate, censor, and ban printed publications and recorded media that contained Nazi propaganda, especially Holocaust denial, and to protect minors against images of extreme violence, hard pornography, and hate speech.[20] For broadcast media, the *Landesmedienanstalten* (German state media agencies) has carried out similar tasks at the

federal-state level since the 1980s. However the Internet posed new challenges to the German legislation and administration to enforce existing national law of information regulation and create new rules of interaction to regulate the supranational realm of the Internet.

In Germany, Internet content filtering and blocking emerged on the political agenda for the first time in 1995, when Bavarian prosecutors pressured the U.S. company CompuServe to block access to 200 electronic message boards that dealt with images of hard pornography and images of child abuse illegal in Germany (Stadler, 1998).[21] Since that time, several attempts were made both at the national and federal states (*Länder*) levels to deal with illegal Internet content with varying results.

The next sections will focus more specifically on how the competencies for online content have been settled between the national and federal states' levels, and how the organization and interaction of a variety of interests influenced the German blocking regime. Furthermore, we show how the attempt by the federal government to introduce a mandatory blocking mechanism of child pornographic content in 2009 failed due to constitutional and political reasons, and settled at a cooperating solution between state and Internet industry in form of "regulated self-regulation."

Competency for online content

Due to Germany's federal structure (Lijphart, 2012), the main challenge at stake with regard to Internet content regulation consisted of determining whether the federal states or the national level were legally and politically responsible for regulating online content. The question remained unsolved for a long time. The first cases of blocking Internet content in 1995 and 1996 relied on existing German criminal legislation and were enforced by individual federal state police and courts (Kossel & Möcke, 1996). Above all, it was unclear whether the Internet had to be considered similar to broadcasting media or not. As mentioned previously, the regulation of broadcast media issues traditionally falls within the responsibilities of the federal states and the *Landesmedienanstalten*, while youth protection in distributable media such as printed or taped media is part of the national jurisdiction practiced by the BPjS using age classification and banning.

Between 1997 and 2007 legislative efforts on the federal state and national levels were made to clear these jurisdictional problems. The federal states asserted in 1997 their regulatory competency regarding online youth protection by adopting the *Mediendienste-Staatsvertrag* (MDStV, Media Service Treaty). The same year, jugendschutz.net was launched as a "central federal agency" (Hans-Bredow-Institut, 2007, p. 177) with special competencies in controlling and evaluating Internet content with regard to youth protection and hate speech.

At the national level, the revision of the *Jugendschutzgesetz* (JuSchG, Youth Protection Act) in 2002 and the adoption of the *Jugendmedienschutz-Staatsvertrag* (JMStV, Youth Media Protection Treaty) in 2003 confirmed the competency of the federal states, but also aimed to coordinate both levels to work together on Internet content regulation. In order to centralize and coordinate action, the 16 federal state agencies were concentrated in one single institution, the *Kommission für Jugendmedienschutz der Landesmedienanstalten* (KJM). The KJM and jugendschutz.net work on finding and collecting Internet content that is harmful to minors. At the national level, the then-called BPjM[22] gained competence for banning not just printed and recorded media, but also digital media such as computer games and Internet content by placing these on an index.

Another legal problem was the question as to whether ISPs were liable for the content to which they provide access. While the European Union clarified in its E-Commerce Directive (2000) that ISPs were not liable for the content they enable access to, as long as they are not aware of the illegal or harmful nature of the content, several German courts had questioned this principle.[23] The *Telemediengesetz* (TMG, Telecommunication Media Law) of 2007 finally solved this problem of legal uncertainty in favor of the ISPs. Until then, attempts to make ISPs liable failed, but they raised ISPs awareness to find their own solutions to prevent stricter judiciary enforcement and legislation in the future.

As a consequence, self-regulation became an attractive solution to prevent legislation and to ensure against infringing on existing content regulation.

Internet interest groups, civil society, and political parties

Germany is a state with a traditionally high grade of organized interests under a corporatist system (Lijphart, 2012). Political parties generally negotiate with industry representatives, trade unions, and/or civil society actors before proposing legislation. The Internet industry, at a very early stage, founded associations to represent and lobby for its interests. Unlike other German industry sectors, Internet industry associations tended, because of their relatively late establishment in the early 1990s, to be more pluralistic structures with high degrees of competition and lacking hierarchical structure (Lang, 2006). Nevertheless the industry's biggest interest groups, BITKOM and eco, established a system of self-regulation in anticipation of governmental attempts to regulate the sector under probably worse conditions for providers, and managed to integrate their solutions in later governmental attempts at Internet regulation. The early and relatively good grade of organization could thus be seen as an advantage of the IT industry over the political sector where interest and competence for regulating Internet issues was late to develop.

In 1997, the major ISPs and Internet industry syndicates founded their own regulatory agency: the *Freiwillige Selbstkontrolle Multimedia-Dienstanbieter* (FSM, Voluntary Self-Regulation of Multimedia Service Providers). Through the legislations of 2002 and 2003, the FSM was legally accepted as an adequate tool for Internet content regulation. In 2005, the major search engines (Google Germany, Lycos Europe, MSN Germany, AOL Germany, Yahoo!, and T-Online) joined the FSM and started officially filtering their search results (Deibert et al., 2008). The filtering targeted content according to the German laws of youth protection and criminal legislation, such as pornography, hate speech, violence, and images of child abuse. In practice, filtering meant that search engines would change their results, making it impossible to find such sites using the service, without however blocking the content, but simply making it inaccessible to users.

Similarly, well organized structures and public interest groups developed from within civil society. Rapidly, groups emerged and organized against the introduction of Internet censorship in Germany. Some of them already had been formed as part of the peace movement in the early 1980s, such as the *Forum InformatikerInnen für Frieden und gesellschaftliche Verantwortung* (FIfF, Forum of Computer Scientists for Peace and Societal Accountability), or as part of the privacy debate in the context of the national census of 1987,[24] such as the *Verein zur Förderung des öffentlichen bewegten und unbewegten Datenverkehrs* (Föbud, Association for Promoting Public Moved and Unmoved Data Traffic).[25] Others, such as the Chaos Computer Club (CCC), were born as the organizational unit of the European hacker scene in the early 1980s. Over time, new groups emerged, such as the *Förderverein Informationstechnik und Gesellschaft* (FITUG, Association Information Technology and Society) and the *Online-Demonstations-Plattform für Menschen- und Bürgerrechte im digitalen Zeitalter* (ODEM, Online Demonstration Platform for Human and Civil Rights in the Digital Age), which were founded in reaction to the first governmental blocking attempts through courts in the mid-1990s and early 2000s. The most recent groups emerged during protests against the implementation of the data retention directive (e.g., the *Arbeitskreis gegen Vorratsdatenspeicherung*, AK Vorrat, working group against data retention) and in opposition against the Access Impediment Act of 2009 (e.g., the *Arbeitskreis gegen Internet-Sperren und Zensur*, AK Zensur, Working Group Against Internet-Blocking and Censorship). These various networks represented a platform for creating public awareness of the Internet blocking issue and of mobilizing protest against governmental attempts to hinder online access to information. It was impressively shown at that time to be the biggest online petition against the access impediment act (see the next section, The Access Impediment Act).

While in Germany, private and public interest groups focused very early on Internet issues in general and Internet blocking in particular, political parties did not engage in these topics for some time. When they did, they were unable to find clear and consistent positions within their own parties and in response to political opponents. The unclear competences between the national and federal state levels made it difficult to establish a coherent Internet regulation program. When, in 2002, the social democrat district governor of the German Federal State of Nordrhein-Westfalen, Jörgen Büssow, implemented blocking measures (*Sperrverfügung*) for local ISPs, he found himself criticized by his own party's new-media representative on the national level, Jörg Tauss, while gaining support of the Bavarian Christian-Democrat's speaker for media issues, Martin Mayer (Rötzer, 2002). The party lines on Internet blocking were still unclear when the German federal government proposed a nationwide blocking system in 2009.

The Access Impediment Act

In early 2009, a federal election year, the Ministry of Family Affairs, which was chaired by the Christian-Democrat Minister Ursula von der Leyen, initiated an agreement with all German ISPs to "voluntarily" block child abuse–related material. The five major ISPs signed the agreement, but the debate heated up as ISPs, the social-democrat coalition partners, and civil society voices criticized the measure for lacking a coherent legal framework and posing serious civil liberties issues. Therefore, the government proposed the *Zugangserschwerungsgesetz* (ZugErschwG, Access Impediment Act), a law establishing a DNS-tampering Internet blocking system to block access to images of child abuse, a procedure which was supported by the German criminal police and child protection groups. The law was adopted in June 2009, two months before the federal election, with the support by the then-coalition partner, the social democrats.

However, the law was never implemented. The Internet industry opposed the law, which would broadly intervene in its business interests of a liberal market of information such as the

Internet.[26] Also, broad public protests emerged against the government's bill carried by well-organized groups of citizen's rights activists and the Internet community (Meister, 2011). The early coordination and previous engagement in Internet policy issues, particularly through the established media channels (Löblich & Wendelin, 2012), provided the grounds for the development of new civil society organizations (e.g., AK Zensur) and the rise of the German section of the Pirate Party leading to a broad mobilization of the public against the governmental blocking legislation. The mobilization crystallized as the largest online petition in Germany's parliamentary history, with more than 130,000 signatories. The federal elections of September 2009 led to the formation of a coalition between Christian-Democrats and the Liberal Party, the latter of which opposed the Internet blocking measures. The bill was never implemented, and eventually was revoked in December 2011.

"Regulated self-regulation"

After the failure of creating a state-mandated Internet blocking system through the Access Impediment Act, the regulation of online content in Germany remains based on the approach of "regulated self-regulation" by the Internet industry in close cooperation with state regulatory agencies such as the BPjM and jugendschutz.net. A report, which was ordered by the German government in 2002 about the efficiency of this form of regulatory regime, came to the conclusion that "regulated self-regulation" could be an attractive alternative to top-down governance in cases where "fast changes and complex structures of the regulatory field" could be found and "governmental agencies of surveillance" were confronted with "the problem of gaining information" or "juridical limitations of state action" (Schulz & Held, 2002, p. D-2). With the Internet being a fast-growing and decentralized media, and the state holding limited influence on the media sector, all these conditions applied to the case of online content regulation.

Furthermore, it was also considered as very important that similar interests and a "culture of cooperation" could be found in the industry sectors concerned (Schulz & Held, 2002, p. D-3). At the time it was set up, in 2002, the Internet industry had more to offer than just a "culture of cooperation," as it had established an already working self-regulatory agency, the FSM. Existing governmental structures of youth protection such as the BPjS and new agencies, which were created in the aftermath of the battle for competency between the national and federal state level, such as jugendschutz.net, were coordinated and created the framework of the government-supported "regulated self-regulation" of Germany's Internet industry.

As McIntyre (2012) mentions, self-regulation offers benefits to both the government by "outsourcing enforcement and minimizing the accompanying costs" and to the Internet industry by "the promise of flexible and light touch regulatory regime" (pp. 2–3). However, Brown (2010) stresses the disadvantages of such systems through the "lack [of] procedural fairness and protection for fundamental rights that are encouraged by independent judicial and parliamentary scrutiny" (p. 98). The German solution can thus provide a "third way," as it combines the advantages of self-regulatory regimes with the legitimacy provided by oversight through and cooperation with public bodies (see also Marsden, 2011). The particular circumstances and structures posed by the institutional framework and the actor's constellations led to the establishment in Germany of the "regulated self-regulation" model, providing a practicable method for dealing with the problem of Internet content regulation. The existing system made it difficult, then, to introduce other types of solutions, such as state-mandated blocking.

DISCUSSION

This article reviewed Internet content regulation in France and Germany, in particular through technical filtering mechanisms. In adopting technology-aware, actor-centered institutionalism (Bendrath & Mueller, 2011; Mayntz & Scharpf, 1995), both case studies focus on the networks of actors and interests in two particular policy settings that led to regulatory innovation in the domain of Internet content regulation.

The Internet has posed new challenges to the enforcement of content regulation. In France and Germany, it is generally accepted that democracy is best served when the state restricts particular types of content, such as speech contesting the rule of law and constitutional values, and protects the most vulnerable sections of the population such as children and minorities. Restrictions on content are thus not new and are generally considered legitimate state interventions. It is the enforcement of existing content regulation that constitutes a new challenge on the decentralized and global Internet. The issues posed by digital content are similar in both countries, in particular in regard to child pornography, copyright, or gambling legislation that we examined in this article.

If content disputes were resolved by the courts in both countries in the mid-1990s and early 2000s, France has more recently chosen a legislative path for dealing with problematic content, while in Germany a system of "regulated self-regulation" has emerged, in which private actors are invited to "self-regulate" to enforce legal requirements with limited public oversight. As exemplified by our case studies, the divergence in regulatory paths can be principally explained by the institutional settings of both countries and the actor constellations surrounding legislative efforts to introduce Internet blocking mechanisms.

First, the role of the judiciary needs to be highlighted for interpreting existing content regulations with regard to the digital realms and limiting legislators in their efforts to introduce specific Internet regulatory mechanism. Contrary to U.S. courts,[27] German and French judges have never considered freedom of speech to be protected from state intervention in near to all cases. On the contrary, they applied standard criminal law against the U.S. corporations CompuServe in Germany and Yahoo! in France. Because both corporations held assets in the European countries, they could be complied to delete pornographic material in the first case and Nazi memorabilia in the second. As blocking technology was not very sophisticated at the time, the content had to be removed worldwide,

leading, especially in the U.S., to outcries of censorship (Goldsmith & Wu, 2006). Also, the French constitutional court has played an important role in balancing blocking restrictions against economic and civil rights interests.

Second, differences in the institutional systems of both countries provided two different arenas for interaction between political actors aiming to introduce or resist online content regulations. France being a majoritarian type of democracy with a strong unitary state and a reinforced presidential regime since the shortening of the presidential term in 2000, the predominant role played by the government led by president Sarkozy from 2007 to 2012 is not surprising. The government has displayed an early interest in regulating information networks and has generally done so by setting up administrative authorities who would also be in charge of regulating controversial content. The government's central control of the Minitel in the 1980s was challenged by the introduction and adoption of the Internet at the end of the 1990s in France. Although the industry adopted self-regulatory mechanisms, the government kept a close eye on online content through court enforcement and, more recently, by adopting specific legislation. France has adopted three laws that introduce Internet access blocking measures of child pornographic content, illegal online gambling Web sites, and of users who have repeatedly infringed copyright online, although the new socialist government has not yet implemented the extrajudicial blocking mechanism contained in the LOPPSI 2 bill.

In Germany, the desire to restrict particular types of content was similar. However, the federal system posed legislative challenges that the French centralized system did not encounter. While the federal states (*Länder*) and the national level took several years to clarify who was responsible for what type of online content, the Internet sector was able to adopt its own content regulations and convince legislators to minimize direct oversight. Although the Internet industry is more pluralistic than other sectors in the German corporatist system, it organized rapidly to defend its interests, and not only were those interests integrated into policy discussions at an early stage, but the Internet industry created its own instruments of regulation, which were later integrated into legal and administrative solutions of the state.

Third, the actors involved diverged in both countries, which led to different political debates. Breaking with presidential traditions, president Sarkozy's term focused on security frames and demonstrating political will in all realms of society, in order to reinforce the state and state control as part of an all-encompassing security and public order strategy. The government's proximity with the entertainment industry and its obvious desire to block certain types of content could not be countered by other types of actors, such as ISPs or civil society actors who were simply not consulted or listened to on many of these issues (for the case of HADOPI, see for instance Breindl & Briatte, 2013; for LOPPSI 2 see Breindl, 2012). The courts proved to be the only veto player strong enough to defend fundamental values, such as the presumption of innocence, due process, and freedom of expression, as indicated by the Constitutional Court rulings on HADOPI 1 and LOPPSI 2.

In Germany, the position of the Internet industry and civil society was stronger. Aiming to prevent mandatory content regulation, ISPs and content providers established a system of "regulated self-regulation," which mandates that particular types of content should be removed without statutory regulation but with the approval of both the national and federal-state level. All actors had come to a consensus that this system was the best solution to dealing with problematic content. The awkward attempt to introduce a mandatory Internet blocking bill targeting child abuse images in 2009 failed notably because of resistance from the Internet industry and the opposition of a very vocal and well organized civil society. Interestingly, the German debate forced all political parties to take a position on Internet blocking and defend their opposition at the European level, who aimed at introducing a European-wide mandatory blocking scheme in 2010. National debates influenced broader regulatory arrangements at the international level (McNamee, 2011).

CONCLUSIONS

There are many concerns with technical content regulation (Brown, 2010; Mueller, 2010). Because technologies implement automatic and self-enforcing content restrictions (McIntyre & Scott, 2008) that do not leave space for judiciary discretion, they pose a number of constitutional questions, in particular the protection of freedom of expression and privacy as well as the rule of law and due process. At present, there is a "crisis of legitimacy" (Marsden, 2011) regarding these mechanisms, an issue that can only be resolved by introducing and strengthening democratic safeguards (Bambauer, 2009).

State legislation is generally considered as the most accountable and transparent form of regulation because, in liberal democracies, it necessarily requires a democratic process. However, regulation can be captured by special interests and fail to effectively regulate a fast-changing, global, and complex technology such as the Internet. Furthermore, state legislation is likely to disrupt the global flow of information the Internet facilitated in the first place (Mueller, 2010). Self-regulation effectively outsources the states' regulation of constitutionally protected fundamental rights to private actors with little accountability mechanisms.

A third way is emerging, associating public and private actors as in the case of the German "regulated self-regulation" or other forms of co-regulatory mechanisms in place in a number of European countries (Marsden, 2011). However, even in systems where private actors' self-regulation is subject to public oversight, as is the case in Germany, accountability mechanisms are generally lacking, and users are rarely informed about the extent of content restrictions that are applied to their connections. The situation is particularly alarming in light of the rapid technological development and convergence, leading to new shared interests in the use of deep packet inspection and other privacy-invasive technologies to monitor and control Internet traffic. One of the challenges for researchers and policy-makers in particular is how to measure traffic restrictions and hold accountable those who perform them. More research and data are necessary to confront policy-makers and trigger public dialogue about content restrictions in the digital age.

NOTES

1. In July 2010, Finland, for instance, made broadband Internet access a legal right for all of its citizens ("Finland makes broadband a 'legal right,'" 2010).

2. See, for instance, the November 2011 ECJ decision *Scarlet v. Sabam*, which overturned the injunction by a Belgian court to ISP Scarlet to monitor its users and filter illegal peer-to-peer file-sharing activities.

3. See *Loi n° 49–956 du 16 juillet 1949 sur les publications destinées à la jeunesse*, article 2, modified by *Loi n° 2010-769 du 9 juillet 2010*, article 27.

4. The *loi Toubon* mandates the use of the French language in a broad array of public communications, while the "*exception culturelle française*" is the basis for large funding of the cultural sector in France.

5. In the 2000 ruling *LICRA v. Yahoo! Inc.*, the *Tribunal de Grande Instance* of Paris exercised territorial jurisdiction on the grounds that the prejudice of the content hosted abroad took place on French territory. The Court required Yahoo! to prevent French users from accessing Nazi memorabilia on its auction Web site. The company complied with the judgment, even though a U.S. District Court judge considered in 2001 that Yahoo! could not be forced to comply with French laws that were contrary to the First Amendment. The ruling was reversed in 2006 by a U.S. Court of Appeals (Goldsmith & Wu, 2006).

6. A 2008 ruling by a Parisian tribunal has condemned French Web sites for linking to another Web site containing defamatory material (EDRi, 2008).

7. AFA Website, *Association des Fournisseurs d'Accès et de Services Internet*: http://www.afa-france.com/.

8. A special Internet crime police unit coordinates the Internet-signalement.gouv.fr Web site.

9. Translation by the author. Original text last accessed from http://www.legifrance.gouv.fr/affichTexte.do?cidTexte=JORFTEXT000000402408&dateTexte=&categorieLien=id.

10. In fact, French *droit d'auteur* developed independently from UK copyright law in the 18th century, focusing on the "right of the author" instead of the "right to copy." While copyright traditionally grants proprietary rights, the *droit d'auteur* also grants a moral and inalienable right to the author for his work. For more information, see for instance Horten (2011).

11. DADVSI stands for *loi relative au droit d'auteur et aux droits voisins dans la société de l'information* (2006-961). In English, "Law on authors' rights and related rights in the information society."

12. HADOPI stands for *Haute Autorité pour la diffusion des oeuvres et la protection des droits sur Internet*, "the high authority for the dissemination of creation and the protection of rights on the Internet in charge of monitoring and prosecuting online copyright infringement." The bill is also known as the "Creation and Internet" bill "for the diffusion and protection of creation on the Internet" (2009-669).

13. The French position on online copyright enforcement became particularly clear when its minister of foreign affairs announced in August 2011 that France would not sign the UN Report on Freedom of Expression (La Rue, 2011), which was signed by 41 countries including many Western states, as long as there would be no "consensus on the fact that freedom of expression and communication is not superior to other rights, in particular intellectual property rights" (Champeau, 2011).

14. Graduated response is a mechanism involving generalized monitoring of Internet traffic to detect unauthorized file-sharing of copyrighted material followed by a series of notifications to alleged copyright infringers. The punishment varies from suspension or termination of service to the reduction of bandwidth (or "throttling") or the blocking of particular sites or portals (Yu, 2010).

15. Constitutional Council ruling from June 10, 2009, on HADOPI 1 (art. 12): "Taking into account the terms of article 11 of the Declaration of the rights of man and citizens of 1789: 'The free communication of ideas and opinions is one of the most precious of the rights of man. Every citizen may, accordingly, speak, write, print freely, except that he must answer for abuse of this freedom as determined by law'; and that nowadays, in light of the development of communication means and the generalized development auf online public communication services as well as the importance of these services for participation in democratic life and the expression of ideas and opinions, such right implies the online public's freedom to access these communication services" (Translation by the author. Original text available at: http://www.conseil-constitutionnel.fr/conseil-constitutionnel/francais/les-decisions/2009/decisions-par-date/2009/2009-580-dc/decision-n-2009-580-dc-du-10-juin-2009.42666.html).

16. *Loi 2010-476 du 12 May 2010 relative à l'ouverture à la concurrence et à la régulation du secteur des jeux d'argent et de hasard en ligne*, in English "law on the opening to competition and regulation of the gambling sector."

17. The introduction of blocking measures of unlicensed gambling Web sites can thus be interpreted as a way of controlling the market and securing tax revenue to the French state.

18. *Loi (2011-267) d'orientation et de programmation pour la performance de la sécurité intérieure*. The bill updates the 2002 LOPSI bill.

19. Conseil Constitutionnel. Loi d'orientation et de programmation pour la performance de la sécurité intérieure [loppsi 2]: Décision numéro 2011-625. Retrieved February 19, 2012, from: http://www. conseil-constitutionnel.fr/conseil-constitutionnel/ francais/actualites/2011/seance-du-10-mars-2011-[loppsi-2].94818.html.

20. BPjM, last accessed from: http://www. bundespruefstelle.de/bpjm/Die-Bundespruefstelle/ geschichte.html

21. Because the company did not have the technical means to block the newsgroups only in Germany, these were removed worldwide. The court issued a warrant on CompuServe's Munich office, which led the company to block access to the groups. In 1998, after CompuServe had reopened the newsgroups, its general manager was convicted for introducing child pornography to Germany. He was later on acquitted on appeal.

22. BPjS changed its name to BPjM replacing Schriften (Writings) by Medien (Media).

23. E.g., while the Federal district government in Duesseldorf ordered ISPs to block Nazi propaganda sites, the administrative courts of Muenster and Duesseldorf affirmed the blocking orders under the suggestion of the ISP's liability for the content it transmitted. See http:// heise.de/-122463, last accessed 19 February 2013.

24. From 1983 to 1987, the German government's plans to carry out a full population census by registering personal information of all German citizens caused an important wave of protest, which led to the first declaration of a right of informational self-determination by the German Constitutional Court.

25. Föbud's "Big Brother Award," held each year, is given to companies with the worst privacy and data protection measures.

26. See BITKOM Stellungnahme (http://www. bitkom.org/files/documents/090205_BITKOM-Stellungn ahme_Expertengespraech_UA_neue_Medien_12_2_2009. pdf).

27. See, for instance, the U.S. Supreme Courts' *Reno v. Amercian Civil Liberties Union* (1997), which stroke down as unconstitutional the anti-indecency provisions of the Communications Decency Act (1996).

REFERENCES

Akdeniz, Y. (2010). To block or not to block: European approaches to content regulation, and implications for freedom of expression. *Computer Law & Security Review, 26*, 260–272.

Axelrod, R. (1979). *Structure of decision. The cognitive maps of political elites.* Princeton, NJ: Princeton University Press.

Bambauer, D. E. (2009). Guiding the censor's scissors: A framework to assess Internet filtering. *Brooklyn Law School. Legal Studies paper*, 149, 1–72.

Bendrath, R., & Mueller, M. (2011). The end of the Net as we know it? Deep packet inspection and Internet governance. *New Media & Society, 13*(7),1142–1160.

Breindl, Y. (2012). Assessing success in Internet campaigning: The case of digital rights advocacy in the European Union. *Information, Communication & Society.* Advance online publication. doi:10.1080/ 1369118X.2012.707673

Breindl, Y., & Briatte, F. (2013). Digital protest skills and online activism against copyright reform in France and the European Union. *Policy & Internet, 5*(1), 27–55.

Briatte, F. (2008, February). *Parliamentary controversy expansion over digital rights management in France.* Paper presented at the ECPR Joint Sessions, Rennes, France.

Brown, I. (2010). Internet self-regulation and fundamental rights. *Index on Censorship, 1*, 98–106.

Brown, I., & Marsden, C. (2013). *Regulating code: Good governance and better regulation in the Information Age.* Cambridge, MA: MIT Press.

Champeau, G. (2011, August 18). La France prétend défendre les libertés sur Internet, mais . . . [France pretends to defend freedoms on the Internet, but . . .]. *Numerama.* Retrieved from http://www.numerama. com/magazine/19589-la-france-pretend-defendre-les-libertes-sur-Internet-mais.html

Dahl, R. A. (1971). *Polyarchy: Participation and opposition.* New Haven, CT: Yale University Press.

DeBeer, J. F., & Clemmer, C. D. (2009). Global trends in online copyright enforcement: A non-neutral role for network intermediaries. *Jurmetrics, 49*(4), 375–409.

Deibert, R. J., & Crete-Nishihata, M. (2012). Global governance and the spread of cyberspace controls. *Global Governance, 18*(3), 339–361.

Deibert, R. J., Palfrey, J. G., Rohozinski, R., & Zittrain, J. (2008). *Access denied: The practice and policy of global Internet filtering.* Cambridge, MA: MIT Press.

Deibert, R. J., Palfrey, J. G., Rohozinski, R., & Zittrain, J. (2010). *Access controlled: The shaping of power, rights, and rule in cyberspace.* Cambridge, MA: MIT Press.

Deibert, R. J., Palfrey, J. G., Rohozinski, R., & Zittrain, J. (2011). *Access contested: Security, identity, and resistance in Asian cyberspace.* Cambridge, MA: MIT Press.

DeNardis, L. (2012). Hidden levers of Internet control. *Information, Communication & Society, 15*(5), 720–738.

Dix-huit lois sur la sécurité depuis 2001. (2009, February 5). *Le Monde.* Retrieved from http://www.lemonde.fr/ societe/article/2009/02/04/dix-huit-lois-sur-la-securite-depuis-2001_1150563_3224.html#ens_id=1150640

EDRi. (2008, April 9). *France: Linking can be damaging to your pockets.* Retrieved from http://www.edri. org/edrigram/number6.7/linking-decison-france

European Commission. (2012). *Towards a comprehensive framework for online gambling.* Retrieved from http:// ec.europa.eu/internal_market/services/docs/gambling/ comm_121023_onlinegambling_en.pdf

Exception culturelle: La mission Lescure fera ses propositions en mars 2013 [Cultural exception: The Lescure mission will make its propositions in March 2013]. (2012, July 18). *Le Monde.* Retrieved from http://www.lemonde.fr/politique/article/2012/07/18/exception-culturelle-la-mission-lescure-fera-ses-propositions-en-mars-2013_1735295_823448.html

Finland makes broadband a "legal right." (2010, July 1). *BBC.* Retrieved from http://www.bbc.co.uk/news/10461048

Freedom House. (2012). *Freedom on the Net 2012. A global assessment of Internet and digital media* [Technical Report]. Retrieved from http://www.freedomhouse.org/report/freedom-net/freedom-net-2012

Froomkin, M. (2011). *Lessons learned too well: The evolution of Internet regulation* [Technical report]. CDT Fellows Focus series. Retrieved from https://www.cdt.org/blogs/lessons-learned-too-well-evolution-internet-regulation

Goldsmith, J. L. (1997/1998). The Internet and the abiding significance of territorial souvereignty. *Indiana Journal of Global Legal Studies, 5,* 475–491.

Goldsmith, J. L., & Wu, T. (2006). *Who controls the Internet? Illusions of a borderless world.* Oxford, England: Oxford University Press.

Hans-Bredow-Institut. (2007). *Analyse des Jugendmedienschutzsystems Jugendschutzgesetz und Jugendmedienschutz-Staatsvertrag* [Analysis of the youth media protection system, the youth protection law and the youth media protection state contract]. Retrieved from http://www.hans-bredow-institut.de/webfm_send/104

Horten, M. (2011). *The copyright enforcement enigma: Internet politics and the telecoms package.* Basingstoke, England: Palgrave Macmillan.

Hutchison, S., & Minton, S. (n.d.). ".fr." Cambridge, MA: Berkman Center for Internet and Society, Harvard Law School. Retrieved from http://cyber.law.harvard.edu/itg/libpubs/France.pdf

Johnston, D. R., & Post, D. (1996). Law and borders—the rise of law in cyberspace. *Stanford Law Review, 48,* 1367–1402.

Kossel, A., & Möcke, F. (1996). Pornowächter versus Internet: Proteste gegen bayerische Datensperre [Pornowatchers versus Internet: Protests against Bavarian datablocking]. *C't* 2/96, 14. Retrieved from http://www.heise.de/ct/artikel/Pornowaechter-versus-Internet-284398.html

La fin de L'Hadopi reportée à mars 2013 [The end of Hadopi is delayed until March 2013]. (2012, July 19). *Le Nouvel Observateur.* Retrieved from http://obsession.nouvelobs.com/high-tech/20120718.OBS7565/la-fin-de-l-Hadopi-reportee-a-mars-2013.html

La Rue, F. (2011). *Report of the special rapporteur on the promotion and protection of the right to freedom of opinion and expression.* Technical Report A/HRC/17/27, Human Rights Council Seventeenth session Agenda item 3. Retrieved from http://www.ohchr.org/EN/Issues/FreedomOpinion/Pages/Annual.aspx

Lang, A. (2006). *Die Evolution sektoraler Wirtschaftsverbände: Informations- und Kommunikationsverbände in Deutschland, Großbritannien und Spanien* [The evolution of sectoral industry associations: Information and communication associations in Germany, Great Britain and Spain]. Ph.D. dissertation, University of Konstanz. Forschung Politik. VS Verl. für Sozialwissenschaften, Wiesbaden, Germany.

Lapousterle, J. (2009). *L'influences des groupes de pression sur l'élaboration des normes: Illustration à partir du droit de la propriété littéraire et artistique* [The influence of pressure groups on the development of norms: Illustration on the case of literary and artistic property]. Paris: Nouvelle Bibliothèque de Thèses, Dalloz.

Lausson, J. (2012, July 25). Loppsi: Le décret sur le blocage des sites sans juge est abandonné [Loppsi: Decree for blocking sites without court order is not implemented]. *Numerama.* Retrieved from http://www.numerama.com/magazine/23260-loppsi-le-decret-sur-le-blocage-des-sites-sans-juge-est-abandonne.html

Le budget de la Hadopi passe à 8 millions d'euros [The budget of Hadopi reaches 8 million euros]. (2012, October 3). *Le Monde.* Retrieved from http://www.lemonde.fr/technologies/article/2012/10/03/le-budget-de-la-Hadopi-reduit-a-8-millions-d-euros_1769154_651865.html?xtmc=Hadopi&xtcr=1

Lessig, L. (2006). *Code: And other laws of cyberspace, version 2.0.* New York: Basic Books.

Lijphart, A. (2012). *Patterns of democracy: Government forms and performance in thirty-six countries* (2nd ed.). New Haven, CT: Yale University Press.

Löblich, M., & Wendelin, M. (2012). ICT policy activism on a national level: Ideas, resources and strategies of German civil society in governance processes. *New Media & Society, 14*(3), 899–915.

Mailland, J. (2010). Freedom of speech, the Internet, and the costs of control: The French example. *New York University Journal of International Law & Politics, 33,* 1179–1234.

Margetts, H. (2009). The Internet and public policy. *Policy & Internet, 1*(1), 1–21.

Marsden, C. T. (2011). *Internet co-regulation: European law, regulatory governance and legitimacy in cyberspace.* Cambridge, England: Cambridge University Press.

Mayntz, R., & Scharpf, F. W. (1995). Der Ansatz des akteurzentrierten Institutionalismus [The actor-centred institutionalism approach]. In R. Mayntz & F. W. Scharpf (Eds.), *Gesellschaftliche Selbstregelung und politische Steuerung* [Societal self-regulation and political steering] (pp. 39–72). Frankfurt am Main, Germany: Campus Verlag.

McIntyre, T. (2012). Child abuse images and clean-feeds: Assessing Internet blocking systems. In I. Brown (Ed.), *Research handbook on governance of the Internet* (pp. 277–308). Cheltenham, England: Edward Elgar.

McIntyre, T. J., & Scott, C. (2008). Internet filtering: Rhetoric, legitimacy, accountability and responsibility. In R. Brownsword & K. Yeung (Eds.), *Regulating technologies: Legal futures, regulatory frames and technological fixes* (pp. 109–124). Oxford, England: Hart Publishing.

McNamee, J. (2011, July 13). ENDitorial: Why it was good to propose Web blocking for child abuse images. *EDRi*. Retrieved from http://www.edri.org/edrigram/number9.14/blocking-debate-good

Meister, A. (2011). *Zugangserschwerungsgesetz: Eine Policy-Analyse zum Access-Blocking in Deutschland* [The Access Impediment Act: A policy analysis on access-blocking in Germany]. Master of Arts Thesis, Humboldt Universität zu Berlin, Berlin, Germany.

Mueller, M. L. (2010). *Networks and states: The global politics of Internet governance*. Cambridge, MA: MIT Press.

Murdoch, S. J., & Anderson, R. (2008). Tools and technology of Internet filtering. In R. J. Deibert, J. G. Palfrey, R. Rohozinski, & J. Zittrain (Eds.), *Access denied: The practice and policy of global Internet filtering* (pp. 29–56). Cambridge, MA: MIT Press.

Murray, A. D. (2007). *The regulation of cyberspace: Control in the online environment*. Oxford, England: Routledge Cavendish.

Olivennes, D. (2007, November). *Le développement et la protection des oeuvres culturelles sur les nouveaux réseaux* [The development and protection of cultural works on new networks]. Report to the Minister of Culture and Communication. Retrieved from http://www.culture.gouv.fr/culture/actualites/conferen/albanel/rapportolivennes231107.pdf

Pfanner, E. (2010, July 27). Europe unleashes online gambling to fill coffers. *New York Times*. Retrieved from https://www.nytimes.com/2010/07/28/technology/28eurogamble.html?r=0

Pourquoi nous ne participerons pas à la mission lescure [Why we will not participate in the Lescure mission].

(2012, September 25). *La Quadrature du Net*. Retrieved from http://www.laquadrature.net/fr/pourquoi-nous-ne-participerons-pas-a-la-mission-lescure

Rees, M. (2010, August 7). ARJEL: les FAI français astreints à filtrer un site par tous moyens [ARJEL: French ISPs obliged to filter sites by all means]. *PCINpact*. Retrieved from http://www.pcinpact.com/news/58678-arjel-blocage-filtrage-fai-jeux.htm

Reporters Without Borders. (2012). *Internet enemies report 2012*. Retrieved from http://en.rsf.org/IMG/pdf/rapport-internet2012_ang.pdf Rötzer, F. (2002, June 15). *Büssow und die CSU*. Retrieved from http://www.heise.de/tp/artikel/12/12733/1.html

Saurugger, S., & Grossman, E. (2006). Les groupes d'intérêt français: Transformations des rôles et des enjeux politiques [French interest groups: Transformation of political roles and issues]. *Revue Française de Science Politique*, 56(2), 197–203.

Scharpf, F. W. (1997). *Games real actors play: Actor-centered institutionalism in policy research*. Oxford, England: Westview Press.

Schimank, U. (1991). Politische Steuerung in der Organisationsgesellschaft am Beispiel der Forschungspolitik [Political steering in the organisation society, the case of research policy]. In W. Zapf (Ed.), *Die Modernisierung moderner Gesellschaften* [The modernisation of modern societies] (pp. 505–516). Frankfurt, Germany: Campus Verlag.

Schulz, W., & Held, T. (2002). Regulierte Selbstregulierung als Form modernen Regierens [Regulated self-regulation as a form of modern government]. Im *Auftrag des Bundesbeauftragten für Angelegenheiten der Kultur und Medien*. Hamburg, Germany: Verlag Hans-Bredow-Institut.

Stadler, T. (1998). *Der Fall Somm (Compuserve)*. Retrieved from http://www.afs-rechtsanwaelte.de/urteile/artikel06-somm-compuserve1.php

Yu, P. K. (2004). The escalating copyright wars. *Hofstra Law Review, 32*, 907–951.

Yu, P. K. (2010). The graduated response. *Florida Law Review, 62*, 1373–1430.

Zeno-Zencovich, V. (2009). *Freedom of expression: A critical and comparative analysis*. Abingdon, England: Routledge-Cavendish.

Zittrain, J. (2003). Internet points of control. *Boston College Law Review, 43*(1), 1–36.

Governing Internet Expression: How Public and Private Regulation Shape Expression Governance

Ben Wagner

ABSTRACT. Governing public expression has historically constituted a key element of public policy, and in the 20th and the 21st century has remained an important tool for both state and nonstate actors. The following article will look at two specific cases of expression governance—the content regulatory regimes in the U.S. and on Facebook—in order to understand how the process of content regulation plays out in public and private contexts. This institutional distinction between public and private, and the manner in which content regulatory practices traverse it, has important implications for both outcomes and process of content regulation.

Governing the expression of citizens has historically constituted a key element of public policy and can be traced back to the birth of the first states in antiquity (Bowman & Woolf, 1994). In ancient China, control of writing played an important role in the formation of the Chinese Empire (Lewis, 1999), and during the Renaissance and the early Modern period various states developed extensive censorship regimes (Horodowich, 2008; Lambert, 1992; Lyons, 2009). In the 20th and the 21st century, the governance of expression remains an important tool of public policy for all states, including liberal democracies (Castells, 2008; Garry, 1993; Price, 1942). In historical terms, the vast majority of states have attempted to exert some form of control over the expression of their citizens (Jones, 2001).

From a historical perspective, waves of disruptive communications technology are closely linked to waves of expression control. The printing press was possibly the first technology of this kind, and brought with it a new era of civilization (Robertson, 1998, p. 20). Later inventions such as the radio (Wu, 2010, p. 74) and the television (Wu, 2010, p. 136) have all been faced with similar waves of regulation and control from both the public and the private sector. In this sense, the Internet is just the latest in a long line of disruptive media and communications technologies (Klang, 2006) for which regulatory regimes and governance structures have been developed and are continuing to develop over time (Wu, 2010).

The emergence of the Internet as a media and communications technology has been a

Ben Wagner is currently completing his Ph.D. as a researcher at European University Institute in Florence, Italy. He works on the transnational governance of Freedom of Expression, state regulation and control of the Internet and the role of Internet governance in foreign policy. His work has been published by *Telecommunications Policy, International Journal of Communications*, UNESCO and the European Parliament.

transformative and disruptive phenomenon for societies across the world (Klang, 2006). One of the main consequences is the redistribution of governance capacity over media and communications technology, with a distinct redistribution of governance capacity away from states (Knill & Lehmkuhl, 2002). The disruption of public power over communications has been further increased by the global infrastructure of the Internet. This makes it both difficult to define the applicable legal jurisdictions by which the power of sovereign states is generally bound, as well as limiting the actual coercive power of any one state over technical Internet infrastructure. As was noted by the German Minister of Justice on March 9, 2011: "With classic regulatory mechanisms—making laws, banning something, breaking up a company—you encounter boundaries of this approach far more quickly than one would believe . . . a company like Facebook can't be regulated by the German State" (Hildebrandt & Wefing, 2011, translation by the author).

This poses a particular dilemma for liberal democracies as, unlike authoritarian states, they are typically constrained from exerting direct control over the content of media and communications technologies (Tambini, Leonardi, & Marsden, 2008, p. 284); this limits the tools liberal democracies have at their disposal to govern the Internet (Hood & Margetts, 2007). This is not to suggest that liberal democracies are powerless to govern the Internet—far from it (Drezner, 2004). However their capacity to govern the Internet is substantially lower than for previous media and communications technologies such as the telephone, the radio, or the television (Wu, 2010), and the nature of their regulatory practices is equally distinct. Notably, the U.S. government has also chosen to respond to this challenge in its foreign policy by promoting the First Amendment as a global speech norm (Wagner, 2012). However, cases such as the U.S. public sector's response to the organization Wikileaks (Daly, 2012) suggest that despite these attempts to globalize the First Amendment, tensions remain between the U.S. approach to free expression within its own borders, despite its very public support of the principle (Morozov, 2011).

Furthermore the Internet has led to an enormous expansion of expression, thereby disrupting and calling into question the established boundaries defining permissible communication (Hamilton, 2005). The "vibrant culture of freedom of expression . . . on the Internet" (Balkin, 2008, p. 108) as disseminated through the global architecture of the Internet collides with cultures of free expression, which typically develop in national contexts (Mueller, 2010; Zeno-Zencovich, 2008). However the Internet also provides a space for "activities" that most states and their citizens would typically deem worthy of regulation. Such activities range from pervasive objectification and Internet misogyny (Nussbaum, 2011), a systemic cybersecurity risk (Sommer & Brown, 2011), or the perceived role of Internet "technology-inducing perversity" (Chun, 2006, p. 97)—a common techno-deterministic narrative that sees technology as responsible for negatively affecting social norms and public morality, all of which directly relate to questions of expression on the Internet.

This article will explore two crucial cases that can both assist in providing a better understanding of the challenges in this area. It will attempt to understand how the boundaries of Internet expression were defined in the U.S. regulatory context during the past two decades, since the emergence of the public Internet, and how these boundaries have been defined in more recent years by the online service provider (OSP) Facebook. Here it is important to look at public and private actors, as both play a role in governing Internet expression while employing distinct strategies of content regulation and control. The U.S. is a crucial case, because it was the first mover in regard to the regulation of Internet expression; the first country in the world faced with the "regulatory challenge" of having 10% of its populace online, it continues to have the strongest global Internet economy. Facebook has become an equally crucial case in recent years by attaining a de-facto monopoly in online social networking in most parts of the world (Kiss, 2012; York, 2010). As a space in which Internet users spend a considerable amount of their time and share vast amounts of content, it is a crucial hub of social interaction and content creation, both of which are highly important dimensions of human expression online.

Importantly, although the private regulatory model is linked to the public U.S. regulatory model and its context, it is distinct from it. Moreover, the effect of the U.S. regulatory context is not uniform. Rather it has produced many distinct private regulatory regimes such as those created by Twitter and Google, to name but two. Also, the effects of the U.S. regulatory context are not limited to United States corporations, but apply far beyond it, even if not always in equal measure. The U.S. Internet market remains too big to ignore, as a result of which products are typically tailored to suit the speech norms of this market and have been tailored in this manner for almost two decades. As such, the U.S. remains a key norm setter for private regulatory speech regimes globally and is clearly a crucial case.

While not all conclusions about these two crucial cases can be generalized, the existing academic literature suggests that the U.S. regulatory environment and Facebook's private regulation constitute two key regulations of Internet expression (MacKinnon, 2012; Pariser, 2011; Wu, 2010; York, 2010). The method used in this article is explorative and attempts to provide an accurate, but by no means exhaustive, overview of the boundary-drawing processes in both cases. It will specifically focus on the role of power as constitutive in defining the boundaries of Internet expression and the gatekeepers that exercise forms of boundary creation (Barzilai-Nahon, 2008; Birnhack & Niva Elkin-Koren, 2003). The analysis of the cases will explore the types of governance employed, the dynamics of expression boundary creation, and the key discursive frames and scripts that are present, as well as specific types of regulatory and governance practices used to implement these boundaries.

PUBLIC SECTOR REGULATION: EXPRESSION GOVERNANCE IN THE U.S.

Information and communications technologies have a long history of content regulation in the United States. While the print medium was typically protected by stronger free speech protections, broadcasting of radio and television programs was subject to a more stringent regulatory regime (Hazlett, 1990). In the U.S. the regulation of broadcasting and telecommunications is mostly organized at the federal level, with the exception of cable television, which is typically regulated by states (Hoffmann-Riem, 1996, p. 18). The federal agency responsible for a large part of this regulation is the Federal Communications Commission (FCC). Created in 1934, the FCC has a broad "technology-agnostic" regulatory remit over radio, television, and telecommunications, which, in the 1990s, evolved to cover the Internet. Notably a similarly converged communications regulatory authority did not exist in Europe until the Office of Communications (OFCOM) was created in 2003 in the UK. By contrast, European media and communications regulators have historically been linked to a specific type of technology, regulating only television broadcasting or only telecommunications.

The FCC has historically engaged in a number of important content regulatory decisions in the U.S. media landscape. One of the most important examples is the "Fairness Doctrine," which was developed in 1949 to promote "fair" political reporting and played an important role in chilling and restricting political speech (Hazlett & Sosa, 1997). It was extensively used by both Democrat and Republican presidents to restrict reporting that was critical of their own policies. Another feature of U.S. government regulation was framework restrictions on public broadcasting, including a minimum amount of "information content" or restrictions on certain types of content such as sex and violence (Hoffmann-Riem, 1996, p. 32). It was not until a Supreme Court decision in 1976 that commercial speech was considered protected by the First Amendment, which in turn limited constitutional protections for the speech of commercial broadcasters. Following the U.S. Supreme Court decision, commercial speech increasingly came to be seen as also worthy of protection (Sunstein, 2007, p. 167).

Importantly these decisions are not only significant within U.S. borders. Indeed, writing the history of the Internet is, in many ways, similar to writing the history of an American network. While many different parts of the world were involved in the various research projects that eventually spawned the publicly available Internet, and there were a variety of communication networks linking computers to each other that have existed around the world since the 1970s, the locus of research, development, and private corporate activity that took place at the beginning of what we now have come to know as the public Internet took place in the U.S. This has led to the, perhaps slightly envious, European perception of a "special relationship between the U.S. and cyberspace" (Mayer, 2000).

Although Internet access was offered by a number of Internet service providers (ISPs) before 1992, it was not until then that restrictions on commercial uses of the Internet were removed in the U.S. (Leiner et al., 2011). What was previously a research network became available to any customer willing to pay (Sunstein, 2007, p. 158). From 1992 to 1995, the number of Internet users grew from 4,453,200 to 24,600,557, which in 1995 represented around 9% of the U.S. population. In the late 1990s, the number of Internet users expanded massively to 121,697,045 users online in 2000, 201,742,976 in 2005 and 245,203,319 in 2010.[1] See Figure 1.

The explosion of users and the size of the Internet brought with it all manner of regulatory debates. These were strongly shaped by the U.S. media, which ran a succession of stories on the dangers of the Internet for children. One such story was prominently placed in *Time* magazine in 1995. While *Time* was later forced to retract many of the claims in the story about the pervasiveness of pornography on the Internet, the discursive frame was powerfully set (Hazlett & Sosa, 1997). Nevertheless the extensive public debates that followed spurred on legislation "reflecting a desire on the part of lawmakers to avoid being labeled 'pro-smut'" (Hazlett & Sosa, 1997). As a result, the U.S. Congress passed the Communications Decency Act (CDA; passed in 1996), which served to criminalize "any communication which is obscene, lewd, lascivious, filthy, or indecent with the intent to annoy, abuse, threaten, or

harass" (Edick, 1998; 47 U.S.C. §§ 223(a)(1)). Criminal penalties were to be enforced by law enforcement, with heavy fines and imprisonment up to two years considered appropriate. Notably the Communications Decency Act created "chilling effects" on Internet communications before it was even passed. America Online (AOL) began to "clean up" its services, removing user profiles and chat rooms that went so far as to include "chat room titles devoted to breast cancer survivors" (Hazlett & Sosa, 1997). Before any legislation had been passed, AOL was already making an "effort to comply with the anticipated indecency standard" (Hazlett & Sosa, 1997). Pre-empting legal restrictions served to shield AOL from future liability, while ensuring that AOL protected its reputation as a "family ISP." Evidently the threat of legislation casts a long shadow of hierarchy, even when the respective measures do not become law.

Within minutes of the CDA passing into law, the American Civil Liberties Union (ACLU) filed a constitutional challenge against the CDA and was eventually successful; the CDA was struck down in court (Edick, 1998). While obscenity and child abuse images remained illegal, other types of content were considered to be protected by the First Amendment. However a less broad version of the CDA, with a similar discursive thrust, but focused exclusively on children in schools and libraries, the Children's Internet Protection Act (CIPA), was passed by the U.S. Congress in 1999 and was able to survive a challenge in the Supreme Court by the American Library Association in 2003 (Marwick, 2008). It was also American Librarians who were central in challenging the provisions of the USA-PATRIOT Act, which they believed would infringe on their readers' First Amendment and privacy rights (Jones, 2009). Notably, both Supreme Court decisions on the boundaries of digital speech emphasized that some, but by no means all, speech would be considered protected.

Another important result of the debates on CDA and CIPA is the close discursive linkages between child sexual abuse images, child abuse, protection of children from adult pornography, and the regulation of adult pornography in the wider interests of society. These debates fused

FIGURE 1. Internet users as percentage of the U.S. population (color figure available online).[2]

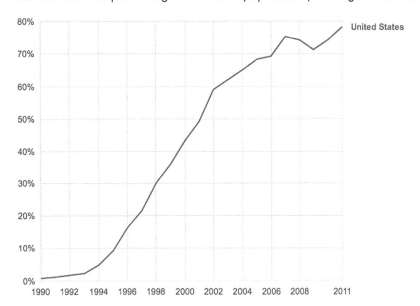

together in the context of a wider scale moral panic about the content available on the Internet (Jenkins, 2001). The seemingly endlessly constructed cyberspace provided an unlimited expanse of supposedly regulable frontiers in urgent need of re-bordering. It is therefore important to understand the relevance of debates about pornography in order to understand that wider evolution of the regulation of the Internet:

> Pornography therefore was, and still is, central to the two issues that map the uneasy boundary between public and private: regulation and commerce. The Internet's privatization paved the way for cyberporn to the extent that it made digital pornography a hypervisible threat/phenomenon and cyberporn paved the way for the "Information Superhighway" to the extent that it . . . caused media, government, and commercial companies to debate seriously and publicly the status of the Internet as a mass medium. (Chun, 2006, p. 79)

It is in this context that the National Center for Missing and Exploited Children (NCMEC) launched its CyberTipline in 1998. NCMEC is a private, not-for-profit organization that was established in 1984. It sees its mission

as providing information about missing and sexually exploited children across the U.S. Although the timing might suggest recourse to a British-style Internet Watch Foundation (IWF) institutional model, the establishment of the CyberTipline actually represents the transfer of an existing U.S. institutional model for dealing with missing children and child abuse. NCMEC had operated an offline National Child Pornography Tipline in conjunction with the United States Customs Service and the United States Postal Inspection Service since 1987. Consequently the existing institutional structure provided by the Tipline was simply used to produce an institution for the Internet.

NCMEC is also extraordinarily interesting as a "site" of knowledge production. The organization operates from the International Children's House, which is located opposite the Arlington, Virginia, courthouse. The building was financed by Computer Associates and several other private donors (Monaco, 2000). The values the organization stands for seem almost literally fused into concrete, with an extraordinarily strong mission and message present throughout the building. The walls of the lobby and entrance to the NCMEC building are covered in the badges of the many law enforcement agencies NCMEC has worked with in the past. Due to the huge number of law enforcement agencies in the U.S., there are literally thousands of badges on display. These aspects all suggest a close relationship between NCMEC and U.S. law enforcement agencies. By their own admission, their capacity to do so stems from weak U.S. privacy regulations, which allows NCMEC to take the role of assisting and providing services (Martinez, 2007, p. 94) to law enforcement investigations. However it should also be noted that NCMEC has access to internal law enforcement information and communications systems, such as the "National Crime Information Center and the National Law Enforcement Telecommunications System" (Martinez, 2007, p. 94). As a consequence, it seems perhaps unsurprising that the vast majority of the operational funding for NCMEC comes from the U.S. Department of Justice.

As an organization, NCMEC is essentially a trusted actor within law enforcement circles. Both in the U.S. and internationally, it provides information, training, and knowledge to law enforcement agencies. In this sense, NCMEC is a key actor in governmental capacity building, as it assists U.S. law enforcement in building its own capacity to deal with the Internet. The existence of an organization such as NCMEC, however, suggests that, in many situations, such experience and training are lacking, and that U.S. law enforcement and prosecutors would not necessarily have the capacity to act in the same way without NCMEC's expertise. At the same time, NCMEC serves to raise the profile of the role of child abuse–related material on the Internet, while disseminating it within a community of practitioners with the capacity to act. Equally interesting is NCMEC's extraordinary ability to react to child abuse reports, with a hotline that is manned 24 hours a day by specially trained call-center staff. These operators code incoming calls in a "triage-style process" according to the likely danger to the child involved.

Another important aspect of NCMEC's work is related to its staff of analysts, who spend their time poring over individual images of child sexual abuse to find clues as to where these children might be located. The information gathered from such analysis is then forwarded to law enforcement agents, who use the information in their inquiries. Separately, NCMEC attempts to ensure that the images themselves are removed from the public Internet, either by contacting the host provider directly, or in the case of the internationally hosted content, the respective national Internet hotlines are contacted through the EU-funded INHOPE network of Internet hotlines. When looking at the language and actual practices of NCMEC more closely, the boundary between NCMEC and law enforcement agencies blurs considerably. The organization is designed to support police who are investigating highly sensitive crimes of child sexual abuse. Content regulation pales in comparison. While the removal of child abuse material from the Internet is clearly still important to NCMEC, it is far less of a concern than rescuing children.

The institutional role of NCMEC reflects the wider debate on content regulation in the U.S. This debate mainly operates through criminalization of a relatively limited type of content, which is comparatively easy to define. The high level of legitimacy of NCMEC and its existing historical role as a child protection nongovernmental organization (NGO) means that it is also relatively resistant to "mission creep." It seems highly unlikely that NCMEC would begin regulating other kinds of content, which is often suggested as a danger of Internet hotlines (McIntyre, 2012). Indeed it seems reasonable to argue the historical pre-Internet role of NCMEC led naturally to the creation of the CyberTipline as an actor regulating Internet content.

Beyond NCMEC, there is also extensive self-regulation of content on the U.S. Internet. This form of communications governance has substantial historical precedent in the U.S. Indeed the strict First Amendment restrictions on speech regulation by the state have historically meant that private rather than public actors are engaged in greater levels of speech regulation (Pariser, 2011). As a result of the birth of the Internet in the U.S., pre-existing norms on the appropriateness of private regulation of speech were transferred to the Internet. The U.S. government has attempted to encourage this, and similar measures, by exempting intermediaries from liability under section 230 of the Communications Decency Act (CDA), insofar as they fulfill certain conditions (Balkin, 2008, p. 110).

This process of private liability and enforcement has been reinforced by the creation of the Digital Millennium Copyright Act (DMCA), which provides OSPs with considerable incentives by exempting them from liability if they follow strict notice and takedown procedures (Birnhack & Niva Elkin-Koren, 2003). These conditions typically ensure that the offending material is swiftly removed, allowing Internet intermediaries to reside in a "'safe harbor' from liability" (Zuckerman, 2010, p. 79). But they also induce the creation of private regulatory instruments within OSPs to ensure the private regulation of content. While the DMCA was specifically created to ensure the protection of copyright, there are numerous examples that suggest that takedown requests have included political speech (Lee, 2012).

Following the lead of the private sector, additional legislation was passed in 2006 to build on the model pioneered by the Internet service provider AOL, by requiring "electronic communication service providers" to notify NCMEC when a service provider "obtains actual knowledge of any facts or circumstances . . . that involves child pornography" (McIntyre, 2012, p. 11). An additional step toward propagating the AOL model and reinforcing NCMEC's central role in the self-regulatory model was taken by Congress in 2008 with the PROTECT Our Children Act. This Act "specifically authorizes NCMEC to provide hash values to ISPs for the purpose of detecting and blocking child pornography" (McIntyre, 2012, p. 11). This was seen as a way of "adding to pressures to turn Internet service providers into cops examining all Internet traffic for child pornography" (Dedman & Sullivan, 2008). An associated public campaign was also initiated by "the office of New York Attorney General Andrew M. Cuomo, who has been calling out ISPs that won't agree to block sites with illegal images, and Ernest E. Allen, the president and CEO of [NCMEC]" (Dedman & Sullivan, 2008).

U.S. expression governance is pervaded by self-regulation. The private sector takes the lead on content regulation on the Internet, at the express wish of both legislative and executive branches of government. This regulatory paradigm was challenged by the CDA, and it took a crucial Supreme Court decision in 1996 to reinstate the old regulatory settlement. Characteristic of such a model of Internet content regulation is that changes to the system are initiated by private actors who are also responsible for implementation of the regime. Another important characteristic is that public sector organizations remain at the fringes of the debate, only regulating the most extreme forms of content where there is broad public consensus that this kind of content is not only just not permissible but morally wrong (Kierkegaard, 2011). Finally, private sector–led Internet content regulatory regimes are characterized by giving implementing organizations greater discretionary power in regulating content than would be the case with comparable public sector organizations. This self-regulatory focus does not, however, mean that the U.S. government has been inactive. Rather, Congress has allowed private companies to take the lead and then imposed the regulatory models created by innovative companies on other private companies.

Looking more closely at the dynamics of boundary creation regarding expression, these revolve around public debate that gains critical momentum to the point at which numerous elements of "regulable content" forge together around a single agenda. The U.S. debate on the CDA in the mid-1990s in the U.S., which initially focused on the removal of child sexual abuse material from the Internet, quickly expanded to encompass forms of obscenity and online sexuality. At the same time, it is notable that advocacy campaigns and widespread public debates tend to become key instruments of boundary creation, while strongly shaping the resulting boundaries. At the same time, the frames used within these debates are heavily centered on public values and morality. While this has led some authors to speak of moral panics in public debates (Boyd & Ellison, 2008; Jenkins, 2001), others argue that certain arguments are simply morally wrong (Kierkegaard, 2011).

Finally, within the governance practices used to implement this model, there is a clear focus on non-public institutions regulating content, either through separate publicly funded NGOs, such as NCMEC, or organizations that are embedded within other private sector organizations, such as Facebook's Hate and Harassment team. From a public perspective, NCMEC and its CyberTipline play a crucial role, both by providing an institutional model that could also be transported to the Internet and by engaging in government capacity building. Importantly, the overwhelming focus of content regulation by NCMEC has been on child abuse material, which has insulated it from much potential criticism about restricting speech or harming First Amendment rights. Insofar as additional Internet speech has been regulated, this was done by private actors. Again, this is not to say that the public sector has been inactive. Indeed, "State attorneys-general, acting through quasi-private foundations such as NCMEC, have been able to impose regulations on expression that could fail to pass constitutional muster" (Mueller, 2010, p. 213). That the enforcement mechanisms are in the hands of private actors does not mean that states are not involved. Moreover, such shifts in power are not entirely unusual, and there are many precedents both in U.S. media and communications regulation and in other globalized regulatory domains (Cafaggi, 2011; Wu, 2010).

PRIVATE SECTOR REGULATION—EXPRESSION GOVERNANCE BY FACEBOOK

Having discussed the role of expression governance from a public perspective, I will now turn to the private model of Internet content regulation and its most prominent example found in the form of Facebook. It is important to note in this context that the explosion of social networks as a business model in the late 2000s has changed many of the regulatory assumptions about the Internet as a whole. Facebook is the dominant player in social networking space and may well have succeeded in not only becoming a de facto monopolist, but also in becoming essentially indispensable to many of its users (York, 2010).

This shift is part of wider developments in Internet markets, moving direction from the provision of unidirectional services to interaction as part of an Internet trend known as "Web 2.0." Although social networking sites existed on the Internet as early as 1997, it was not until 2003 that there was an explosion of creative activity in the social networking space (Boyd & Ellison, 2008). Since then, "social network sites (SNSs) such as MySpace, Facebook, Cyworld, and Bebo have attracted millions of users, many of whom have integrated these sites into their daily practices" (Boyd & Ellison, 2008, p. 210). Notably, that Facebook would eventually expand beyond its early university networks was by no means certain. A Web site that in 2007 had 30 million users, of which the overwhelming number were U.S. college students, now has more than 1 billion users worldwide (Kiss, 2012; Phillips, 2007). The dominance of one actor is not, however, unusual in the evolution of social networks in general. Historically it was not uncommon for one social network to dominate for several years before being replaced by another dominant social network (Boyd & Ellison, 2008).

Much has been written about the early history of Facebook and disputes on ownership of the company, but there has been less debate about the organizational evolution of the company (Phillips, 2007). Indeed, until recently there has been almost no information provided about this, as there was very little information published about the finer details of Facebook's corporate culture (Levin, 2012). Documents published in the course of its initial public offering in April 2012 suggest an engineer-run company, which thrives on "taking risks [and] breaking things" (Levin, 2012). Most notable in this context is the simple and straightforward formula "code wins arguments" (Levin, 2012), which seems to be the key part of the company's philosophy. The argument emphasizes the primacy of technical solutions, where technology has the capacity and the performativity to solve all problems within the platform.

Facebook's increasingly central role in content regulation stems from an ability to attract users to its Web site, keep them on the site, and get them to share content there. With over

1 billion users worldwide using its service, Facebook's role as a central player in Internet content regulation is evident (Kiss, 2012; York, 2010). This is particularly relevant, as Facebook is far more restrictive of content than Google. While Google wishes to assist any user to find almost anything they are looking for, Facebook is designed as a network in which deliberation is possible for anyone aged 13 and older. As the product was developed for the U.S. market, it is designed to be safe for any 13-year-old in the U.S. This is a direct, although probably unintended, result of U.S. legislation, the "Children's Online Privacy Protection" Act (COPPA). COPPA prohibits Web sites from collecting personal information from children under the age of 13 without parental consent. This in turn leads Facebook to ban any individual under the age of 13 from its Web site, regardless of where they are in the world. At the same time, these regulations have not been particularly effective at protecting children under 13; indeed recent scholarship suggests that the average age in which U.S. children are joining Facebook is 12 (Boyd, Hargittai, Schultz, & Palfrey, 2011). However as an unintended consequence of COPPA and the lack of content or age differentiation within Facebook, all Facebook content is evaluated to the standards of a 13-year-old American teenager (Helft, 2010).

The resulting norm generation process needs to be seen in this context, as regulating content by standards that would be considered acceptable for American teenagers—or their parents. Consequently, content regulation has continued to focus on sexual content, removing any references to sexual language or pictures, including—like AOL—pictures of breastfeeding mothers. Here the regulation of everyday depictions of human bodies returns as an element of content regulation, and the inability to differentiate between actors but instead creating a globally applied-rule stratifies appropriate depictions of the human body as sanitized objects of Internet content (Blumberg, 1984). The process of norm generation—while considering the protection of its users in certain elements—still seems closely aligned with the interests of Facebook as a business. The process described seems to suggest that the goal

of reputation management plays a role from the very beginning of the Facebook incident response process. Notably, U.S. child privacy regulation (COPPA) has also left a substantial imprint in Facebook's Terms of Service and heavily influenced the design of the site, even if this influence works in unintended ways of making all Facebook users the moral equivalents of 13-year-old American teenagers. That their sensibilities—or those of their parents—should not be offended is at the core of Facebook's norm generation process. The norm generation process at Facebook is also influenced by the fact that the company has recruited members of its content regulation team from law enforcement circles.[3] They bring with them norms and assumptions about regulable content and act as norm transmitters from organizations such as NCMEC and the wider law enforcement community.

Similarly to Google's content regulatory regimes, users are directly involved in Facebook's attempts to regulate content. They are asked by Facebook to "flag" any types of content that they consider inappropriate, essentially co-producing Facebook's content categorization through their own selection of content. In this sense, the Facebook "community" participates in identification of illegal content, but is not able to influence the vast majority of the norms behind the platform (Newland, Nolan, Wong, & York, 2011). Facebook itself follows the following process in regulating content: "Our intent is to triage to make sure we get to the high-priority, high-risk and high-visibility items most quickly" (Helft, 2010).

Notable here is the attempt to ensure not just that risk—presumably to Facebook users—is minimized, but also that "high-visibility items" are removed swiftly. This suggests less of a process of user protection than of reputation management, ensuring that the overall damage to Facebook's reputation is not harmed by high-profile public incidents. While it is clear that Facebook is a private company that is interested in earning money, the extent to which reputation management comes through from the earliest stages of the incident response process is surprising. The process described is also remarkably similar to NCMEC's triage process discussed in the previous section. Indeed it seems that Facebook has copied many procedures from the U.S. child protection organization discussed in the previous section. This may be in part because Facebook's chief security officer is a former federal prosecutor who was likely to have been familiar with the workings of NCMEC. More generally, this form of norm and process diffusion suggests that in generating norms and implementation mechanisms for their own spaces, Facebook relies heavily on existing values and structures provided by U.S. law enforcement. In this sense, they do create parallel norm spaces, but these spaces rely heavily on what is already there.

Facebook's response to the challenge of expression governance on its platform clearly represents a specific form of private regulation. At the same time, what is considered to be the "Facebook model" is still very much under construction. Facebook's current practices suggest that it intends to emulate AOL, following similarly restrictive practices with a very narrow definition of "protected political" speech. What is particularly notable within Facebook and seems typical for private regulation in general is the extraordinary level of discretion left to the Facebook content regulators. Moreover, the rules around the governance of expression on the platform—the Facebook Term of Service (ToS)—are so over-broad and general as to allow almost any kind of regulation that Facebook considers fit. The result is a private regulatory system that is centered around the COPPA regulatory framework, rather than the First Amendment, and while considering forms of expression protection in a relatively narrow set of cases, the design of the overall system is primarily oriented to creating a profitable service to Facebook users.

The dynamics of boundary creation in Facebook are—analogously to the U.S.—centered on public campaigns. It has become common for both state and nonstate actors to use public campaigns to coerce Facebook into changing its forms of content regulation (Williams, 2009). Those wishing to change the nature of content regulation online have identified Facebook's expression governance as a

key site of contesting existing forms of free expression online. Facebook is criticized both from supporters of free expression (York, 2010) and those calling for greater limitation of content online (Kierkegaard, 2011). The discursive scripts employed are manifold: Facebook is both a censor and endangering children, both limiting speech and not doing enough to prevent suicides on its platform (Helft, 2010; Ruder, Hatch, Ampanozi, Thali, & Fischer, 2011; Williams, 2009). One could almost say that the sum of human behavior in some form or another is communicated on Facebook.

This tension is particularly difficult for Facebook to resolve, as the organization, despite its size and importance for free speech online, has had significant difficulties converting its user base into actual revenues (Hof, 2012). While there is no need to mourn for Facebook's business model, the massive reliance on Web-based advertising for income has consequences for speech online. Attempts by Facebook to resolve this conflict has led it to provide streams of pictures from Facebook to low paid employees in call-centers around the world (Webster, 2012). Through an outsourcing partner, the operators were used as additional taggers of images following strict criteria to augment the capacity of Facebook to find "problematic content." When the practice was publicized, Facebook was accused of exploiting the Third World and quickly ended this method of tagging pictures (Webster, 2012).

Another area in which Facebook has received considerable pressure relates to the protection children and sexual predators on Facebook. The UK Child Exploitation & Online Protection Centre (CEOP) used this and other means of public coercion to pressure Facebook into cooperating more closely with the police agency (Williams, 2009). CEOP wanted Facebook to insert a button into its online platform that would forward all complaints from Facebook users in the UK directly to CEOP. What seems like a trivial battle about a small button on a Web site goes to the heart of the debate on the governance of social networks. Which institution is provided with content that is flagged by a user, and which institution is able to respond? By integrating such a button by default, Facebook would cede control over escalation procedures and instead place these in the hands of a UK police agency (CEOP). A compromise was since reached, and CEOP developed its own Facebook application that allowed users to add a "CEOP button." However, the addition to Facebook is purely on a voluntary basis, leading to relatively low user take-up of only a few thousand users in the UK.

At the same time, Facebook and other social networks have also become sites of regulatory contestation. As a result, interested parties have employed numerous regulatory practices in order to shift the boundaries of content regulation practices on Facebook. As previously noted, public campaigns form one means of exerting pressure on and attempting to regulate Facebook. Another avenue that was previously discussed is the attempt to actually regulate Facebook's code by inserting a reporting button created by public actors. In the endeavors to protect children, regulators have attempted not only to change the site's behavior, but also to change its operative procedures and reporting mechanisms. A third avenue that is less prevalent in speech regulation, but far more common in regard to privacy and data protection, is the threat of regulation by state actors. Fourth and most infrequent are court orders that require Facebook to remove certain kinds of content from its servers.

In a more general sense, the focus on nonjudicial content regulation rather than the use of established legal procedures to regulate content is one of the hallmarks of expression governance on the Internet. This is particularly important, as many free speech protections that would be relevant for public spaces and actors do not apply in private spaces and for private actors. Even given the de facto monopoly status of Facebook, private users are not able to exercise their full First Amendment rights on the platform. There are obvious reasons for this: (a) Facebook is a private and not a public platform, (b) the sheer amount of content on the platform makes agile public sector responses highly unlikely, and (c) private regulation of speech is a widely accepted norm in the U.S.

In consequence, it is not unreasonable to suggest that private regulation of content is the preferred form of controlling content in which

individual gatekeepers such as Facebook play a key role (Barzilai-Nahon, 2008). Of course, such a central role in speech governance is also in the interest of the private actors being asked to regulate speech, as this allows them to mold the speech on their platforms not only to the demands of third parties attempting to regulate speech, but also to their own commercial needs. As regulating these actors is faster and allows for forms of regulation that they could not otherwise engage in themselves, it should not be surprising that this regulatory settlement persists (Birnhack & Niva Elkin-Koren, 2003).

However this regulatory settlement also comes with considerable consequences, not just at the individual level, but also at the macrosocietal level. Ceding control over key communications infrastructure poses considerable risks to democratic societies. The Internet is the central converged communications platform of modern societies, and if the boundaries of what is permissible speech are drawn by private actors, they will do so in their own interests. Particularly if oligopolistic online services markets persist, actors such as Facebook will in time become more relevant decision makers in content regulation than states. It might even be plausible to argue that in regard to some small states with high Internet penetration and Facebook usage, this is already the case. To the extent that Facebook is perceived as a positive force within society or as the instigator of "democratic" "Facebook revolutions," they are unlikely to face much scrutiny. But the more that public regulators and civil society realize that without decisions, they are losing any remaining control over the boundaries of permissible speech, the more likely they are to contest Facebook's power and legitimacy in expression governance.

CONCLUSION

The U.S. was faced with massive growth in the level of Internet penetration and the number of Internet users in its respective jurisdictions. This brought with it all manner of regulatory and governance challenges, particularly regarding Internet content regulation, which had been substantively liberalized between the 1960s and 1980s long before the Internet (Hoffmann-Riem, 1996; Sunstein, 2007). Still, states have a long history of attempting to control information, communications, and media, and the Internet cannot escape this trend.

The initial response was to transfer their existing institutional models for dealing with content regulation to a new technological context. This generally led to copying media regulations or providing institutional outgrowths of institutions and agencies to govern the Internet. The key question in this context was what the highly convergent Internet actually was, and by extension, which regulator, regulatory regime, and historical regulatory paradigm should be applied. In the U.S., the purely industry-based model of content regulation was by far the most prominent. Even in areas where the government later became involved, industry players were the innovative force. This is in line with the historical First Amendment trend, where the U.S. government remains overwhelmingly "neutral on speech," and nonstate actors fill this regulatory void.

The obvious exception to this trend is of course the Communications Decency Act (CDA), which, while in part pushing self-regulation by private actors, also attempted to criminalize indecent communications—an element that was swiftly struck down by the Supreme Court. This regulatory reflex by Congress can in part be explained by the moral panic at the time, as well as the novelty of the problem faced by the U.S.: In 1995/1996, the U.S. was the first country in the world where 10% of its population had access to the Internet. However, the Supreme Court decision served to reinstitute the regulatory settlement whereby the U.S. public sector generally stays out of speech regulation, and nonstate actors regulate speech instead. Importantly, this decision removed any credible threat of legislation that the American state previously had.

Within the private sector, there are certain key actors and pressure points that develop over time and become relevant in previously unexpected ways. This is particularly the case when private companies such as Facebook develop into near monopolies in their respective sectors, leading

users to become massively locked in (Vasile, 2011). In the private regulatory model of speech as developed by Facebook, markets of speech and expression begin to develop, and Facebook in turn needs to develop transnational regulatory regimes for these content markets. Importantly, although we are talking about private regulation (Cafaggi, 2011), this private regulation is still influenced by public regulation as many of the preceding examples have shown. However, the "market makers" in these cases are no longer public authorities, but private corporations. Indeed they generate much of their value not by creating content and services, but by providing platforms for others to do so within markets they create, of which content regulatory boundaries are a crucial component.

These changes go hand in hand with a shift away from providing human-driven content regulation and direct customer interaction to algorithm-driven content regulation that is primarily an automated procedure within a computer system. This process, while not overtly pushed by individual organizations, is evidently driven by market powers, as it allows a lowering of staffing costs and greater predictability and consistency of the content regulatory process. Facebook seems to be pushing this model of content regulation forward, although there are still examples of outsourcing certain content regulatory functions to low paid workers in Southeast Asia (Hardy, 2011).

At the same time, Facebook has also chosen to include social identification and social enforcement within its content regulatory procedures, with users co-producing the content regulation that governs the network. In the context of Google's platform, this has been described as the "decidedly more democratic path" (Bennett, 2010). However, it is questionable what kind of "democracy" or even deliberation such decisions represent in substantive terms. Indeed, users' choice is notional, and while users can vote with their feet, but do not actually make decisions, it seems more reasonable to describe users as "test subjects" within large global experiments conducted by both Google and Facebook. Even if deliberation is introduced, actual choice about content regulation remains firmly with the respective companies, who like to create imagined communities but prefer not to give them any substantive power within their community spaces.

Both of the cases discussed here suggest a strong embedding of norm generation processes in existing social and political institutions. Speech on the Internet is by no means "unregulable" (Clinton, quoted in Goldsmith & Wu, 2006, p. 90), although the effects of regulation do not always have the intended consequences (i.e., COPPA). More generally, the United States still remains the key norm setter for corporate definitions of appropriate expression norms, as the products they develop are typically developed first for the U.S. market and later pushed into other markets. This trend is accentuated the less Internet corporations decide to localize their products and the less vulnerable they become to regulation in non-U.S. jurisdictions. As transnationalization and delocalization are ongoing phenomena in the wider evolution of the Internet industry, the effects may become even greater in years to come. Importantly, neither of the actors discussed here has the capacity to regulate Internet content alone. Power is dispersed across the Internet and works in ways that make implementation of policy decisions uncertain. The result has been a widespread reliance on private implementation of Internet content regulation coupled to a proliferation of self-regulatory regimes to ensure such compliance. However the extensive use of public sector coercion to induce such regimes has important consequences for democratic legitimacy in Internet governance.

NOTES

1. Data from World Bank, World Development Indicators. Last updated: January 24, 2012. The data can be accessed here:http://data.worldbank.org/data-catalog/world-development-indicators?cid=GPD_WDI

2. Data are taken from World Development Indicators. The original graphics was generated by Google and can be accessed here: http://www.google.com/publicdata/explore?ds=d5bncppjof8f9_&ctype=l&strail=false&bcs=d&nselm=h&met_y=it_net_user_p2&scale_y=lin&ind_y=false&rdim=country&idim=country:USA&ifdim=country:income_level:OEC&tstart=632358000000&tend=1231974000000&hl=en&dl=en&icfg&iconSize=0.5

3. This is based on interviews with individuals familiar with the matter and Helft (2010).

REFERENCES

Balkin, J. M. (2008). *The future of free expression in a digital age.* Faculty Scholarship Series. Paper 223. Retrieved from http://digitalcommons.law.yale.edu/fss_papers/223

Barzilai-Nahon, K. (2008). Toward a theory of network gatekeeping: A framework for exploring information control. *Journal of the American Society for Information Science and Technology, 59*(9), 1493–1512.

Bennett, B. (2010, December 12). YouTube is letting users decide on terrorism-related videos. *Los Angeles Times.* Retrieved from http://articles.latimes.com/2010/dec/12/nation/la-na-youtube-terror-20101213

Birnhack, M., & Elkin-Koren, N. (2003). The invisible handshake: The reemergence of the state in the digital environment. *Virginia Journal of Law & Technology, 8*(6).

Blumberg, R. L. (1984). A general theory of gender stratification. *Sociological Theory, 2,* 23–101.

Bowman, A. K., & Woolf, G. (1994). *Literacy and power in the ancient world.* Cambridge, England: Cambridge University Press.

Boyd, D. M., & Ellison, N. B. (2008). Social network sites: Definition, history, and scholarship. *Journal of Computer-Mediated Communication, 13*(1), 210–230.

Boyd, D., Hargittai, E., Schultz, J., & Palfrey, J. (2011). Why parents help their children lie to Facebook about age: Unintended consequences of the "Children's Online Privacy Protection Act." *First Monday, 16*(11). Retrieved from http://firstmonday.org/ojs/index.php/fm/article/view/3850/3075

Cafaggi, F. (2011). New foundations of transnational private regulation. *Journal of Law and Society, 38*(1), 20–49.

Castells, M. (2008). The new public sphere: Global civil society, communication networks, and global governance. *The ANNALS of the American Academy of Political and Social Science, 616*(1), 78–93.

Chun, W. (2006). *Control and freedom: Power and paranoia in the age of fiber optics.* Cambridge, MA: MIT Press.

Daly, A. (2012). Private power and new media: The case of the corporate suppression of WikiLeaks and its implications for the exercise of fundamental rights on the Internet. In C. M. Akrivopoulou & N. Garipidis (Eds.), *Human rights and risks in the digital era: Globalization and the effects of information technologies* (pp. 81–96). Hershey, PA: Information Science Reference.

Dedman, B., & Sullivan, B. (2008). ISPs pressed to become child porn cops. *MSNBC.* Retrieved from http://www.msnbc.msn.com/id/27198621/ns/technology_and_

science-security/t/isps-are-pressed-become-child-porn-cops/#.TxMfQUpzCpI

Drezner, D. (2004). The global governance of the Internet: Bringing the state back in. *Political Science Quarterly, 119*(3), 477–498.

Edick, D. A. (1998). Regulation of pornography on the Internet in the United States and the United Kingdom: A comparative analysis. *Boston College International and Comparative Law Review, 21*(2), 437–460.

Fund Raising Management. Retrieved from http://www.highbeam.com/doc/1G1-60582603.html

Garry, P. (1993). *An American paradox: Censorship in a nation of free speech.* Westport, CT: Praeger.

Goldsmith, J. L., & Wu, T. (2006). *Who controls the Internet? Illusions of a borderless world.* New York: Oxford University Press.

Hamilton, S. (2005). *To what extent can libraries ensure free, equal and unhampered access to Internet-accessible information resources from a global perspective?* Copenhagen: Department of Library and Information Management Royal School of Library and Information Science.

Hardy, Q. (2011, December 5). Spot pornography on Facebook for a quarter-cent an image. *New York Times.* Retrieved from http://bits.blogs.nytimes.com/2011/12/05/spot-porn-on-facebook-for-a-quarter-cent-an-image/

Hazlett, T. (1990). The rationality of U.S. regulation of the broadcast spectrum. *Journal of Law and Economics, 33*(1), 133–175.

Hazlett, T., & Sosa, D. W. (1997). *Chilling the Internet? Lessons from FCC regulation of radio broadcasting.* Washington, DC: Cato Institute.

Helft, M. (2010, December 13). Facebook wrestles with free speech and civility. *New York Times.* Retrieved from http://www.nytimes.com/2010/12/13/technology/13facebook.html

Hildebrandt, T., & Wefing, H. (2011). Bundesjustizministerin sieht kaum staatliche Regulierungsmöglichkeiten im Netz [German Federal Minister of Justice hardly sees any public regulatory options on the Internet]. *BMJ.* Retrieved from http://www.zeitverlag.de/vorabmeldungen/bundesjustizministerin-sieht-kaum-staatliche-regulierungsmoglichkeiten-im-netz/

Hof, R. (2012, August 30). Poof! $1 billion slashed from 2012 Facebook revenue forecast. *Forbes.* Retrieved from http://www.forbes.com/sites/roberthof/2012/08/30/poof-1-billion-slashed-from-2012-facebook-revenue-forecast/

Hoffmann-Riem, W. (1996). *Regulating media: The licensing and supervision of broadcasting in six countries.* New York: Guilford Press.

Hood, C., & Margetts, H. (2007). The tools of government in the digital age. Basingstoke, England: Palgrave Macmillan.

Horodowich, E. (2008). *Language and statecraft in early modern Venice.* New York: Cambridge University Press.

Jenkins, P. (2001). How Europe discovered its sex offender crisis. In J. Best (Ed.), *How claims spread: Cross-national diffusion of social problems.* New York: Aldine de Gruyter.

Jones, B. M. (2009). "Librarians shushed no more": The USA PATRIOT Act, The "Connecticut Four," and professional ethics. *Newsletter on Intellectual Freedom, 58*(6).

Jones, D. (2001). *Censorship: A world encyclopedia.* London: Fitzroy Dearborn Publishers.

Kierkegaard, S. (2011). To block or not to block—European child porno law in question. *Computer Law & Security Review, 27*(6), 573–584.

Kiss, J. (2012, October 4). Facebook hits 1 billion users a month. *The Guardian.* Retrieved from http://www.guardian.co.uk/technology/2012/oct/04/facebook-hits-billion-users-a-month

Klang, M. (2006). *Disruptive technology: Effects of technology regulation on democracy.* Dissertation, Department of Applied Information Technology, Göteborg University, Göteborg, Sweden.

Knill, C., & Lehmkuhl, D. (2002). Private actors and the state: Internationalization and changing patterns of governance. *Governance, 15*(1), 41–63.

Lambert, S. (1992). State control of the press in theory and practise: The role of Stationers' Company before 1640. In R. Myers & M. Harris (Eds.), *Censorship and the control of print in England and France, 1600–1910* (pp. 1–32). Winchester, England: The British Library Publishing Division.

Lee, T. B. (2012, July 19). YouTube restores Obama videos, refuses to explain takedown policies. *ArsTechnica.* Retrieved from http://arstechnica.com/tech-policy/2012/07/youtube-restores-obama-videos-refuses-to-explain-takedown-policies/

Leiner, B. M., Cerf, V. G., Clark, D. D., Kahn, R. E., Kleinrock, L., Lynch, D. C., et al. (2011). Brief history of the Internet. *The Internet Society (ISOC).* Retrieved from http://www.internetsociety.org/internet/internet-51/history-internet/brief-history-internet

Levin, J. (2012, December 12). Facebook's IPO filing reveals how Zuckerberg and his employees talk. *Slate Magazine.* Retrieved from http://www.slate.com/blogs/browbeat/2012/02/01/facebook_s_ipo_filing_reveals_how_zuckerberg_and_his_employees_talk.html

Lewis, M. (1999). *Writing and authority in early China.* Albany: State University of New York Press.

Lyons, M. (2009). *A history of reading and writing: In the Western World.* Basingstoke, England: Palgrave Macmillan.

MacKinnon, R. (2012). *Consent of the networked: The world-wide struggle for Internet freedom.* New York: Basic Books.

Martinez, L. (2007). Best kept secret in law enforcement. *Law Enforcement Technology, 34*(5), 92–94.

Marwick, A. (2008). To catch a predator? The MySpace moral panic. *First Monday*, *13*(6). Retrieved from http://firstmonday.org/ojs/index.php/fm/article/viewArticle/2152

Mayer, F. (2000). Europe and the Internet: The old world and the new medium. *European Journal of International Law*, *11*(1), 149–169.

McIntyre, T. (2012). Child abuse images and cleanfeeds: Assessing Internet blocking systems. In I. Brown (Ed.), *Research handbook on governance of the Internet* (pp. 277–308). Cheltenham, England: Edward Elgar.

Monaco, C. (2000, January). Contributions open doors to international children's building. *Fund Raising Management*. Retrieved from http://www.highbeam.com/doc/1G1-60582603.html

Morozov, E. (2011). *The Net delusion: The dark side of Internet freedom*. New York: PublicAffairs.

Mueller, M. L. (2010). *Networks and states: The global politics of Internet governance*. Cambridge, MA: MIT Press.

Newland, E., Nolan, C., Wong, C., & York, J. (2011). *Account deactivation and content removal: Guiding principles and practices for companies and users*. Cambridge, MA: The Berkman Center for Internet & Society and The Center for Democracy & Technology. Retrieved from http://cyber.law.harvard.edu/sites/cyber.law.harvard.edu/files/Final_Report_on_Account_Deactivation_and_Content_Removal.pdf

Nussbaum, M. C. (2011). Objectification and Internet misogyny. In S. Levmore & M. C. Nussbaum (Eds.), *The offensive Internet: Privacy, speech, and reputation*. Cambridge, MA: Harvard University Press.

Pariser, E. (2011). *The filter bubble: What the Internet is hiding from you*. New York: Penguin Press.

Phillips, S. (2007, July 25). A brief history of Facebook. *The Guardian*. Retrieved from http://www.guardian.co.uk/technology/2007/jul/25/media.newmedia

Price, B. (1942). Governmental censorship in wartime. *The American Political Science Review*, *36*(5), 837–849.

Robertson, D. S. (1998). *The new renaissance: Computers and the next level of civilization*. New York: Oxford University Press.

Ruder, T., Hatch, G. M., Ampanozi, G., Thali, M. J., & Fischer, N. (2011). Suicide announcement on Facebook. *Crisis: The Journal of Crisis Intervention and Suicide Prevention*, *32*(5), 280–282.

Sommer, P., & Brown, I. (2011). *Reducing systemic cyber-security risk*. London: OECD, Global Futures Program. Retrieved from http://www.oecd.org/dataoecd/57/44/46889922.pdf

Sunstein, C. (2007). *Republic.com 2.0*. Princeton, NJ: Princeton University Press.

Tambini, D., Leonardi, D., & Marsden, C. (2008). *Codifying cyberspace: Communications self-regulation in the age of internet convergence*. London: Routledge.

Vasile, J. (2011). Presentation of the FreedomBox. In *Elevate 2011—Music, Arts and Political Discourse*. Graz, Austria: Verein zur Förderung des gesellschaftspolitischen und kulturellen Austausches.

Wagner, B. (2012). *After the Arab spring: New paths for human rights and the Internet in European foreign policy*. Brussels, Belgium: European Commission, Directorate-General for Economic and Financial Affairs.

Webster, S. C. (2012, February 22). Low-wage Facebook contractor leaks secret censorship list. *The Raw Story*. Retrieved from http://www.rawstory.com/rs/2012/02/22/low-wage-facebook-contractor-leaks-secret-censorship-list/

Williams, C. (2009, November 18). Facebook battles attack by child protection chief. *The Register*. Retrieved from http://www.theregister.co.uk/2009/11/18/ceop_button/

Wu, T. (2010). *The master switch: The rise and fall of information empires* (1st ed.). New York: Alfred A. Knopf.

York, J. C. (2010). *Policing content in the quasi-public sphere*. Boston, MA: Open Net Initiative Bulletin, Berkman Center, Harvard University.

Zeno-Zencovich, V. (2008). *Freedom of expression: A critical and comparative analysis*. Abingdon, England: Routledge-Cavendish.

Zuckerman, E. (2010). Intermediary liability. In R. J. Deibert, J. G. Palfrey, R. Rohozinski, & J. Zittrain (Eds.), *Access controlled: The shaping of power, rights, and rule in cyberspace* (pp. 71–86). Cambridge, MA: MIT Press.

Regulatory Capitalism, Decentered Enforcement, and its Legal Consequences for Digital Expression: The Use of Copyright Law to Restrict Freedom of Speech Online

Benjamin Farrand

ABSTRACT. Copyright, as currently understood, is justified by the belief that the protection it grants to creators incentivizes the continued creation of works deemed culturally beneficial to society. However, its use can be less altruistic, as a means of suppressing embarrassing or controversial information. The ability to disseminate sensitive material quickly through the Internet concerns both state and non-state actors, and there are indications that, through the use of private intermediaries, copyright can be used to suppress speech. This article seeks to explain how the current neoliberal system of governance blurs the line between public and private actors, creating a diffused and decentralized system of copyright enforcement that allows for the suppression of speech in a way that avoids discussion of censorship.

The regulation of the content of published and disseminated material is a constant source of debate and controversy throughout the world, irrespective of cultural or linguistic difference, governmental structure or legal system. Questions regarding free speech and censorship on the Internet are not new, but constitute new facets of an ongoing debate on the limits of expression. Although not widely known as a regulatory mechanism to oversee the boundaries of permitted and prohibited speech, one of the first tools of legal censorship over broadly disseminated written works was the system of copyright. Originating in Renaissance Europe with the invention of the printing press, the use of copyright as a means of suppressing unfavorable speech was an explicit means of state and/or religious censorship. However, copyright today is purported to exist for the protection of creative artists and the incentivization of creation for the benefit of society. Indeed, copyright is predominantly associated with economic issues, such as questions over the economic harm caused by Internet-based piracy of cultural works. However, there is evidence to suggest that copyright law can be used, particularly on the Internet, to control or suppress speech by a range of state and non-state actors. With the

Benjamin Farrand is Lecturer in Intellectual Property Law and Policy at the University of Strathclyde in Glasgow, Scotland. He holds a Ph.D. in law from the European University Institute in Florence, Italy, on the cross-border regulation of digital copyright. His current research focuses on lobbying processes in the field of intellectual property law, in addition to the law, philosophy, and governance of human enhancement technologies.

ability to disseminate material quickly over the Internet, potentially being able to reach a greater number of people than ever before possible and with fewer barriers to reproduction or dissemination, actors have been forced to respond with various regulatory techniques in order to suppress content deemed unfavorable. Whereas this is achieved through explicit means that are acknowledged as forms of censorship in certain autocratic regimes such as Saudi Arabia, Iran, and China (Deibert, Palfrey, Rohozinski, & Zittrain, 2010; Mueller, 2010, p. 10), such active means may not fit effectively within discourses of Western liberal democracy. Take, for example, U.S. Secretary of state Hillary Clinton's address to the Newseum in New York in 2010, where she stated that the U.S. government took the view that it is critical that Internet users are assured certain basic freedoms. In her speech, Clinton stated that blogs, e-mails, social networks, and text messages have opened up new forums for exchanging ideas, and also created new targets for censorship. Nevertheless, the U.S. and others have been involved in the suppression of embarrassing and critical information, such as in the case of the release of diplomatic cables by WikiLeaks (an issue that will be considered in greater detail at a later point in this article). This suppression of information is achieved by indirect rather than direct means, in part perhaps to avoid allegations of censorship. One means of achieving this indirect suppression is through the use of copyright law.

The purpose of this article is to explore further the use of copyright law as a means of suppressing speech on the Internet through the application of a theory of regulation that can aid in explaining how such use is possible. In particular, this article seeks to demonstrate how neoliberalism and the associated regime of self-regulation have impacted the regulation of speech online in a way that requires that the traditional perception of the state as the entity with the power to censor be re-examined. This article will argue that neoliberal theories have allowed for the suppression of speech through the twin effects of the proliferation of self- and intermediary-based regulation, described by some authors as "regulatory capitalism," and the primacy of property protection

as a regulatory goal (in general and within copyright law), which allows for the control of information through its treatment as a form of property. Through a process of "intermediarization" and the decentralization of regulation, in which responsibility for assessing breaches of copyright and the removal of infringing content is held by different Internet intermediaries, state and non-state actors such as transnational corporations are able to suppress speech that they find embarrassing, critical, or otherwise unfavorable, while being able to both avoid allegations of censorship and limit accountability. This article argues that the perception of copyright as bestowing a strong property right in the neoliberal tradition over created works makes enforcing copyright through intermediarization a particularly effective tool in suppressing speech. This will be done through briefly tracing the evolution of copyright law as a means of controlling expression, by analyzing the interaction between copyright law and censorship, and by applying of the theory of intermediarization to a number of case studies that demonstrate the usage of copyright as a means of suppressing information. The difference between this approach and more traditional approaches to Internet regulation, and indeed, the original contribution this article aims to make, is that while traditional analysis focuses on how infrastructure determines how access is permitted or restricted, either through code (Lessig, 2006) or through the creation of closed systems that offer stability in exchange for flexibility (Zittrain, 2008), this article approaches the issue differently by assessing how a general regulatory theory that explains contemporary regulatory environments and relationships between actors can determine both infrastructure and response to regulatory challenges on the Internet. Whereas the theories of Lessig and Zittrain are technology-specific, the theory of regulatory capitalism applied is an overarching theory that can nevertheless provide insight into Internet-based regulation. The originality of this article is in its assessment and application of this theoretical framework to the use of copyright law enforcement mechanisms as a way of suppressing embarrassing content.

The structure of this article therefore is as follows. The main body of the article comprises three sections. In the first section, the theoretical underpinnings of this research are expanded upon, providing the frame of reference for the rest of the article. This section will both define and assess, with reference to relevant literature, the concepts of neoliberalism and regulatory capitalism, and their applicability to the issue of free speech online. The second section will consider the interaction between copyright and the First Amendment, detailing the view of the U.S. courts that there is little (if any) incompatibility between the two legal principles. In particular, the view that the First Amendment is predominantly concerned with state censorship, rather than private censorship, will be addressed. The third section begins by discussing how the modern copyright system brings this perception into question, as copyright enforcement on the Internet has developed in such a way that it may be used for the purpose of private censorship through the assignment of enforcement powers to intermediary non-state organizations. It will argue that the influence of neoliberal conceptions of property have had a demonstrable impact on the development of copyright law, and how the conception of copyrighted works as a form of absolute property has resulted in far-reaching legislation that can impact freedom of expression. The third section of the article will also consider the role of copyright as a tool of decentered censorship in more detail, expanding upon the findings of the second section. This section will exemplify this censorship ability through three case studies that demonstrate the use of copyright to censor material by a state/public actor, a transnational corporation, and by individuals, all through the use of a private regulatory mechanism. This final section will demonstrate the importance of intermediaries in achieving this censorship, due to both the takedown of material under the authorization of private actors rather than judicial authorities, and the difficulties in having removed content reinstated. The article will conclude by arguing that the combination of regulatory capitalist systems of governance combined with a neoliberal conceptualization of copyright have allowed for the use of copyright law as a decentralized means of suppressing unfavorable speech. This article will focus in particular on the effect of notice and takedown requests as a means of removing content alleged to infringe copyright.

NEOLIBERALISM AND REGULATORY CAPITALISM: THE CREATION OF A "DECENTRALIZED" REGULATION SYSTEM

In this section, I will demonstrate how neoliberalism and regulatory capitalism provide a useful framework for assessing the way in which copyright law can be used as a means of suppressing speech on the Internet. There are three main ways in which regulatory capitalism can contribute to the study of this issue: First, regulatory capitalism in its encapsulation of decentralized, nonhierarchical, and self-governing regulatory systems accurately reflects the decentralized nature of Internet-based regulation, and can bring new insight into existing theories of internet governance. Second, the approach to regulation in regulatory capitalism as constituting relationships between informational nodes mirrors the nodal structure of the Internet, which ultimately constitutes a network of networks. Finally, taking the view that regulatory capitalism does not stand opposed to neoliberalism as an explanation for the development of private and self-regulatory systems, then the regulatory capitalism theory may help to explain how precisely copyright as conceived as a property right can allow for censorship by state and non-state actors online through diffused self-regulatory enforcement. In order to demonstrate how this is the case, it is necessary to expand on the theory of neoliberalism, and its relation to regulatory capitalism.

Neoliberalism, according to Harvey (2007b), is a theory of political economic practices that proposes "that human well-being can best be advanced by the maximization of entrepreneurial freedoms within an institutional framework characterized by private property rights . . . the role of the state is to create and preserve an institutional framework appropriate to such practices" (p. 22). As a result of the promotion of this ideology, Harvey argues, a property discourse has become hegemonic. This has largely been achieved through the dispersal of neoliberal thinkers throughout educational, financial, state, and international institutions (such as the International Monetary Fund and World Trade Organisation), sweeping "across the world like a vast tidal wave of institutional reform" (Harvey, 2007b, p. 23). In turn, this has had significant impact on political and economic thought, to the extent that neoliberalism "has become incorporated into the common-sense way we interpret, live in, and understand the world" (Harvey, 2007b, p. 23). In terms of practical effect, neoliberalism is both a return to, and an expansion of, "classical liberalism, entailing limited government, unregulated free markets and the sanctity of private property" (Robertson, 2008, p. 27), which is based heavily on the work of Friedrich von Hayek, author of *The Road to Serfdom* , and Milton Friedman, author of *Capitalism and Freedom.*

Whereas Hayek was much more influential in European politics, Friedman was highly influential in the United States, where his work in economics, particularly *Capitalism and Freedom*, resulted in the University of Chicago and Chicago School Economics dominating U.S. political-economic thought from the late 1970s onward (Birch & Tickell, 2010, p. 50). Through the combination of the election of the Thatcher and Reagan governments in the UK and U.S., respectively, and the support of these governments for the policies of Hayek and Friedman, policies of "privatization, marketization and deregulation have opened up the state to profit-making activities . . . and lifted restrictions on businesses operating within and across national borders" (Cahill, 2010, p. 298). This process is often conceptualized through the word "neoliberalism." It is worth noting that privatization refers both to the act of the state placing once-public property into the hands of private actors, and to the act of outsourcing traditionally public regulatory functions to private entities.

However, the adoption of neoliberal policies does not appear to result in a significant reduction in the number of regulatory institutions; instead, regulatory bodies appear to have proliferated. For this reason, Levi-Faur and Jordana

(2005) and Braithwaite (2008) see regulatory capitalism as a critique of neoliberalism, providing explanation for the increased number of regulatory structures. According to Levi-Faur and Jordana (2005), while "conventional wisdom holds that we live in a neoliberal era and under neoliberal hegemony, the reality is significantly different and much more complex" (p. 6). After all, it is reasoned, the prime motivations of neoliberalism as envisioned by thinkers such as Friedman were the shrinking of the state, deregulation, and the free market forming the basis of societal and economic relations. Given the substantial increase in regulations and regulatory bodies since the 1980s, neoliberalism would appear to have failed as a doctrine: "If we were to judge neoliberalism by the degree of 'deregulation' it attained, it would be a failure. If we were to judge it by the degree of 'regulation' it promoted, it would be, on its own terms, a fiasco" (Levi-Faur & Jordana, 2005, p. 7). Braithwaite goes further: Privatization in the UK was combined with the creation of numerous regulatory bodies. Seeing this link between proliferation of regulators both governmental and nongovernmental in the wake of privatizations, Braithwaite (2008) states that neoliberalism is something of a misnomer in explaining these developments: "Markets themselves are regulatory mechanisms, as opposed to the neoliberal schema of markets as the antithesis of regulation" (p. 8). For this reason, academics such as Levi-Faur (2005) and Braithwaite (2008) have argued that "regulatory capitalism" is a more adequate explanation for contemporary regulatory structures, with Levi-Faur (2005) defining it as:

> . . . a distinctive order that critically differs from laissez-faire capitalism. In regulatory capitalism, the state retains responsibility for steering, while business increasingly takes over the functions of service provision and technological innovation. . . . [It entails] a restructuring of the state (through delegation and the creation of regulatory agencies) and the restructuring of business . . . through the creation of internal controls and mechanisms of self-regulation. (p. 15)

Braithwaite has theorized that since the 1980s, states have become rather more preoccupied with the regulation of governance structures and less with taking a direct hand in the provision of that governance. The number of non-state regulatory bodies has grown at an impressive rate, Braithwaite (2008) has argued, "so it is best not to conceive of the era in which we live as one of the regulatory state but of regulatory capitalism" (p. 1).

Under this theory, "markets and rule-making displace public ownership and centralized administration through privatization and the growth of autonomous regulatory agencies" (Wright, 2011, p. 31). Through the development of these autonomous agencies, Bevir and Rhodes (2003, p. 1) consider that government has shifted from government of a unitary state to governance in and by networks. Lazer (2005, p. 54) expands upon this conceptualization, stating that it is no surprise, and indeed, not coincidental that the regulatory age overlaps with the information age. To regulate requires access to sizeable amounts of information and the ability to process that information. The development and accessibility of information-processing technologies facilitates access and utility of regulatory information. For this reason, Lazer (2005) states, the role of regulators has shifted from one of "primarily being somewhat isolated decision makers to rich informational nodes in an international network" (p. 54). In other words, regulation, and indeed regulatory capitalism, function through networks, in which regulation is decentralized, or in Lazer's (2005) words, "diffused" (p. 55). For the purposes of this work, the conceptualization of regulatory capitalism as a system that functions through networks is a useful one. According to Mueller (2010), the Internet "triggers an explosion of new kinds of network organisation . . . and . . . enables a vast expansion of transnational issue networks or policy networks" (p. 45). In this way, the Internet is something of a "network of networks," a network both by way of its infrastructure and by way of its regulation. Understood in this way, regulatory capitalism can be seen as a networked system of regulation, taking place within the Internet, which is itself a network. In this way, it complements well Castells's (2000) theory of the network society, in which "communication technologies, a virtually indispensible medium in our informational age, [are placed] at the center of human action, which is to rely on processes enacted by organisational forms that are built upon networks, particularly upon information networks" (Miard, 2012, p. 129).

The Internet is a decentralized and diffuse system that is regulated in different ways by different actors. As Mueller (2010) states, "Most of the real world governance of the Internet is decentralized and emergent: it comes from the interactions of tens of thousands of network operators and service providers" (p. 9). In this way, regulation becomes diffused—not performed by one over-arching institution, but by and through networks of intermediaries. Wu (2010) considers the issue with Internet regulation to be one of increased centralization and the problems associated with monopoly, with "the flow and nature of content . . . strictly controlled for reasons of commerce" (p. 6), and control placed in "a few hands" (p. 110). When assessed through the regulatory capitalism model, however, a monopoly is not essential to restricting or suppressing content, as that control can be affected through the network relationships. Or, to put it another way, the diffusion of regulatory control could potentially achieve the same result as monopoly regulatory control.

Regulatory capitalism is a useful theory that helps to explain the proliferation of decentralized, privately enacted regulatory structures over the past few decades, while not being incompatible with the general critique of neoliberalism. Cahill (2010) is supportive of such a view, stating that "clearly there are differences between neoliberal theory and neoliberalism in practice" (p. 305). Whereas neoliberal theory considers that markets are autonomous and any state regulation is considered as interference or intervention, history has demonstrated that states have often regulated in order to ensure certain free-market ideals. Polanyi uses the example of *laissez faire* capitalism in 19th-century England, which was presumed to be a time of minimal regulation or state interference, when in fact the state was involved in continuous, centrally organized, and controlled interventionism (Polanyi, as cited in Cahill, 2010, p. 306). In contrast to regulatory capitalism thinkers, Cahill (2010) suggests that we consider neoliberalism in terms of "actually existing neoliberalism," which corresponds closely with neoliberal theory while recognizing that the neoliberal ideal of the small state has not been eventuated (pp. 306–307). Harvey (2007a) maintains that this is to be expected; the neoliberal project relies on state action to ensure that neoliberal goals are met, creating "the paradox of intense state interventions and government by elites and 'experts' in a world where the state is supposed not to be interventionist" (p. 69). Businesses and corporations often work closely with governments, setting the terms and conditions of regulatory and self-regulatory systems, with legislators producing legislation and regulatory frameworks favorable to particular businesses or industries (Harvey, 2007a, pp. 76–77). In this way, the interests of state and corporation are aligned; in actually existing neoliberalism, state and market are mutually reinforcing, rather than opposed. As shall be demonstrated, the state and market may not be opposed, but align, when considering the suppression of speech through copyright law. Goldsmith and Wu (2006), for example, have considered predominantly the role of the state in Internet regulation, and the impact of territoriality in regulating the Internet along national jurisdictions, referring to how "governments control behavior not individually, but collectively, through intermediaries" (p. 68). However, it is not only governments that are able to exercise this ability to control power through intermediaries; other non-state actors within the network are also able to exert this influence. Furthermore, whereas Goldsmith and Wu (2006) posit that the Internet is a sphere in which government and market are in conflict (see, for example, pp. 29–30), with one seeking to regulate and the other seeking to *avoid* regulation, the regulatory capitalism approach would suggest that both "market" and "state" can be aligned in seeking regulatory approaches.

Cahill (2010) posits two main ways in which regulatory capitalism is used to ensure neoliberal ends; the first is that there has been a significant process of marketization and privatization, particularly of social services. Although they are subject to some form of regulation, the provision of the service is performed by the private entity rather than the state. Cahill reasons that "neoliberal theory has provided a convenient rationale and justification for such policies," based on the idea that the state is an inefficient provider of certain services, which the market is much better able to provide (p. 307). Second, Cahill states that this "actually existing neoliberalism" has facilitated a greater marketization of life, in which an increased number of services, such as childcare provision and education funding, are provided by private, self-regulating entities, "in keeping with the neoliberal argument that markets are the most moral and efficient means of economic organization and . . . should be the primary mechanism through which individuals source their wants and needs" (2010, p. 308). Cahill goes on to state that while there may have been an increase in legislation and regulation, it "has been used to secure the formal freedoms advocated by neoliberal polemicists" (p. 308). This would appear to be in line with Harvey's argument that despite neoliberalism's "small-state" theoretical basis, neoliberalism in fact relies on state intervention in order to achieve its aims.

There is indeed evidence to suggest that this is the case. Numerous writers on the topic of regulation (Jessop, 1997; Ogus, 1995; Scholte, 1997; Shamir, 2011, to name but a few) express a certain cynicism over whether regulatory regimes control private companies or whether private companies control the regulatory regime, particularly with regard to private self-regulation. Ogus (1995), for example, argues that from the early 1980s onward, the UK was (and is) seen as a "bastion" of self-regulation (p. 97), and that fitting with the neoliberal dynamic, the perception is that self-regulation is cheaper and more effective than public regulation, and addresses a "market failure" of information asymmetry, in which private enterprises better understand their business than public regulators (pp. 97–98). However, as Ogus goes on to note, "Private interests that are threatened by regulation may gain considerable benefits if they are allowed themselves to formulate and enforce the relevant controls" (p. 98). Culpepper (2011) in particular has researched this issue extensively, and has determined that where private actors work in areas of low political saliency (i.e., issues that are not particularly mediatized and are unlikely to be "vote winners" in elections, such as corporate directorship), often those private interests are able to direct legislation and/or regulation in a way that suits their business interests in a way that Culpepper refers to as "quiet politics" (see Culpepper, 2011, p. 5–23 for more information). As will be demonstrated in later sections, this perception appears to be relevant and applicable to the case of Internet intermediaries that take on regulatory functions. To give but one example at this stage, MacKinnon (2012) argues that ". . . the geopolitical power of corporations has been growing for decades . . . the conventional power politics of nation-states is disrupted by the emerging power of the private sector. . . . Internet-related companies are even more powerful because not only do they create and sell products, but they also provide and shape the digital spaces upon which citizens increasingly depend" (pp. 10–11). For this reason, I feel that regulatory capitalism theory is not entirely inconsistent with analysis of neoliberalism, and is a useful way of considering the way in which copyright law is used as a means of censorship. Nevertheless, before applying these theories to the issue of online censorship through copyright law, it is useful to consider beforehand the traditional perception of the role of copyright in censorship, the interaction between the First Amendment and copyright, and the inbuilt protections afforded to users of copyrighted work found in the doctrine of fair use.

COPYRIGHT AS THE ENGINE OF EXPRESSION, OR COPYRIGHT AS THE SUPPRESSOR OF EXPRESSION?

The focus of this analysis of "censorship," or rather, suppression, is limited to cases in which the documents under discussion contain information that one party wishes to remain confidential, but nevertheless may be subject to a public interest defense under fair use. In this respect, and as shall be demonstrated, both the ability and desire to "censor" in this manner may be on the part of a state or non-state actor who works through an intermediary in order to suppress that speech. The First Amendment states that: "Congress shall make no law respecting an establishment of religion, or prohibiting the free exercise thereof; or abridging the freedom of speech, or of the press; or the right of the people peaceably to assemble, and to petition the government for a redress of grievances." In this respect, the First Amendment is considered as applying to the U.S. government, and not private actors. The judiciary of the United States does not appear to be favorably predisposed to the argument that copyright can be used as a means of suppressing speech. Birnhack (2002–2003) has gone as far as to state that the U.S. courts' systematic rejections of a conflict between copyright law and freedom of expression constitute a "denial of the conflict" (p. 1282), and Pollack (2004–2005) refers to concerns being "brushed away" (p. 32). In the important (and indeed, controversial) decision Eldred v. Ashcroft (2003), the U.S. Supreme Court ruled that a challenge made by a private actor to a change in copyright law by Congress could not be made on the basis of the First Amendment. The challenge was brought by Eldred (and other petitioners), who runs Eldritch Press. Eldritch Press is a noncommercial enterprise that offers public domain works in digital formats on the Internet. The petition argued that the recently adopted Copyright Term Extension Act (CTEA) was unconstitutional, as the Act extended the term of copyright protection for 20 years (the life of the author plus 70 years, increased from life plus 50) for both existing and new works (Birnhack, 2002–2003, p. 1275). In addition, arguing on the basis of the "limited time" provision of the "Copyright Clause" of the U.S. Constitution (Article 1, S.8), Eldred raised a second argument on the basis that the CTEA as a content-neutral form of regulation of speech failed to comply with the protection of speech provided for by the First Amendment (*Eldred v. Ashcroft*, 2003, p. 2). Content-neutral regulation is regulation that does not discriminate on the basis of the content of the speech; examples provided by Netanel (2008) include decibel limits on rock concerts or permitting broadcasting only within certain frequencies set forth in a Federal Communications Commission license (p. 118). Eisgruber (2003) argues that as copyright protection does not appear to discriminate based on viewpoint or content, even if changes to copyright laws are unwise, they should not necessarily be subject to First Amendment scrutiny (p. 21). The Supreme Court reached a similar conclusion. In the majority opinion given by Justice Ginsburg, it was stated that the Court rejected First Amendment scrutiny of "a copyright scheme that incorporates its own speech-protective purposes and safeguards" (*Eldred v. Ashcroft*, 2003, p. 28), reiterating an earlier statement from Harper & Row (1985) that copyright is the engine of free-expression (*Eldred v. Ashcroft*, 2003, pp. 28–29). Eisgruber agrees (2003), stating that "copyright is not censorious . . . [it] does not pick and choose among ideas and subject-matters" (p. 18). This was a view that was reiterated by the Supreme Court in the case of Golan v. Holder (2012), where it ruled that "by establishing a marketable right to the use of one's expression, copyright supplies the economic incentive to create and disseminate ideas" (pp. 23–24). However, this may be brought into question where copyright is used to *prevent* rather than *promote* dissemination, as shall be expanded upon in the next section of this article.

Birnhack (2002–2003) reasons that this view held by the Supreme Court can be seen in its reference to "the common history of copyright and the First Amendment . . . [and] to their common goal" (p. 1280). In *Eldred v. Ashcroft* (2003), the Court declared that "the Copyright Clause and First Amendment were adopted close in time. This proximity indicates that, in the Framers' view, copyright's limited monopolies are compatible with free speech principles" (p. 28). This is indicative of a view that copyright and the First Amendment are not only compatible, but work harmoniously, with the First Amendment "removing obstacles to the free flow of ideas, [and] copyright adding positives incentives to encourage the flow" (Birnhack, 2002–2003,

p. 1286). Nimmer (1969–1970) argues that the conventional view is that supporting copyright and opposing censorship appear to go hand in hand, and are mutually supportive rather than contradictory (pp. 1180–1181). Preceding analysis by the Courts, Nimmer appears to predict somewhat the reasoning of the Courts when arguing that, in general, copyright's incentivization of the dissemination of knowledge "comports" with freedom of speech (p. 1191). Even if copyright has some ability to restrict free speech through preventing others from copying one's expression of an idea wholesale, it is "far out-balanced by the public benefit that accrues through copyright encouragement of creativity" (Nimmer, 1969–1970, 1192). Pollack (2004) expands upon this, by arguing that the fact that the Copyright Clause was intended only to promote progress (argued by Pollack as being the dissemination of knowledge) and was not aligned with censorship, explaining why the drafters' did not acknowledge any incompatibility between it and the First Amendment (p. 29). Indeed, whereas the First Amendment guaranteed the freedom of speech, copyright would ensure the dissemination of that speech (Pollack, 2004–2005, p. 30). In this way, copyright as established in the U.S. Constitution differed significantly from "pre-modern" copyright, insofar as "pre-modern" copyright was explicitly a tool of censorship (Cotter, 2003, pp. 324–325; Green & Karolides, 2005, p. 111; Witcombe, 2004, p. 59). Cotter (2003) writes that, "In England, the interests of church and state in censoring dangerous ideas, and of the printers and publishers of suppressing competition, coalesced in the development of a quasi-copyright regime that persisted until the 18th century" (p. 326). By focusing on those with the power to disseminate information, rather than those who were able to produce that information, the state was much more able to effectively censor messages. This close relationship between publishers and the State was mutually beneficial; according to Patterson and Lindberg (1991), "By promoting censorship and press control the stationers were utilizing the best means available to protect their 'property.' The government was not really interested in copyright as property, only as an instrument of censorship" (p. 26).

In comparison, in the 18th century, it was the work of Adam Smith and John Locke on the importance of personal property, liberty, and the pursuit of learning that became influential (Deazley, 2004, pp. 1–13), with these works influencing the development of a copyright based on the dissemination of knowledge (Spitzlinger, 2011, p. 273), and therefore a copyright that the drafters considered to be compatible with free speech. Copyright was no longer an explicit means of state censorship, but a tool for economic development and the exchange of ideas (Cotter, 2003, p. 328). For this reason, the First Amendment and copyright could be seen to be compatible, so long as the government did not explicitly interfere. Indeed, government appears to be the particular focus of the First Amendment, as is evidenced in the literature. Netanel (2008) describes freedom of expression as secured "most basically by constitutional constraints on the state's censorial power" (p. 35), and Eisgruber (2003) states that "most of free speech law rests on a concern about censorship . . . on a judgment that government ought not to prohibit the dissemination of ideas because it deems them wrong or harmful" (p. 18). With this in mind, the Supreme Court in *Eldred v. Ashcroft* stated that copyright has "built-in" First Amendment protection, particularly through the doctrine of fair use [*Eldred v. Ashcroft*, 2003, p. 29, reiterating earlier statements in the case of *Harper & Row v. Nation Enterprises* from 1985, and reiterated in *Golan v. Holder* (2012) at p. 24]. With regard to the possibility of private actors having the potential to censor, Birnhack (2002–2003) argues that the view of the courts is that the doctrine of fair use can perform a First Amendment function (p. 1290). The fair use doctrine is laid out in 17 USC §107, in which it is stated that the fair use of a copyrighted work, including such use by reproduction in copies for purposes such as criticism, is not an infringement of copyright. This is subject to four factors being considered, namely the purpose of the use of the work, the nature of the work copied, the amount of the work used, and the effect on the potential market for the work. For example, in the case of Rosemont Enterprises v. Random House Inc. (1966), the notorious tycoon Howard Hughes

sought to block the publication of a biography by John Keats, on the basis that its reliance on portions of a series of articles known as "The Howard Hughes Story" was an infringement of copyright (1966, para. 1). Evidence suggests that Hughes's use of copyright as a means of blocking publication was intended specifically as a means of preventing information from becoming public, including the allegation that Hughes specifically purchased the copyright over the series of articles solely for the purpose of bringing the lawsuit (*Rosemont Enterprises v. Random House Inc.*, 1966, paras. 5–8, 49). The Court of Appeal stated that fair use was a "privilege in others than the owner of a copyright to use copyrighted material in a reasonable manner without his consent" (para. 14), and that in this case, the public interest served by the biography outweighed Hughes' desire for privacy (It is worth noting that this common law approach to fair use predates the current approach, which was laid down in the 1976 Copyright Act). For this reason, Keats could rely on fair use of the copyrighted material in order to publish the biography. In the case of *Harper & Row v. Nation Enterprises* (1985), however, it was held that the publication of sections of Gerald Ford's unpublished manuscript by *The Nation* magazine in such a way as to "scoop" an article appearing in *The Times* did not constitute fair use. The fact that the use of the work was for commercial purposes and intended to preempt publication by another magazine (1985, paras. 32–33), that the manuscript was currently unpublished but subject to contract for publication (paras. 34–36), that the article took only 13% of the manuscript but was almost entirely based around that 13% that the courts considered some of the most important work in the manuscript (paras. 37–39), and that the publication significantly impacted the marketability of the manuscript subject to a contract with another publisher (paras. 40–42) meant that a claim of fair use was negated. With regard to the relationship between fair use and the First Amendment, the Court stated that First Amendment protections were "already embodied in the Copyright Act's . . . latitude for scholarship and comment traditionally afforded by fair use" (para. 28). Eisgruber (2003) comments on this fact that yet another reason why copyright should not be subject to First Amendment scrutiny is that fair use affords "speakers protections comparable to those recommended by the First Amendment itself" (p. 24). In this respect, then, the legal position appears to be that the First Amendment protects from governmental censorship (the government being the body most able to censor or suppress speech), whereas fair use performs the same function *within* copyright with respect to private actors.

REGULATORY CAPITALISM AND THE PRIVATE ENFORCEMENT OF COPYRIGHT: SIDESTEPPING THE FIRST AMENDMENT, SILENCING FAIR USE?

It is submitted that it is here that the theory of regulatory capitalism becomes useful in demonstrating how copyright can be used as a means of suppressing speech. The traditional analysis of the ability to use copyright as a means of censoring content has primarily been undertaken (particularly by the courts) using a state-centered approach, in which the perception is that it is the state that has the power to censor, or perhaps more aptly, the power to regulate (as evidenced by the analysis in the previous section). However, in discussions of the regulation of copyright on the Internet, this state-centered approach is not particularly useful, or enlightening, and is reflective of a traditional view of the state as regulator rather than the model of regulatory capitalism, in which regulation is diffused and regulators are decentralized networks of actors. This traditional approach can be seen in the case of *CBS v. Democratic National Committee* (1973), in which it was stated that "Congress appears to have concluded . . . that of these two choices—private or official censorship—Government censorship would be the most pervasive, the most self-serving, the most difficult to restrain and hence the one most to be avoided" (p. 105). This would suggest that there is a difference in the ability of private and "official" actors to censor, and that both the state and the private sector are distinct

in this respect. Instead, what we have seen since the late 1990s is the de-centering of regulation and regulatory institutions, and the delegation of these powers to private institutions. As goes the theory of regulatory capitalism, governments devolve the power to regulate to private bodies in a form of "self-regulation," predominantly on the neoliberal principle that the private entities are more effectively able to regulate than the government itself. With regard to copyright enforcement on the Internet, these powers have been devolved to Internet intermediaries such as Internet service providers and content-hosting platforms such as YouTube, who effectively self-regulate by removing infringing content. In this way, the regulation of copyright in the online environment has moved from state-centered, public enforcement to decentered, private enforcement through networks of actors. This would appear to fit within the framework of regulatory capitalism as described in the first section of this article.

With regard to copyright enforcement, this is made possible through legislation such as the Digital Millennium Copyright Act (DMCA) in the U.S. and the E-Commerce Directive (Directive 2000/31/EC) in the EU. A framework has been created in which the removal of content from the Internet is not subject to judicial oversight, but only requires requests from rights-holders. This is through the creation of a "notice and takedown" system for regulating copyright infringement online. This legislation in effect outsources the enforcement of copyright online from state actors to private enterprises—in this instance, Internet intermediaries. In the U.S., this power is to be found in section 512 of the DMCA, relating to the liability of service providers online. Section 512 states that a service provider shall not be deemed liable for copyright infringement for material transferred through the Internet connection or stored on a computer system, so long as it removes or restricts access to the infringing content upon receiving a request from the copyright holder. In the E-Commerce Directive, for the purposes of looking at the role of intermediaries, Article 14 is most relevant, as it details the rights and liabilities of content hosting providers. Article 14 states that an information society service that consists of the storage on information provided by a recipient of that service will not be liable for infringement for information held on that service so long as the provider had no actual knowledge of the infringement, and upon being made aware of the infringement, "acts expeditiously to remove or disable access to the information." This means that these service providers are immunized from lawsuits so long as they respond to notices of claimed takedown requests, "and so providers take-down to avoid the risks of suit, even if they would have faced no liability" (Seltzer, 2011, p. 3). Thus forms one type of Internet-based regulatory mechanism that can be explained through regulatory capitalism: Legislation is passed that imposes a regulatory role upon the providers of information hosting services, in exchange for immunity from suit so long as that regulation is performed. The regulators are private, nongovernmental enterprises functioning autonomously within networks, with little if any governmental oversight. This regulation, referring back to the analysis in the first section of this article, works through a decentralized network of nodes: Intermediary content hosts constitute one node within this network, and the node that ultimately makes the decision to remove content, whereas other nodes include the uploader of such content and the entity that makes a copyright infringement claim constituting another inter-relational node. As Mueller (2010) states, "The Internet disperses to millions of private actors the capability to manage and control their own devices and conditions under which they access other networks. It not only makes everyone a potential publisher, it also makes every person a potential censor" (p. 187). Through this decentralized means of regulating copyright enforcement, it becomes possible for private censorship to be fostered, as will be demonstrated by the following case studies. In such a system, the judicial conception of the state being the entity most able to censor, as indicated in the *CBS* case, does not appear to reflect well the contemporary decentralized regulatory system for notice-and-takedown. The relationship is not between the public censor and the private entity censored, but a multilateral relationship, in which either the state or a

private entity can have content removed from the Internet via an intermediary actor. With the final decision being made by that intermediary actor, on the basis of a request by a state or non-state actor, private acts of suppression appear as effective as state-based acts. The following examples seek to show how the regulatory capitalism approach to nodal regulation allows for suppression through copyright infringement accusations, and how this is action that can be taken by both state and non-state actors.

In 2010, it was alleged that Bradley Manning, a private in the U.S. military, leaked sensitive information to WikiLeaks, an organization self-described as a publisher of classified information believed to be in the public interest. The information allegedly passed to WikiLeaks by Manning included over 251,827 diplomatic cables and 8,000 State Department "directives" detailing the opinions of U.S. diplomats regarding certain nations, world leaders, and other government officials (Welch, 2010), revealing potentially embarrassing comments made by official representatives of the U.S. in foreign nations. These cables were released in 2010, along with other sensitive military files such as a video clip showing a U.S. military helicopter firing on civilians in Iraq with the crew "falsely claiming to have encountered a firefight . . . and then laughing at the dead after launching the airstrike" (McGreal, 2010). These leaks proved to be highly frustrating to the U.S. military and government, which considered them to be a threat to national security (McGreal, 2010). The sensitive files were allegedly passed to WikiLeaks, an online host of classified information nevertheless believed to be in the public interest, by U.S. private Bradley Manning. WikiLeaks then worked with several newspapers, including *The New York Times* and *The Guardian*, to search through the cables for information that may be considered to be essential for the public to know. The U.S. government was horrified by the release of this information, and began to apply political pressure to organizations associated with WikiLeaks in order to isolate them politically, financially, and technologically. For example, Visa and MasterCard suspended all payments to the WikiLeaks Web site owners (McCullagh, 2010), and PayPal announced that it was suspending the account used for redirecting funds to WikiLeaks. However, most interestingly, and indeed most worryingly, when WikiLeaks attempted to host its data on Amazon's servers after repeated distributed denial of service (DDOS) attacks rendered its own server unusable, an aide to Senator Joe Lieberman started making enquiries into Amazon's support for WikiLeaks (Vance, 2010), and so Amazon removed the WikiLeaks data from its servers. Denying that this was a result of political pressure, Amazon claimed that the content was removed for a breach of Amazon's terms of service, publicly stating "there have been reports that a government inquiry prompted us not to serve WikiLeaks any longer. That is inaccurate. . . . It's clear that WikiLeaks doesn't own or otherwise control all the rights to this classified content" (Beschizza, 2010). In other words, Amazon justified the removal of the cables from its servers on the grounds that they constituted an infringement of copyright, as WikiLeaks did not hold the "rights" to the content—something that is highly questionable, as according to 17 USC §105, copyright protection is not available for works created by the United States government. Yet Amazon specifically stated that hundreds of people store all sorts of content on their servers, and that "some of this data is controversial, and that's perfectly fine. But, when companies or people go about securing and storing large quantities of data that isn't rightfully theirs . . . it's a violation of our terms of service, and folks need to go operate elsewhere" (Amazon, Message 65348). This appears to indicate that the justification for removing the content was as much about copyright as it was about the sensitivity of the data. Amazon performed an act of self-regulation in response to a political situation, perhaps to avoid being regulated by a state actor: While the controversy relating to the cables had to do with the distribution of confidential (and embarrassing) material, it was "ownership" or "rights" over information that was contested. Through this nodal relationship of power, embarrassing content was removed in a manner compatible with a regulatory capitalism approach. While Eisgruber states that government ought not to

suppress speech because it criticizes government or politicians, or is subversive (2003, p. 18), then if the government had explicitly suppressed the WikiLeaks cables, arguably a First Amendment challenge could have been made. However, in this instance, content was removed from Amazon servers on the basis of copyright infringement. While copyright in itself may not discriminate on the basis of viewpoint or content, in this instance, it is likely that the sensitivity of the documents involved was at the heart of the content removal rather than a desire to protect copyrights. In other words, it is arguable that it is the content of the cables that was the focus of removal, rather than a content-neutral removal of infringing material. Through the decentralization of copyright regulation, and the enforcement capabilities placed in the hands of an intermediary (in this case Amazon by virtue of its position as content host), the suppression of information deemed damaging to a government can be suppressed through the subversive use of copyright, rather than the overt use of governmental demand for removal; in this way "the mechanics of copyright today are the same as when copyright was used as a device of public censorship" (Patterson, 2000–2001, p. 239).

Other examples of such potential acts of censorship exist, in which the state has no direct or indirect involvement. In 2005, analysts from Citigroup wrote a report called "Plutonomy: Buying Luxury, Explaining Global Imbalances." In 2006, a second report, "Plutonomy: The Rich Getting Richer" was written. These two reports detailed the income inequalities rising in the world, while expressing views that cast Citigroup in a bad light and presenting a company unconcerned with, and even appearing to revel in, inequality, in addition to demonstrating a certain amount of hubris. For example, one of the memos stated, "We think the rich are likely to get even wealthier in the coming years. Implication 2: We like companies that sell to or service the rich—luxury goods, private banks, etc." (Kapur, 2006), and in discussion of workers (dubbed "the masses" in the memo), stated that "Capitalists (the rich) get an even bigger share of GDP as a result, principally, of globalization . . . good for the wealth of capitalists, relatively bad for developed market unskilled/outsource-able labor. We expect our Plutonomy basket of stocks . . . to continue performing well in future" (Kapur, 2006). Citigroup was one investment firm that required a bailout from the U.S. government to the tune of $25 billion in October 2008, followed by an additional $20 billion in the following month (McDermid, 2008). Understandably, when the memos were leaked onto the Internet in 2009, they caused a considerable amount of outrage among "Netizens," who shared the memos; the general public had now in effect bailed out a company that had appeared to demonstrate such contempt for that same public. Citigroup, rather than denying the authenticity of the memos, instead attempted to remove them from the Internet. One blog, Political Gates, which documents political scandals, has a page dedicated to attempts by Citigroup to suppress the memos (Patrick, 2011). In particular, it notes that Scribd, a Web site used to host documents, has been subject to repeated takedown notices by lawyers representing Citigroup. For example, if an Internet user attempts to access one Scribd page on which one of the memos was uploaded (http://www.scribd.com/word/removal/6674234), the user is met with a message stating, "This content was removed at the request of Kilpatrick Townsend & Stockton LLP." In fact, the number of takedown notices was so substantial that documents that appear to be one of the Citigroup memos are now automatically removed by Scribd's automated copyright protection system. Files uploaded that appear to be the same as the Citigroup memos are rejected, with Scribd generating an upload error on the basis that they "appear very similar to an unauthorized copyrighted document that was previously removed from Scribd" (see http://www.scribd.com/word/removal/23321255). The error message does however state that if the automated takedown was made in error, the uploader can contact Scribd to report the error (although no guarantee is made that the content will be reuploaded).

This example provides some interesting points for discussion, and once again demonstrates how decentralized regulation, promoted through a regulatory capitalism framework, helps to allow for private censorship in a way

that perhaps was not foreseen by Courts that stated the compatibility of the First Amendment and copyright. Furthermore, it also brings into question the effectiveness of the "built-in" First Amendment protection to be found in fair use. The Citigroup example once again demonstrates suppression on the grounds of copyright infringement, in which enforcement (by means of takedown) is performed by a private entity. In some ways, this case would appear to share similarities with the previously discussed *Random House* case. As was stated earlier, Hughes's intention in bringing an action for copyright infringement was to suppress information that Hughes did not want made public. In the judgment, Chief Judge Lumbard made the observation that Hughes's demand for an injunction could not be granted, as he did not come to the Court with clean hands. Lumbard stated that it "has never been the purpose of the copyright laws to restrict the dissemination of information about persons in the public eye even though those concerned may not welcome the resulting publicity" (*Rosemont Enterprises v. Random House Inc.*, 1966, paragraph 36). Lumbard went on to state that "the spirit of the First Amendment" applies to copyright insofar as courts should not allow for interference with the general public's right to be informed of matters of general interest "when anyone seeks to use the copyright statute which was designed to protect interests of quite a different nature" (1966, para. 37). Arguably, the motivation of Citigroup is similar: copyright is not being protected so as to ensure that Citigroup is able to benefit through the dissemination of its work, but instead used as a means of suppressing the release of embarrassing information. Arguably, this case could be distinguished from that of *Harper & Row*; in that case, the Court determined that the actions by *The Nation* did not constitute fair use. However, in this case, an argument of fair use could potentially be raised. To begin with, the release of the memos was not for commercial purposes, but to instead raise awareness of the actions of Citigroup. The market value of the memos for Citigroup itself is debatable; as given the interest in their suppression, it could be argued that they were more valuable to Citigroup unpublished. While the work had not been previously released, it is arguable that the release of the memo and the criticisms raised regarding Citigroup's conduct could have been found to be in the public interest in a manner similar to *Random House*. Furthermore, 17 USC §107 states that the fact that a work is not published will not in itself prejudice a finding of fair use, particularly in light of the other criteria. While it was stated in *Eldred v. Ashcroft* (2003) that the First Amendment and fair use protection are not as strong when making "other people's speeches" (p. 31), namely by reproducing the work of another author, the uploading of the entirety of the memos for the purposes of criticism and review should at least be analyzed (or capable of analysis) within the context of fair use by the Courts. As Gordon (1990) states, when it comes to the "hostile use" of another's work (in this case, the memos), in order to subject them to criticism or negative review, the user is "unlikely to obtain permission from the prior author" (p. 1033). Indeed, as Gordon goes on to state, "A speaker sometimes needs to use the expressions . . . that represent what he is attempting to rebut . . . or criticize in order to make his point clearly" (p. 1034). This is particularly the case with the memos: If only extracts were provided, the uploader could be accused of presenting quotes out of context. In order for the full import of the memos to be understood, the entirety would need to be presented. For these reasons, fair use analysis would be essential. However, with decentered enforcement of copyright, this analysis does not appear possible. This is because fair use is only a defense to infringement, meaning that an action for infringement must be brought against a defendant before fair use analysis can proceed (Lessig, 2004, pp. 97–99). However, the way in which notice and takedown works under the DMCA and E-Commerce Directive means that no judicial intervention is necessary—the intermediary is informed by the rights-holder that a particular file infringes on copyright, and the file is then removed by that content host. Through the privatization of copyright enforcement, the ability for the courts to intervene and perform a fair use analysis appears to be significantly curtailed. If a fair use defense cannot

be raised, and the Supreme Court has determined that copyright cannot be challenged under the First Amendment, then this gives significant room for private actors to suppress information contrary to their interests. In particular, the use of automated takedowns results in a scenario in which "code is law" (Lessig, 2006). Lessig theorizes that the role that code plays in Internet regulation will result in a shift in the way that copyright is protected: "Code can, and increasingly will, displace law as the primary defense of intellectual property in cyberspace. Private fences, not public law" (p. 175). This appears to be in line with the Citigroup example: An automated takedown/removal process is used to protect the memos, resulting in there being no need for legal action on Citigroup's part in order for the memos to be removed from the server. As there is no need for legal action, fair use cannot be raised as a defense. Because no defense can be raised, and because code is used to automatically remove information deemed as infringing on copyright, the ability of private citizens to censor through the use of intermediaries is significantly increased. As Patterson (2000–2001) warned, "Recall that copyright is a monopoly and that one of the factors of a monopoly is the right of the monopolist to control access" (p. 237).

That both examples deal with confidential information not intended for public release does not impact upon the potential public interest in those documents being released for the purposes of critique, and are at least eligible for consideration under fair use. In the case of Open Policy Group v. Diebold (2004), confidential and private e-mails between employees of Diebold concerning irregularities with the machines used for voting in elections were leaked by an unknown source. These leaked e-mails were then uploaded to a number of Web sites, including that of the Open Policy Group. In order to suppress this information, Diebold sent notice and takedown requests to the intermediaries hosting or linking to these e-mails (Netanel, 2008 p. 115). All complied, with the exception of Open Policy Group. Judge Fogel, presiding, was very critical of Diebold's actions, stating that "the e-mail archive was posted . . . for the purpose of informing the public about the problems associated with Diebold's electronic voting machines. It is hard to imagine a subject the discussion of which could be more in the public interest" (*Open Policy Group v. Diebold*, 2004, p. 10). Similarities can be seen between this case and the WikiLeaks and Citigroup cases. In one, the purpose of the disclosure was to expose the perceived misdoings of the U.S. government, and in the second, the inner workings of a company that received a substantial amount of public funds in order to keep the company afloat. Furthermore, Judge Fogel made additional points that have been argued earlier in this work—that the purpose of Diebold's actions was to use copyright "as a sword to suppress the publication of embarrassing content" (*Open Policy Group v. Diebold*, 2004, p. 13), rather than to protect a commercial interest in copyright, as Diebold had no intention of publishing this information itself. Instead, copyright was being used to prevent publication. Judge Fogel argued that this information was without doubt in the public interest, and copyright could not be used to prevent the publication of this information for the purposes of critique. Arguably, similar findings could be made in the WikiLeaks and Citigroup cases, should they have been in a position to argue a fair use defense.

A final example pertains to the 2008 U.S. Presidential elections. In February 2008, YouTube removed a campaign video by John McCain ostensibly following a request by Warner Bros., on the basis that it used the song "Can't Take My Eyes Off You" (Modine, 2008). According to technology Web site The Register, by October 2008, McCain had several YouTube campaign videos removed on copyright grounds. The McCain campaign team became so frustrated that it sent a letter to YouTube, stating that the site is too quick to remove videos on copyright grounds, "based on overreaching copyright claims" (Modine, 2008). According to the same source, the Obama campaign also suffered from repeated YouTube takedown requests based on allegations of copyright infringement. In *Access Controlled* (Deibert, Palfrey, Rohozinski, & Zittrain, 2010), the authors theorize that "given the rapid-fire nature of political campaigns, the 14 business days it can take to restore a video to

YouTube may effectively constitute censorship" (pp. 79–80). While it may be the case that some of the claims may have been in some way legitimate (although questionable under fair use), it is altogether too likely that at least some of the takedown requests may have been made by members of the opposite campaign group, or individual supporters of either candidate, in order to harm the chances of their political opposition. The authors of *Access Controlled* concur with this view, stating, "It seems likely that we will see political rivals attempt to disable each other's online speech using spurious copyright claims" (2010, p. 80). In this final example, the primacy granted to "property" over "political expression" is indicative of another way in which the decentered enforcement of copyright built on the regulatory capitalism framework can potentially lead to private acts of censorship. In discussions regarding the decision of the Court of Appeal in *Eldred v. Reno* (which led to *Eldred v. Ashcroft* at the Supreme Court), Patterson (2000–2001) states somewhat critically that the courts had not only accepted, but reaffirmed, publishers' arguments that copyright is a form of "garden-variety property ... moreover, copyright is treated as being as the top of the hierarchy of private property" (p. 227). Birnhack (2002–2003) similarly believes that this conceptualization of copyright as property is intimated in the *Eldred v. Ashcroft* decision (p. 1327). This view of copyright as property, it is submitted, is based in neoliberal economic theory and is reflective of the importance placed on property rights more generally. As previously stated, a significant component of neoliberal theory is the increased marketization of life, with the prime role of the state being the protection of property rights. Increased protection of creative works, it is reasoned, would provide wealth not only for the creators of works, but also for society in a form of "trickle down" effect: "Neoliberalism valorized property which was used in the production of goods and services for sale in the market" (Robertson, 2008, p. 218), and through this commodification of creativity, greater general prosperity could be assured, given the neoliberal theory that the best way of distributing that product to the populace would be for intellectual property to be valorized as private property, thereby becoming more marketable. In support of this view is Tyfield, who argues that with the crisis in industrial profitability of the 1970s, capital started finding new areas in which to invest, in particular finance, services, and "cultural industries" (Tyfield, 2010, p. 61).

Yet what does the adoption of a neoliberal conception of copyright mean for the suppression of speech online? According to some authors (Buskirk, 1992; Samuelson, 2002–2003; Zimmerman, 1986), although there may not be an intent upon the part of nations and governments to create a copyright regime that may allow for censorship, increasingly they privilege these property rights to a degree that could foster censorship. For if the copyright holders "are allowed absolute control over the context in which (works) are reproduced, they will also be allowed a form of veto power over criticism by being able to withhold the object of interpretation" (Buskirk, 1992, p. 93). In this respect, the treatment of copyright as giving a strong property right allows rights-holders (and potentially, non-rights-holders) the ability to control use of a copyrighted work as if it were the personal property of the complainant. With regard to the previously mentioned Citigroup memos, it meant that the memos could be treated as personal property and removed from the Scribd server, and in this instance, political ads could be removed from YouTube because of the use of music within those ads. Or, as Patterson (1987) put it, "to view copyright as protecting property is to subject its regulatory aspects to proprietary concepts and thus to minimize, if not defeat, the goal of public access" (p. 9). As cases such as *Hurley v. Irish-American Gay, Lesbian and Bisexual Group of Boston Inc.* (1995) show, the right to speak also includes the right to decide "what not to say" (p. 573). In this instance, this meant that the organizers of a St Patrick's Day Parade could prevent the attendance of a gay rights group on the grounds that they did not want the public to believe that the group's message may have originated with the event organizers. This is the principle, as Netanel (2008) states, that "the government may not compel speech that suggests affirmance of a belief with which the speaker disagrees"

(p. 51). However, Netanel argues that this should not extend to the ability of musicians (and others) to be able to prevent the use of their work in events with which the musician disagrees (p. 51). Netanel makes the example of Nazi band White Pride playing a cover of "Won't Get Fooled Again," suggesting that the playing of this cover by White Pride would not lead the public to conclude that Pete Townshend is a Nazi sympathizer (p. 52). Nevertheless, these are ultimately issues of endorsement, or false endorsement, rather than of copyright and copyright infringement. If a legal action were to be brought by the artist or publisher, it would likely be brought on the grounds of false endorsement or freedom of association rather than on copyright infringement grounds. However, through the use of decentered self-regulatory regimes such as that of notice and takedown, the removal of such content can be more easily achieved by making a request to a content hosting service, rather than having to bring an action to the courts and seek injunction. If the content is removed to avoid appearing to endorse a political campaign through the use of a notice and takedown request, then copyright law, which is intended for the encouragement of the dissemination of information, is being used to suppress information. By treating copyright as property, and allowing for the rights-holder to control it as if it were property, then this allows for the suppression of speech, both by musicians interested in avoiding association with certain politicians, but also potentially by others intent on derailing an opponent's political campaign. As Patterson (1987) states, in the U.S., fair use operates as a "free-floating doctrine of equitable reason" (p. 40). However, if a decentered enforcement system without state control ultimately precludes analysis of fair use, then the potential for inequitable results, and indeed censorship through copyright, is substantially increased.

CONCLUSIONS

What conclusions can be drawn from this analysis? While neoliberal theory would dictate that the number of regulatory institutions and the volume of regulation would decrease through the application of neoliberal policies, the reality has been that regulatory mechanisms have increased in number. However, in line with neoliberal theory, these regulatory institutions are self-regulatory private corporations that are largely able to dictate the terms of their own regulation. Furthermore, the adoption of neoliberal conceptions of property in the field of copyright allows for the treatment of information as an absolute form of property. As the self-regulatory institutions with the ability to remove content from the Internet are under the obligation to remove material that infringes copyright, parties wishing to suppress information are able to do so through the targeting of the Internet intermediaries. As Seltzer (2011) argues, service providers act as effective chokepoints because laws such as the DMCA and E-Commerce Directive shift incentives toward takedown (p. 4). In the environment fostered by regulatory capitalism, in which the ability to regulate is delegated and decentralized, copyright enforcement becomes diffused, operating through networks of actors. Because it takes the form of self-regulation, an approach that is encouraged within neoliberal theory, ultimately the decision to remove embarrassing content that is perceived to infringe on copyright is taken by a private entity. As has been demonstrated, this means that the ability to censor is not one held solely by the state; we have seen that the state can exert indirect influence through a network upon a content host, resulting in removal on the basis of copyright infringement rather than direct state censorship. We have seen private actors use takedown requests to remove embarrassing content hosted by a private content host in a way that limits the ability to raise a public interest fair use defense. Finally, we have seen numerous private actors use takedown requests based in discourse of property protection that can have the potential effect of suppressing campaigns of those running for public office. This demonstrates that this form of regulation is not vertical, but multilateral, and both state and non-state actors can exert this influence through a nodal relationship. However, in all cases, the decision is made through a self-regulatory mechanism, and one that fits effectively into the general theory of regulatory

capitalism. It has been argued that it is wrong to think of neoliberalism as pitting state against market, and that in effect their goals may be aligned; the same may well be said for Internet regulation generally, and copyright enforcement specifically.

REFERENCES

Beschizza, R. (2010, December 2). Amazon: Wikileaks has no right to publish the leaks. *BoingBoing*. Retrieved from http://boingboing.net/2010/12/02/amazon-wikileaks-has.html

Bevir, M., & Rhodes, R. A. (2003). *Interpreting British governance*. London: Routledge.

Birch, K., & Tickell, A. (2010). Making neoliberal order in the United States. In K. Birch & V. Mykhnenko (Eds.), *The rise and fall of neoliberalism: The collapse of an economic order* (pp. 42–59). London: Zed Books.

Birnhack, M. D. (2002–2003) Copyright law and free speech after *Eldred v. Ashcroft. Southern California Law Review*, 76, 1275.

Braithwaite, J. (2008). *Regulatory capitalism: How it works, ideas for making it work better*. Cheltenham, England: Edward Elgar.

Buskirk, M. (1992). Commodification as censor: Copyrights and fair use. *October*, 60, 82–109.

Cahill, C. (2010). "Actually existing neoliberalism" and the global economic crisis. *Labour and Industry*, 20(3), 298–316.

Castells, M. (2000). *The Rise of the Network Society (2nd edition)*. Oxford: Wiley-Blackwell.

CBS v. Democratic National Committee. (1973). 412 US 94.

Cotter, T. F. (2003). Gutenberg's legacy: Copyright, censorship and religious pluralism. *California Law Review*, 91(2), 323–394.

Culpepper, P. (2011). *Quiet politics and business power: Corporate control in Europe and Japan*. Cambridge, England: Cambridge University Press.

Deazley, R. (2004). *On the origin of the right to copy: Charting the movement of copyright law in 18th century Britain (1695–1775)*. Oxford: Hart Publishing.

Deibert, R., Palfrey, J. G., Rohozinski, R., & Zittrain, J. (2010). *Access controlled: The shaping of power, rights, and rule in cyberspace*. Cambridge, MA: MIT Press.

Eisgruber, C. L. (2003). Censorship, copyright and free speech: Some tentative skepticism about the campaign to impose First Amendment restrictions on copyright law. *Journal on Telecommunications & High Tech Law*, 2, 17–32.

Eldred v. Ashcroft. (2003). 537 US 136.

Friedman, M. (2002). *Capitalism and Freedom: Fortieth Anniversary Edition*. Chicago: University of Chicago Press.

Golan v. Holder. (2012). 565 US ___.

Goldsmith, J., & Wu, T. (2006). *Who controls the Internet? Illusions of a borderless world.* Oxford, England: Oxford University Press.

Gordon, W. J. (1990). Towards a jurisprudence of benefits: The norms of copyright and the problem of private censorship. *University of Chicago Law Review, 57,* 1009–1050.

Green, J., & Karolides, N. J. (2005). *Encyclopedia of censorship: New Edition* (2nd ed.). New York: Facts on File.

Harper & Row v. Nation Enterprises. (1985). 471 US 539.

Harvey, D. (2007a). *A brief history of neoliberalism.* Oxford, England: Oxford University Press.

Harvey, D. (2007b). Neoliberalism as creative destruction. *The Annals of the American Academy of Political and Social Science, 610*(1), 21–44.

Hurley v. Irish American Gay, Lesbian, and Bisexual Group of Boston. (1995). 515 U.S. 557.

Jessop, B. (1997). Capitalism and its future: Remarks on regulation, government and governance. *Review of International Political Economy, 4*(3), 561–581.

Kapur, A. (2006). Revisiting plutonomy: The rich getting richer [Citigroup memo]. *Source Watch.* Retrieved from http://www.sourcewatch.org/index.php?title=Citibank

Lazer, D. (2005) Regulatory capitalism as a networked order: The international system as an informational network. *The Annals of the American Academy of Political and Social Science, 598*(1), 52–66.

Lessig, L. (2004). *Free culture: How big media uses technology and the law to lock down culture and control creativity.* New York: Penguin Press.

Lessig, L. (2006). *Code: Version 2.0.* New York: Basic Books.

Levi-Faur, D. (2005). The rise of regulatory capitalism: The global diffusion of a new order. *The Annals of the American Academy of Political and Social Science, 598*(1), 12–32.

Levi-Faur, D., & Jordana, J. (2005). The making of a new regulatory order. *The Annals of the American Academy of Political and Social Science, 598*(1), 6–11.

MacKinnon, R. (2012). *Consent of the networked: the worldwide struggle for internet freedom.* New York: Basic Books.

McCullagh, D. (2010, December 6). MasterCard pulls plug on WikiLeaks payments. *CNET News.* Retrieved from http://news.cnet.com/8301-31921_3-20024776-281.html#ixzz17OXwWn1N

McDermid, B. (2008, November 25). Five questions (and answers) about Citi's bailout. *TIME.* Retrieved from http://www.time.com/time/business/article/0,8599,1861904,00.html

McGreal, C. (2010, April 5). WikiLeaks reveals video showing US air crew shooting down Iraqi civilians. *The Guardian.* Retrieved from http://www.guardian.co.uk/world/2010/apr/05/wikileaks-us-army-iraq-attack

Miard, F. (2012). Call for power? Mobile phones as facilitators of political activism. In S. S. Costigan & J. Perry (Eds.), *Cyberspace and global affairs* (pp. 119–144). Surrey, England: Ashgate Publishing.

Modine, A. (2008, October 15). McCain begs for YouTube takedown immunity. *The Register.* Retrieved from http://www.theregister.co.uk/2008/10/15/mccain_campaign_wants_youtube_dmca_special_treatment/

Mueller, M. L. (2010). *Networks and states.* Cambridge, MA: MIT Press.

Netanel, N. W. (2008). *Copyright's paradox.* New York: Oxford University Press.

Nimmer, M. B. (1969–1970). Does copyright abridge the First Amendment guarantees of free speech and press? *UCLA Law Review, 17,* 1180–1204.

Ogus, A. (1995). Rethinking self-regulation. *Oxford Journal of Legal Studies, 15*(1), 97–108.

Open Policy Group v. Diebold, Inc. (2004). 337 F. Supp. 2d 1195 (N.D. Cal.).

"Patrick." (2011, December 10). The Citigroup plutonomy memos: Two bombshell documents that Citigroup's lawyers try to suppress, describing in detail the rule of the first 1%. *Political Gates.* Retrieved from http://politicalgates.blogspot.it/2011/12/citigroup-plutonomy-memos-two-bombshell.html

Patterson, L. R. (1987). Free speech, copyright and fair use. *Vanderbilt Law Review, 40,* 1–66.

Patterson, L. R. (2000–2001). *Eldred v. Reno:* An example of the law of unintended consequences. *Journal of Intellectual Property Law, 8,* 223–244.

Patterson, L. R., & Lindberg, S. W. (1991). *The nature of copyright: A law of user rights.* Athens, GA: University of Georgia Press.

Pollack, M. (2004–2005). The democratic public domain: Reconnecting the modern First Amendment and the original progress clause (aka copyright and patent clause). *Jurimetrics, 45,* 23–40.

Robertson, M. (2008.) Property and privatization in *RoboCop. International Journal of Law in Context, 4*(3), 217–235.

Rosemont Enterprises, Inc. v. Random House, Inc. (1966). 366 F.2d 303.

Samuelson, P. (2002–2003). Copyright and freedom of expression in historical perspective. *Journal of Intellectual Property Law, 10,* 319–344.

Scholte, J. A. (1997). Global capitalism and the state. *International Affairs, 73*(3), 427–452.

Seltzer, W. (2011). *Infrastructures of censorship and lessons from copyright.* Resistance Paper for USENIX Workshop on Free and Open Communications on the Internet. Retrieved from http://static.usenix.org/event/foci11/tech/final_files/Seltzer.pdf

Shamir, R. (2011). Socially responsible private regulation: World culture of world-capitalism. *Law and Society Review, 45*(2), 313–336.

Spitzlinger, R. (2011). On the idea of owning ideas: Applying Locke's labour appropriation theory to intellectual goods. *Masaryck University Journal of Law and Technology, 5*, 273–287.

Tyfield, D. (2010). Neoliberalism, intellectual property and the global knowledge economy. In K. Birch & V. Mykhnenko (Eds.), *The rise and fall of neoliberalism: The Collapse of an Economic Order* (pp. 60–76). London: Zed Books.

Vance, A. (2010, December 5). WikiLeaks struggles to stay online after attacks. *The New York Times.* Retrieved from http://www.nytimes.com/2010/12/04/world/europe/04domain.html?_r=2&hp

von Hayek, F. (2005). *The Road to Serfdom* (2nd edition). New York: Routledge.

Welch, D. (2010, November 20). US red-faced as "cablegate" sparks global diplomatic crisis, courtesy of Wikileaks. *Sydney Morning Herald.* Retrieved from http://www.smh.com.au/technology/technology-news/us-redfaced-as-cablegate-sparks-global-diplomatic-crisis-courtesy-of-wikileaks-20101128-18ccl.html

Witcombe, C. L. (2004). *Copyright in the Renaissance: Prints and the privilegio in sixteenth-century Venice and Rome.* Leiden, the Netherlands: Koninklijke Brill NV.

Wright, J. S. (2011). Regulatory capitalism and the UK Labour Government's reregulation of commissioning in the English National Health Service. *Law and Policy, 33*(1), 27–59.

Wu, T. (2010). *The master switch: The rise and fall of information empires.* New York: Random House.

Zimmerman, S. S. (1986). A regulatory theory of copyright: Avoiding a First Amendment conflict. *Emory Law Journal, 35*, 163–211.

Zittrain, J. (2008). *The future of the Internet and how to stop it.* New Haven, CT: York University Press.

Speaking for Freedom, Normalizing the Net?

Peter Jay Smith

ABSTRACT. This article focuses on the efforts of large intellectual property exporters, such as the United States, to curtail Net freedoms by means restrictive copyright and anti-circumvention measures through the Anti-Counterfeiting Trade Agreement (ACTA), other international agreements, and reforms of national legislation. These efforts have upset the historical balance between owners and users of copyright, leading to widespread global resistance. The defeat of the ACTA in Europe may represent the last hurrah of the U.S. and the European Union to globalize their norms of digital intellectual property rights. However, the U.S. and EU can still impose their standards on a bilateral basis.

In January 2010, U.S. Secretary of State, Hillary Clinton, made a speech promoting the State Department view that the Internet was an excellent means of promoting democracy and freedom. "Our government," she noted, "is committed to helping promote Internet freedom." Moreover, the intent of the U.S. government was "to put these tools in the hands of people who will use them to advance democracy and human rights" (Clinton, 2010). Here Clinton was endorsing the long-held view that the Internet and digital technologies were technologies of freedom. Yet, at the same time, the Office of the United States Trade Representative (USTR) was attempting to conclude a plurilateral trade agreement, the Anti-Counterfeit Trade Agreement (ACTA), that would restrict Internet freedoms by ratcheting up global norms on intellectual property rights (IPR)—norms based to a considerable extent on the U.S. 1998 Digital Millennium Copyright Act (DMCA). The DMCA, for example, criminalized the access of digitally protected material whether or not copyright itself was infringed. The attempts of the U.S. in this and other global, regional, and bilateral forums to impose its IPR norms represent a long-held view of scholars that the Internet and informational technologies are in the process of being normalized, in essence, put under the control of governments and corporations, reinforcing hierarchies of power, and limiting Internet freedoms.[1]

While the debate between the cyber-optimists of Net freedom and the cyber-pessimists of Net control has been occurring since the first days of the Internet, there is increasing evidence that "the dark side of Internet freedom" (Morozov, 2011) is emerging stronger than ever, aided by

Peter Jay Smith, Ph.D., is professor of political science at Athabasca University, Alberta, Canada. He has published articles recently on his current research interests in new communications technologies, globalization, trade politics, transnational networks, democracy, and citizenship in a variety of international journals and edited works. He currently serves on the editorial board of Athabasca University Press.

The author would like to thank Helena Carrapico, Ben Wagner, Ken Rogerson, and the reviewers of this manuscript for their constructive comments.

governments and corporations that are using a variety of regulations, controls, and means of surveillance. For some, attention is focused on increasing Internet control with reliance on censorship in countries such as China, Iran, and Saudi Arabia, thus making the issue one of authoritarian rule. This article, however, will focus primarily on the efforts of liberal democracies, in particular, large intellectual property exporters such as the United States, to curtail Net freedoms by means of more restrictive copyright and anti-circumvention measures through the Anti-Counterfeiting Trade Agreement, recent bilateral trade agreements between the U.S. and other countries, and other forms of national legislation. These efforts have intensified the concern over the growing imbalance between owners, primarily corporate, and users of copyright that has been evident since the 1994 World Trade Organization agreement Trade Related Aspects of Intellectual Property Rights (TRIPS). This growing imbalance has led to widespread global resistance and demands that the Internet and knowledge remain free, in the public domain, and accessible to the maximum number of people.

This resistance from civil society, social movement organizations, and a number of governments poses a growing challenge to U.S. hegemony over IPR at the global level, but because of asymmetries of power leaves considerable ability of the U.S. to impose its standards on a country by country bilateral basis.

The article will be developed as follows. First, I will outline the debate over the Internet as a space of freedom versus a space of control and surveillance. Second, I will then discuss the increasing salience of copyright issues, particularly digital copyright, and the growing interest of states, particularly the United States, in regulation and control. I will then outline the theoretical framework used to analyze the political dynamics of these restrictions on Internet and copyright freedom. I refer, in particular, to the literature in terms of risk, security, insecurity, framing, and the phenomenon of forum shifting. Forum shifting and the use of language and discourse have a similar purpose—to construct and maintain power relations of domination and exclusion. In terms of forum shifting

I discuss how the United States and also the European Union (EU) use a variety of venues—global, regional, plurilateral, bilateral—to shape and impose their norms of IPR. Forum shifting, in considerable part, is due to strong counter-hegemonic resistance, a growing phenomenon I discuss in detail later in the article. As Foucault reminds us, "Where there is power, there is resistance." Finally, I ask does this resistance and a decline of U.S. hegemony mean that the U.S can prevail only in situations where it retains overwhelming asymmetries of power, and, if so, what are the implications? In terms of methodology, this article utilizes existing secondary literature, online primary documents, issue network, and blog and Web site analyses.

In addressing the above, the article makes a contribution to the literature in three ways. First, while many analysts refer to uncertainty in terms of digital copyright (May, 2010), they do not necessarily ground this and similar concepts in the burgeoning literature on risk and security. Second, while others (Drahos, 2004) discuss the significance of power in the imposition of norms of IPR, this article burrows deeper and wider highlighting three dimensions of power in this regard: (a) instrumental power (e.g., forum shifting), (b) discursive power (framing), and (c) structural power (the influence that states and corporations have over the formulation of proposals, agendas, and norms governing IPR).[2] Third, while others (Sell, 2013) have focused on aspects of resistance to encroachments on digital copyright, this article discusses the full arc of this resistance from TRIPS through ACTA, highlighting its diversity, growth, and increasing success.

CYBER-TECHNOLOGIES— TECHNOLOGIES OF FREEDOM OR TECHNOLOGIES OF CONTROL?

For approximately four decades, the debate over what I describe as cyber-technologies, in particular the Internet, has been cast in somewhat oversimplified terms as a dichotomy of freedom versus control. On the one hand there are those who argue that cyber-technologies are technologies of freedom. The idea of technologies of freedom was first articulated in the rallying cry of hackers (not criminals or crackers[3]) that "information wants to be free." According to Castells (2001), for hackers, freedom means the "freedom to create, freedom to appropriate whatever knowledge is available, and freedom to redistribute this knowledge under any form and channel chosen by the hacker" (pp. 46–47). It is this ethos with the emphasis on the user that underpins the open source software movement—a fundamental source of opposition to greater control and regulation of copyright by corporations and government. Here, the notion is one of cyberspace as nonregulated and decentralized with a minimal role for the state.

Counter to the notion of cyberspace as liberating is the normalization thesis, which argues that "pre-Internet power brokers [state and corporate] will come to define the online world autonomously of technological change" (Anstead & Chadwick, 2008, p. 58). Deibert and Rohozinski (2010a) argue that, "Whereas it was once considered impossible for governments to control cyberspace, there are now a wide variety of technical and nontechnical means at their disposal to shape and limit the online flow of information" (p. 49). As the Internet has become ever more accessible, it reveals a darker side of crime, theft, risk, espionage, hate, extremism, terrorism, and pornography. In essence, the Net becomes increasingly viewed as being in a Hobbesian state of nature and, hence, needing control and regulation. According to Deibert and Rohozinski (2010b), "As the Internet has grown in political significance, an architecture of control—through technology, regulation, norms, and political calculus—has emerged to shape a new geopolitical information landscape" (p. 4). It would be a mistake, however, to view these regulations as directly enforced by the state. Rather the state prefers to work through private nodes of power, for example Internet service providers (ISPs), to perform its policing functions, providing increased intellectual property protection. This public–private nexus of power in regulation has been described as the "invisible handshake" (Birnhack & Elkin-Koren, 2003).

These increasing security measures and regulations need to be placed within the growing literature on security and risk, which has moved beyond military concerns to focus on economic, ecological, and cultural concerns. Here the work of Michel Foucault is useful. For Foucault, risk is socially produced and is subject to surveillance, discipline, and control by means of governmentality—an ensemble of various societal components, public and private (Foucault, 1991). According to Foucault, knowledge in the form of institutions, techniques, practices, procedures, and analysis is used to govern (shape, discipline, and control) the entire population. The purpose is not so much to tame risk but to attribute a quantifiable degree of risk to different subgroups to render them manageable. Foucault's approach lends itself to recognizing not only the social construction of security and risk but, as I will shortly explain, the social construction of the source of risk in intellectual property protection and the risk-group (pirates) needing to be brought under social control. This construction also lends itself to understanding how the debate about the need for IP enforcement has been framed.

To this analysis, I add a related notion— the politics of collective insecurity. That is, risk and insecurity may not originate so much from a risk-group as be deliberately fostered by political and societal leaders to bring about desired policy outcomes. Sell (2010), for example, argues that "advocates of the IP enforcement agenda have engaged in a shrill public relations campaign to frighten people into accepting their agenda" (p. 22). Here the social construction of insecurity is intended to heighten the sense of risk, even though the actual risk may be quite low. Collective insecurity is thus a "social and political construction" that focuses on "particular segments of the population or even society as a whole" (Béland, 2007, p. 320). Béland argues that "political leaders often play a major role in shaping the perception of collective threats" by means of framing (p. 321). Once identified as collective threats, they then may become part of the policy agenda.

Intellectual-Property Property at Risk

Since the 1980s, the United States has viewed the expansion of intellectual-property protection as imperative in asserting its economic hegemony and protecting its competitive position in terms of global trade.[4] In a world where digital products and services are of increasing economic importance, the United States has an overwhelming competitive advantage. According to Simons (1999), "The export of intellectual property is believed to be one of the most important economic factors in the future of the United States" (p. 67). In 2000, the United States had a 51% share of exports of royalties and license fees—by far the largest in the world, but this share declined in relative terms over the next decade, dropping to 39% by 2012.[5] While still large in relative terms, the European Union was in the ascendancy. For the United States, the imperative of maintaining its competitive advantage has led, in cooperation with the other major exporters of intellectual property, the European Union and Japan, to efforts to ratchet up and impose its domestic norms of IPR on a global basis.

For those exporters of intellectual property, there has been a sense that their IPR are at risk. Here, one must have some sense of how IPR are created. The essential purpose of IPR is to construct "a scarce resource from knowledge or information that is not formally scarce" (May, 2006, p. 5). Unlike scarcity in the material world, scarcity in terms of knowledge and information has to be created, which is a role historically of the state. The argument is that without security for economic rewards, there would be little incentive to innovate within a capitalist society.

However, IPR have never been absolute. According to May (2010), there has been, in principle, a balance between the rewards that result from private ownership and the public interest or benefit. However, depending on time and place, technological changes, and legal reform, the balance of interests in intellectual property (IP) has shifted. In the 19th century, for example, while the United States protected the copyrights of Americans until 1891, the rights of foreigners were considered to be in the public domain. Indeed, the U.S. may have benefitted from piracy (Khan, 2008). One hundred years later, piracy in intellectual property had become a primary concern of the U.S. government. Today, the introduction of digital technologies poses a challenge to owners of copyright, particularly in the U.S. The ease with which anyone with a computer can reproduce high quality digital copies of digital artifacts means that copyright owners no longer have a monopoly on high quality reproduction (May, 2007). This fosters a sense of a loss of control, which, in turn, has led to increasing anxiety by corporate owners of copyright over potential theft and digital piracy. According to May (2010), "the discourse of 'piracy' and 'theft' dominates the discussion of copyright in the global political economy" (p. 151) and has led to an ongoing effort to establish and strengthen the international enforcement of IPR.

Selective Strategies for Advocates of IPR—Forum Shifting and Framing

Those campaigning for enhanced protection have used two primary methods: forum shifting and framing. Forum shifting is a process by which a negotiating agenda is moved from one venue or organization to another friendly venue or organization, often, but not always, due to increased resistance. Forum shifting is also an example of instrumental power—the exercise of direct influence of one actor or actors over another. What is significant here is the ability of a set of actors—the U.S., the EU, and allied corporations—to select venues to achieve desired policy outcomes—outcomes that would not have been possible in another venue. As Drahos (2004) notes, "The basic reason for forum-shifting is that it increases the forum-shifter's chances of victory. . . . Forum-shifting is a way of constituting a new game" (p. 55). Facing defeat or a sub-optimal result in one forum, a state may gain a better result by shifting its agenda to a new forum, for example, from one multilateral forum to another, from the World Intellectual Property Organization (WIPO) to the World Trade Organization (WTO) back to WIPO and then later to ACTA . Or the shift can be vertical, for example, from a state to a multilateral forum or from a multilateral forum to the use of bilateral and regional free-trade agreements to secure

IPR in countries (Drahos, 2004, pp. 55–56). This is a cat and mouse game—one of power relations, exercised by those seeking to maximize IP protection. Today, there is an increasing shift from multilateral to bilateral forums, suggesting the simultaneous use of multiple forums to obtain desired results.

Framing, on the other hand, represents an attempt to establish a dominant narrative and is often a terrain of struggle, because those who successfully frame the issue can define the terms of debate and possibly policy solutions, that is, desired outcomes. In other words, framing represents another dimension of power, that of discursive power. In the increasingly contested world of copyright protection, forums can become sites or political opportunity structures of contestation over framing. Initially, however, in terms of IPR in the United States, government agencies, corporations, and other states were particularly successful in framing the issue in terms of a discourse of piracy and theft. According to Patricia Loughlan (2006), "pirates" has become the dominant "metaphor" in intellectual property discourse.[6] The choice of the piracy/pirates framing not only arises from a sense of risk and uncertainty but also serves as a means of creating a sense of collective insecurity. The result, Loughlan argues, is that the "piracy" metaphor has set the "agenda and the normative framework for interpreting the issues in international trade treaty negotiations over copyright and patent rights . . ." (2006, p. 226). In brief, the discourse of piracy becomes a means by which states and corporations can impose disciplinary power on "social deviants" in cyberspace who file-share or otherwise are seen to be infringing on copyright (Denegri-Knott, 2004).

Piracy, then, became a discursive power advantage that the United States used to help convince other countries that more intellectual property protection was needed—a discourse that at times was imposed upon countries seen by the USTR as deviant. These countries imposed, in turn, greater protection of IPR on their populations by means of accession to global and bilateral agreements. In June 1988, a U.S. trade representative put it this way:

. . . we have made a good start at putting pirates out of business. . . . But many countries are yet to act, and many others still need to improve binding multilateral obligations which will ensure that nations maintain adequate and effective protection. We continue to seek this goal, through the GATT [General Agreements on Tariffs and Trade], which complements our bilateral efforts and provides an excellent opportunity for us to drive pirates out of business. . . . (Quoted in Simons, 1999, pp. 9–10)

Yet, for all its profession of concern over piracy and pirates, neither the U.S. nor other states or corporations have produced convincing evidence that a severe problem exists, at least in terms of online piracy (Huygen et al., 2009; U.S. Government Accountability Office, 2010). Regardless, there is a perceived, if not socially constructed, risk by corporations and governments, primarily economic, due to piracy.

Global Governance and Intellectual Property

In a digital age, risks to IPR are no longer perceived to be manageable within a single state, hence the need for institutions of global governance to address problems and transcending borders. Manuel Castells (2010) refers to global governance in terms of networks whereby private nonstate actors, nongovernmental organizations (NGOs), and, in particular, corporations play an increasing important role in decision-making. So intertwined have the participants in global governance become "that governance activity is neither 'public' nor 'private' in character," in effect, exhibiting the characteristics of governmentality discussed by Foucault (Haufler, 2006, p. 87). That said, network governance requires a leading role by the state. Particularly, in terms of IPR, the private sector needs the state to formally create and enforce desired international norms, albeit frequently by means of the "invisible handshake."

Global governance is dispersed, multilateral, plurilateral, regional, and bilateral in nature and interwoven in many respects. Bilateral and regional agreements between countries can be used as precedents to secure multilateral agreements, such as the 1994 WTO (TRIPS) agreement which, in turn, can be used as a means to impose disciplinary power on nation-states. TRIPS, in fact, became a model by which a small number of states and corporations could cooperate to set norms of IP protection and harmonization on a global scale. As I note later, this was the intention of the ACTA.

Given its importance, TRIPS merits a brief discussion. TRIPS was negotiated during the Uruguay Round of the General Agreement on Tariffs and Trade (GATT) in 1994 and is administered by the WTO, the successor to the GATT. As Archibugi and Filippetti (2010) note, "TRIPS constitutes the most important attempt to establish a global harmonisation of Intellectual Property (IP) protection and enforcement, creating international standards for the protection of patents, copyrights, trademarks and design" (p. 138). It also includes a dispute settlement mechanism and enforcement procedures. TRIPS, however, was not negotiated at the WIPO because the WIPO was viewed, in terms of its instrumental power, as "toothless in the face of 'piracy' and infringement" (May, 2010, p. 366). Sell (1999) makes clear, however, that while it was the U.S. government that formally facilitated the shift in forums, the impetus for the shift came from 12 corporations, which, in cooperation with the USTR, the EU, and Japan, "made public law for the world" (p. 172).[7] This represents a third dimension of power, structural power, whereby states and corporations have the ability to set agendas and rules. In sum, in a good example of governmentality in action, influential U.S. firms with high stakes in the intellectual property sector mobilized an international coalition of U.S., European, and Japanese firms and the U.S., the EU, and Japanese governments to protect their competitive advantage in IP in terms of trade. The corporate executives of 12 U.S. firms identified a problem (piracy) in the U.S.'s growing trade deficit and framed a solution to impose disciplinary power over deviants by means of TRIPS (Drahos & Braithwaite, 2002). Disciplinary power in this instance represents another aspect of structural power, whereby

dominant states and transnational corporations have the ability to reward, punish, and influence weaker states, whether it is by means of dominant states providing improved access to their markets or corporate decisions to invest and provide jobs.

TRIPS, in brief, gave most of what its corporate proponents asked for (Sell, 1999), requiring all members of the WTO to take positive action to enforce minimal standards of intellectual property protection. Yet, its bias in favor of the exporters of intellectual property was obvious from the start. According to Henry and Stiglitz (2010), "From the outset, it was recognized that the TRIPS agreement was unbalanced, with costs imposed on developing countries almost surely greater than the benefits, and with intellectual property protection concerns of developing countries being given short shrift" (p. 244). This was particularly the case in terms of drugs needed to fight HIV/AIDS in Africa.

Almost immediately after TRIPS was passed, corporations began to press for further protection of IPR particularly in terms of digital regulation, which was seen as a weaker aspect of TRIPS. By the mid-1990s, the emergence of the World Wide Web, along with its ability to easily reproduce and distribute digital products, had heightened the sense of insecurity and risk by exporting countries and corporate owners of these products. Once again the social construction of risk and the increasing emphasis on fear of piracy and theft underlay the rhetoric of corporations apprehensive at the increasing ease by which digital artifacts could be reproduced by ever increasing numbers of people (May, 2010). The WIPO, which had been eclipsed by TRIPS, had sought to re-establish itself in terms of IPR and enforcement. In another example of forum shifting, WIPO became the venue in which the WIPO Copyright Treaties (WCT) were approved in 1996. In essence, WCT provided another layer of protection for copyright, particularly in terms of the legal recognition and protection of digital rights management (DRM). DRM is a technological means by which either software or hardware can be employed by IP owners to prevent unauthorized access, use, or distribution of digital content. The WCT effectively prohibits the circumvention of DRM, but at the same time it did affirm "the need to maintain a balance between the interests of authors and the larger public interest, particularly education, research and access to information," otherwise known as fair dealing (Samuelson, 1997, p. 375).

However, to be effective, the WCT had to be ratified by member countries. In 1998, the United States Congress passed the Digital Management Copyright Act (DMCA) as part of its ratifying and enabling legislation of the WCT.[8] The DMCA provides strict and sweeping protection for digital property, effectively limiting the fair dealing provisions of the WCT noted above. Particularly controversial were digital rights management provisions. According to Reichman and Uhlir:

> In effect, the DMCA allows copyright owners to surround their collection of data with technological fences and electronic identity marks buttressed by encryption and digital controls that force would-be-users to enter the system through an electronic gateway. To pass through the gateway, users must accede to nonnegotiable electronic contracts, which impose the copyright owner's terms and conditions without regard to the traditional defenses and statutory immunities of copyright law. (p. 378, as quoted in May & Sell, 2006, p. 182)

In an example of the "invisible handshake," a transfer of the policing function from the public to private nodes of power, Section 512 of the DMCA had a notice-and-takedown provision that granted service providers liability protection for removing content claimed to be infringing on the right of copyright owners. In May 2001, the European Union followed with approval of the European Copyright Directive with little public upset, although there was strong academic opposition, which is often the forerunner of more popular opposition later.[9] The ECD also prohibits circumvention of DRM. Its adoption, however, has been slow in Europe (May, 2010).

Still concerned about potential infringement and the need for additional enforcement, particularly in terms of digital property, the United States and Japan opted in 2007 to negotiate a plurilateral agreement to establish additional standards on intellectual property rights enforcement. In essence, the U.S. and Japan were opting out of the WTO as well as the WIPO as negotiating fora. The U.S., in particular, no longer saw them as convivial spaces to negotiate, although enforcement has continued to be discussed in these organizations.

Backlash—The Rise of Resistance

The WTO and WIPO were no longer friendly forums because of growing resistance from an eclectic mixture of nongovernmental organizations, academics, individuals, and governments. In retrospect, TRIPS and the WCT represent the high water mark in terms of the ability of the U.S., the EU, and Japan to expand IPR in multilateral forums, although they have had more success in bilateral agreements. This resistance can be located in a growing, amorphous series of movements against the ratcheting up of protections on patents and copyright. By the late 1990s, improvements in communications technologies had greatly increased the capacity of social movements to organize both domestically and across borders, providing new opportunities and resources for protest and influencing policy. These movements can be characterized by their heterogeneity, diversity, overlapping membership, and their network form with groups and individuals linked horizontally through multiple ties (della Porta, Andretta, Mosca, & Reiter, 2006). They represent a globalization from below to protest corporate globalization from above, for example, the WTO and WIPO.

Since the late 1990s, a shifting series of movements with overlapping interests and memberships have challenged growing protection of IPR at various venues, including the WTO, WIPO, and ACTA. The emphasis of each movement differed, for example, on patents versus copyright, or digital media users rights, but they all shared a common objective in stopping, if not reversing, the increasing expansion of intellectual property rights, which was seen as upsetting the balance between owners and users. In terms of digital copyright, corporate owners became alarmed with advances in digital technology and the ability of users to reproduce and disseminate digital artifacts. They demanded that governments give them greater protection—protection that was perceived as further upsetting the balance between users and owners, ratcheting up further resistance, all of which challenged the ability of the U.S., EU, and corporations to manage risk in digital copyright.

One of the first movements to challenge the ratcheting up of IPR, in particular patents, was the Access to Knowledge (A2K) movement, which includes AIDS activists, open source software programmers, educators, librarians, NGOs, and developing countries. According to Kapczynski (2010), A2K is (a) "a reaction to structural trends in technologies of information processing and in law" and (b) "an emerging conceptual critique of the narrative that legitimates the dramatic expansion in intellectual property rights that we have witnessed over the past several decades" (p. 18). Underlying the A2K is a strong belief that knowledge should belong in the commons.

The A2K movement played a vital role in de-legitimizing both the WTO and the WIPO as venues for the expansion of IPR. The rapidly rising costs of pharmaceuticals led to an access-to-medicines campaign, which, with some degree of success, discursively re-framed intellectual property as an issue of access to health (Henry & Stiglitiz, 2010; Sell, 2010). The overall result was much greater awareness of the one-sided nature of changes in practices in IPR that were imposed by a few developed countries. One result is that at the WTO Brazil and India, both part of the A2K movement, exercised instrumental power and "have consistently blocked the inclusion of enforcement as a permanent agenda item" (Sanders, Shabalala, Moerland, Pugatch, & Vergano, 2011, p. 8).

By the late 1990s, the WTO was no longer a friendly venue for the expansion of IPR. Seeking further patent protection, the U.S., Europe, and Japan returned to the WIPO with an agenda designed to harmonize global patent law that principally benefitted developed countries (Shashikant, 2005). The WIPO's strong IP protectionist position alienated many developing countries, in particular, Brazil and Argentina, key players in what is now known as the A2K movement. In 2004, led by Brazil and Argentina, a group of 14 developing countries including India formed what has become known as the "Friends of Development" (FOD), which called for a WIPO Development Agenda. This call received wide support from civil society, including economists, Nobel laureates, and NGOs (Shashikant, 2005). The U.S. resisted the FOD demands that the Development Agenda take priority over discussion on patents. By 2004, the WTO and WIPO were no longer friendly spaces for the negotiation of enhanced protection of IPR. Another venue would have to be found.

Growing resistance at the WTO and WIPO paralleled growing resistance to restrictions on digital technologies and both domestically, for example, to the DMCA in the U.S., and internationally as well. A key part of this resistance has been the open source movement (OSM) with its hacker culture described previously.

The emphasis of open source is on user control of digital technologies. With an expanding number of corporations incorporating open source into their industrial operations, the OSM is acquiring economic prominence. Google, for example, uses open source software extensively and even has an Open Source Programs Office that is "tasked with maintaining a healthy relationship with the open source software development community" (Google, 2012).

The OSM's emphasis on freedom, openness, and user control has played a key role in energizing what has become known as the digital rights movement. It is described by Postigo (2009) as "a concerted international effort by activists, hackers, student groups, academics and social movement organizations [SMOs] to ensure digital media users rights" (p. 3). This movement, while it overlaps with the A2K and OSM, differs from both. Like the A2K, it believes that knowledge should belong to the commons but does not emphasize patents. According to Postigo (2006), the digital rights movement combines elements of the OSM with its focus on the user, freedom, and openness, with the concept of fair use or fair dealing whereby users, whether as consumers or producers of content, can freely "access and use copyright content for creative and personal purposes" (p. 3).

The movement is an amalgam of SMOs, for example, the Electronic Frontier Foundation and the Free Software Foundation, as well as key individuals such as Richard Stallman, of F2F; Lawrence Lessig, creator of the Creative Commons license; and John Perry Barlow, who serves on a number of boards of SMOs, and a host of European digital advocacy organizations such as La Quadrature du Net. Hackers, while not a part of the SMOs per se, serve a vital role in providing technological resistance to restrictions on copyright use. These SMOs utilize a variety of political opportunity structures, including courts, legislatures, protests, and, increasingly, transnational meetings. As Sell (2010) notes, the movement was unable to stop the enactment of the DMCA. However, the movement has continued to grow and offers increasingly potent resistance at various levels of governance to new restrictions on digital media use, particularly as perceived in the ACTA.

The Anti-Counterfeiting Trade Agreement (ACTA)

The digital rights movement was to enjoy greater success in its resistance to the ACTA. An EU analysis notes that the ACTA "was born out of the frustration of the major industrialized economies with progress . . . on the enforcement of intellectual property rights in multilateral fora" (Sanders et al., 2011, p. 8). So, once again there was a shift to a new negotiating space, this time completely outside existing multilateral organizations. According to the USTR, the ACTA was "envisioned as a leadership effort among countries that will raise the international standard for IPR enforcement to address today's challenges of counterfeiting and piracy," particularly counterfeit medicines (USTR, 2010).[10] According to one IP analyst, the lumping together of counterfeit and physical goods with digital copyright infringement produces a heightened sense of risk and collective insecurity and:

. . . is a very common tactic for folks trying to pass massively draconian, expansionary, copyright laws. You lump them in with physical counterfeiting for two key reasons: (1) If you include physical counterfeiting, even though it's a relatively small issue, you can talk about fake drugs and military equipment that kill people— so you can create a moral panic. (2) You can then use the (questionable) large numbers about digital copyright infringement, and then lump those two things together, so you can claim both "big and a danger to health." Without counterfeiting, the "danger" part is missing. Without copyright, the "big" part is missing. The fact that these are two extremely different issues with extremely different possible solutions, becomes a minor fact that gets left on the side of the road. (Masnick, 2012)

In addition not only would ACTA establish new standards for IPR enforcement, it promised to improve international cooperation in the enforcement of IPR (Weatherall, 2011).

In October 2007, the United States, the European Union, Switzerland, and Japan announced they would negotiate the ACTA. They were soon joined by Australia, Canada, Jordan, Mexico, Morocco, New Zealand, Republic of Korea, Singapore, and the United Arab Emirates along with select corporations.[11] Given their position as IP producers and exporters, the logic of the original four participants is obvious, but on what basis were the other parties invited to participant? None are significant IP producers or exporters. What they have in common is that they were either Free Trade Agreement (FTA) partners with the United States [Canada and Mexico via NAFTA (1994), Jordan (2001), Australia (2004), Singapore (2004), Morocco (2006)], awaiting approval [Republic of Korea (2010)], in the process of negotiating a treaty (United Arab Emirates), or were intending to, as in the case of New Zealand. According to Gathii (2011), the "countries chosen by the United States . . . for regional and bilateral agreements are generally those with which they have a trade surplus— countries over which they exercise great market power" (p. 437). The U.S. employs its greater structural power to include in these agreements provisions to be negotiated at another level, and even requires countries such as Australia, in the case of the Australia–U.S. FTA (2004), to participate in these negotiations (Morin, 2010). In brief, ACTA was intended to incorporate stronger IPR provisions in these agreements, or as the USTR (2008) put it, "ACTA will build upon the Administration's prior bilateral and regional cooperation successes." The process was intended to model the TRIPS process, where a select group of like-minded countries and corporations negotiate to reach a consensus among themselves (the proposed ACTA) and later include other countries on a take or leave it basis.[12]

Almost immediately, the ACTA process was strongly criticized for its almost complete secrecy. The USTR attempted to maintain secrecy by means of a confidentiality agreement that it prepared and required all participants, states, and a select number of corporations with access to documents to sign before negotiations began. These corporations included companies such as Sony Pictures, Time Warner, and, interestingly enough, Google, a leading user and producer of open source software, who in 2011 was to become a vocal opponent of proposed restrictive U.S. copyright legislation. Other large intellectual property organizations, including the Recording Industry Association of America, the Motion Picture Association, the Pharmaceutical Research and Manufacturers of America, and the Business Software alliance, were consulted on the draft treaty. The process was exclusive in terms of negotiations, in so far as it left out most developing countries, in particular those seen as infringers of IPR, China, India, and Brazil. The process was also exclusive in terms of consultations, in the sense that most civil society organizations were not consulted.

The negotiations soon became subject to recurring leaks of key documents. Beyond process, there were grave concerns about substance, particularly in terms of digital enforcement. A leaked document of July 1, 2010, called upon the private sector to enforce key provisions of the treaty, in effect, engaging in the "invisible handshake" between public and private power characteristic of copyright enforcement. These provisions included the following:

- Liability of online services providers raising the fear that they would have to monitor the Internet communications of their customers raising issues of privacy and institute measures to disconnect customers infringing IP
- Provisions for a three strikes and you are out rule—cut off from the Internet—if, for example, one person in the household at a particular Internet address file shared copyrighted material
- ISPs would also have to enforce what is known as provisions for "notice and takedown."[13] These are provisions of the DMCA, which permit a copyright owner to request Web sites to take down infringing material in order to avoid liability.

Other key elements of the proposed treaty that caused alarm included the following:

- Stricter provisions on technological protection measures (TPMs) or digital locks modeling the DMCA. In this case, circumvention will apply to any hacking, not necessarily copyright infringement. A person could be held criminally liable for deliberately circumventing a locked down device and accessing legally useable material (Kaminski, 2010).
- Criminal responsibility for IPR infringement "for purposes of commercial advantage or private financial gain (no matter how low the number)." Criminal liability could include willful infringements without intent of financial gain if they negatively affected the owner of copyright (Weatherall, 2009, p. 12).

Thus a person downloading a CD or DVD or portion thereof to avoid paying for it could be subject to criminal liability. The result, Kaminski (2009) claims, is that this standard had "the potential to criminalize the behavior of an enormous number of individuals, worldwide"

(p. 253). The overall tilt in favor of corporate owners of digital copyright served to mobilize resistance.

Unlike the negotiation of TRIPS, which the U.S. was attempting to emulate in terms of its secrecy, its club-like atmosphere of select countries and corporate insiders, this time the opposition consisting of a mix of NGOs and states were prepared, much more critical and willing to mobilize. The result was a two-stage backlash. The first stage primarily dominated by U.S. SMOs put considerable pressure on the negotiators to be more open and transparent and to drop offending provisions, which ultimately occurred in the fall of 2010. The second stage was European centered and was inspired by the successful resistance in the U.S. to the Stop Online Piracy Act (SOPA) and Protect Intellectual Property Act (PIPA) that were introduced in the U.S. House of Representatives and Senate, respectively, in 2011. European resistance grew despite the diluted content of the ACTA. It culminated in the overwhelming rejection of the ACTA in July 2012. Clearly resistance to enhanced IPR had moved from obscurity to a movement that politicians could no longer ignore.

The Backlash—Growing Resistance

Overall, participants in the countermovement share a common desire to have a free, unencumbered Internet and keep knowledge in the public domain. In a sense, the digital rights movement, itself a countermovement to governments, corporations, and institutions of global governance, can be seen as a movement of movements, as it includes those engaged in the access to knowledge (A2K) and open source movements. In terms of power, it relies heavily on discursive power, in particular its ability to re-frame the debate over copyright in terms of digital freedom, openness, innovation, and privacy. In some instances, it employs instrumental power, for example, the ability to raise issues in parliamentary bodies or of certain governments to block negotiations at international fora, or as in the case of the European Parliament, the ability to defeat a treaty.

The ACTA Backlash—Stage One

Many (but not all) of the key organizations in the first stage of the countermovement were found in the United States, with the key nodal actor in the issue network[14] (see below) being the Electronic Frontier Foundation (EFF), an organization that was co-founded by John Perry Barlow and was dedicated to defending the public interest in terms of digital rights. Today, the EFF's primary interest is fighting the efforts of the movie and recording industries to manipulate "copyright laws to tip the delicate balance toward intellectual property ownership and away from the right to think and speak freely" (EFF, 2012). As the network analysis in Figure 1 indicates, the EFF has been joined in this effort by a variety of SMOs, including the Electronic Privacy Information Center and Public Knowledge, the latter dedicated to "the openness of the Internet and the public's access to knowledge" (Public Knowledge, 2012), as well as the Berkman Center for Internet Study and Law at Harvard and the Freedom Software Foundation, all of which were key players in the digital rights movement. They were joined by key European SMOs, Privacy International, and La Quadrature du Net.

While spearheaded by U.S. SMOs, the movement included civil society organizations and individuals from all continents who demanded that the process be made transparent and key concerns over substance be addressed. Included were growing numbers of civil society and political organizations, as well as ISPs from countries participating in the ACTA negotiations, including New Zealand, Australia, Canada, and the European Union. In Australia, a diverse coalition of organizations consisting of the Australian Digital Alliance (a public interest organization), the Australian Library and Information Association, Choice (a consumer organization), and the Internet Industry Association made a submission to the Australian Department of Foreign Affairs and Trade. The submission raised a number of concerns, including the need for transparency and accountability in negotiations, presumption of innocence, the need to balance the rights of owners and users and to "avoid promoting a surveillance culture,"

FIGURE 1. ACTA issue network, January 2010 (color figure available online).

and the need for safeguards against liability for intermediaries such as educational institutions, libraries, and ISPs (Australian Digital Alliance, 2010). In New Zealand, a coalition of NGOs including the NZ Open Source Society, the Internet Service Providers of NZ, and the Creative Freedom Foundation NZ, among others, demanded greater transparency in the negotiations (ACTA New Zealand, 2010). In Canada, opposition centered around the blog of the leading critic of ACTA, Michael Geist.

In Europe, resistance led to growing support for the Pirate Party, itself a worldwide movement. In 2009, the Swedish Pirate Party contested the European Parliamentary elections and won 7.13% of the vote in Sweden and two seats in the European Parliament (Gagatek, 2010). Pirate Parties have been sprouting up since 2006, when it was founded internationally.

The 40 Pirate Parties around the world support free sharing of knowledge (open content), data privacy, transparency, freedom of information, and the reform of laws regarding copyright and patents. As to the label, "pirate," according to the Pirate Party (UK), "We have taken this label and made it our own," re-framing the word positively as a rallying cry of opposition (Pirate Party UK (2010).

Elsewhere in Europe on March 10, 2010, the European Parliament, by a margin of 663 to 13, passed a resolution strongly criticizing ACTA (European Parliament, 2010). The resolution was concerned that the ACTA could violate EU laws and stated that the European Parliament could go to court if ACTA contained any disciplinary provisions, such as cutting off users from the Internet for downloading copyrighted material. The resolution also spoke to the need for transparency and to include more developing countries in the negotiations.

Exactly what influence this opposition had is unclear, but pressure was visibly building, and in October 2010, the negotiators of ACTA made a *volte face* and dropped their most offensive digital enforcement provisions. According to one study, "What we have now in the agreement does not bear out any of the fears regarding this section [on digital enforcement]" (Sanders et al., 2011). A detailed study of the agreement by Australian copyright scholar and critic of the ACTA, Kimberlee Weatherall, argues that in terms of achieving its two primary goals, establishing a new standard of IP enforcement and improving international cooperation in IP enforcement ACTA failed "to succeed on its own terms" (Weatherall, 2011, p. 231). Moreover, in the area of digital enforcement, the "most ambitious proposed texts of ACTA were gradually reduced to an uncertain and vague shadow of their earlier selves, and . . . highly specified provisions found in early drafts were, in the end, whittled down to little more than aspirational statements about ensuring that enforcement procedures are available and encouraging business entities to cooperate" (Weatherall, 2011, p. 260). Despite the watered down content, fears associated with ACTA's secretive process and its original vision persisted in Europe.

What was achieved, according to the Japanese government was, "ACTA Lite." "Lite" or not, on October 1, 2011, a signing ceremony for ACTA was held in Tokyo with the United States, Australia, Canada, Japan, Morocco, New Zealand, and Singapore. The European Union, Mexico, and 22 member states of the EU signed in 2012. However,

> The signing of the agreement does not mean the agreement is enforceable yet. ACTA stipulates that it takes effect when six countries have deposited instruments of ratification, acceptance, or approval. In other words, most countries must still ratify the agreement (much like the WIPO Internet treaties, signing indicates general approval of an agreement but being bound

> by the terms requires ratification). (Geist, 2011)

To date, only Japan has ratified the treaty.

ACTA Backlash—Stage Two

The second stage of resistance occurred in Europe during the ratification process. Resistance by the time of the signing ceremony had waned considerably. Yet, it was to erupt stronger than ever in Europe in January and February 2012. In part, resistance was stimulated by the fierce reaction to the proposed SOPA and PIPA introduced in the U.S. House of Representatives and Senate, respectively, in 2011 (Sell, 2013). SOPA and PIPA had a similar purpose: to make it more difficult for sites, particularly those outside the U.S., to traffic in U.S. copyrighted material such as movies or counterfeit products (e.g., drugs, watches). Once again, the familiar framing of the language of threats, theft, and piracy was employed by both Democrats and Republicans, who, before the resistance began, were overwhelmingly in favor of the proposed legislation. There were risks posed to "our intellectual property" by "international criminals" who threatened the loss of American jobs. According to Democratic Senator Al Franken, "We cannot simply shrug off the threat of online piracy. We cannot do nothing" (Brainwrap, 2012).

The list of supporters of the legislation was huge, including media companies, the Recording Industry Association of America (RIAA), the pharmaceutical company Pfizer, TV networks (CBS), movie studios, and book publishers, many of whom were supporters of ACTA as well (Newman, 2012). Service providers would be required to prevent subscribers from linking to any site anywhere "dedicated to the theft of U.S. property" (Magid, 2012). All companies would be prevented from placing material on these sites, and payment companies such as PayPal and Visa would be prevented from transferring money to these sites. To ensure compliance, host-users would need to closely monitor the behavior of their users. Corporate supporters stressed that the Internet was a wild and wooly place, a

Hobbesian world, where Congress, in the words of the CEO of the RIAA, "must bring the rule of law to the Internet" (Sherman, 2012).

Yet, where there is power there is resistance. On January 18, 2012, there was a massive online backlash by Web sites large and small who feared censorship and encroachments on freedom of speech. Wikipedia, Reddit, and approximately 7,000 other sites organized a service blackout. In addition, there were massive petition drives, boycotts of companies supporting the bills, and denial of service attacks on corporate proponents of the legislation (e.g., RIAA). Significantly, corporate America was divided on the legislation. Online companies such as Craigslist, eBay, Google, Mozilla, and Twitter signed an open letter opposing the proposed legislation. Politicians who had not previously faced resistance to legislation or international treaty-making on IPR—including the White House, House of Representatives, and Senate—were stunned at the response and soon abandoned the bills. This was the first successful use in the United States of instrumental power by opponents to the ratcheting up of protection to digital IPR.

For those who had opposed the one-sided construction of bills and international agreements on ratcheting up norms of IPR, this was a seminal moment in the self-realization of their own power, their ability to exercise discursive power and provide a counter-frame of freedom of speech and openness of the Internet, and, for Europeans opposed to ACTA, an inspiration that governing bodies might be moved by democratic forces to defeat the treaty. Despite repeated assurances that ACTA was no longer a hoary monster, that its most controversial elements had been watered down or simply deleted, fears lingered in European civil society over ACTA's implications as the ratification process in Europe got underway.

In the end, perceptions trumped reality, and the European resistance movement went into high gear. First, there was a perception that provisions in ACTA could provide for a low threshold for imposing criminal sanctions, even for a person who unintentionally infringes copyright. In addition, other seemingly inoffensive provisions were seen as having potentially ominous

implications. Thus, while the final version of ACTA made many of its "provisions permissive rather than mandatory . . . the experience with other treaties indicates that permissive language is gradually transformed into mandatory, best-practice language" (Geist, 2012). ISPs could then be required to disclose information about subscribers. As a consequence, there was a fear that ACTA might lead to the "unnoticed monitoring of millions of individuals and all users, irrespective of whether or not they are under suspicion. . . ." Thus the interests of rights holders would be placed "ahead of free speech, privacy, and other fundamental rights" (European Digital Rights, 2012).

As recently as December 2011, there was considerable optimism among its proponents that ACTA would be approved by the EU and all 27 EU member states. Indeed, by February 2012, ACTA in Europe only required the approval of the EU and a handful of states. Yet, by late February that optimism had evaporated. What happened? In part inspired by the SOPA–PIPA uprising in the U.S., Europeans began taking to the streets, particularly in Eastern Europe. In late January, there was a week of massive street demonstrations in Poland, whose government had signed the treaty on January 26, 2012, over the objections of opposition politicians wearing the ubiquitous Guy Fawkes mask of protest.

Initially, the Polish Prime Minister, Donald Tusk, said he would not cave into anti-ACTA "blackmail" (RT Question More, 2012). Continued demonstrations led Tusk to suspend ratification of the treaty for a year to study it further, and on February 17, 2012, Tusk completely capitulated stating, "I was wrong. . . . It would be a sin to maintain a mistaken belief . . . the agreement does not correspond to the reality of the 21st century. The battle for the right to property should also respect the right to freedom" (Tusk, 2012). Unrest across Europe led Germany to delay ratification, along with Latvia, the Czech Republic, and Slovakia.

To cap the protests off, there was a massive STOP ACTA day on February 11, 2012, that was organized by means of Facebook and Twitter and which attracted hundreds of thousands of people (see Figure 2). Prior to and subsequent

FIGURE 2. Anti-ACTA protests in Europe, February 11, 2012. Map courtesy of Wikimedia Commons (http://commons.wikimedia.org/wiki/File:AntiACTA_11012012.png) (color figure available online).

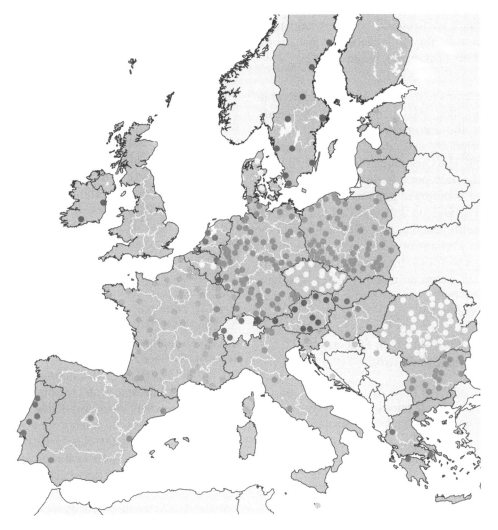

to the STOP ACTA protests, ACTA faced an onslaught of rebuffs. Almost immediately after the European Commission and other EU countries approved ACTA in late January 2012, Kader Arif, the EU's rapporteur on ACTA, resigned, labeling ACTA a "masquerade." The Slovenian diplomat, who signed the ACTA in Japan, described her behavior as an act of "civic carelessness." The Romanian Prime Minister, now resigned, stated he did not know why Romania had signed ACTA. Elsewhere, over 2 million Europeans signed a petition protesting ACTA, and groups associated with the "hacktivist" site Anonymous hacked into government Web sites in the Czech Republic and Poland.

The immense pressure forced the European Commission to backtrack. A European Commissioner for the Digital Agenda recognized the legitimacy of the alternative discursive framing of opponents of ACTA and went so far as to suggest that the ACTA should not come into effect, stating:

We have recently seen how many thousands of people are willing to protest against rules which they see as constraining the openness and innovation of the Internet. This is a strong new political voice. And as a force for openness, I welcome it, even if I do not always agree with everything it says on every subject.

We are now likely to be in a world without SOPA and without ACTA. Now we need to find solutions to make the Internet a place of freedom, openness, and innovation fit for all citizens, not just for the techno avant-garde. (Kroes, 2012)

The result was a growing confidence among its opponents that "ACTA may already be dead," and that the European "Parliament and the Commission are now afraid of citizens and of the streets" (La Quadrature du Net, 2012). If not afraid, the European Parliament was respectful of the widespread popular backlash against the ACTA, and on July 4, 2012, in an exercise of instrumental power, 478 members of the European Parliament voted against the treaty, 39 in favor with 146 abstentions. The vote means that the 22 European member states who have signed the treaty cannot ratify ACTA as their local sovereign law.

What Is Left in the U.S. IPR Arsenal? Bilateralism and Beyond

ACTA may not be dead yet, but it is on life support. The implications for the U.S. and the EU are significant. Cracks are appearing in their dominance over IPR, and the goal of imposing their domestic norms on enforcement globally are perhaps fading. In terms of the three dimensions of power referenced previously, the EU and the U.S. have lost ground. Discursively, the framing of the Internet as a space of freedom, openness, innovation, and privacy is gaining traction. In addition, the EU and the U.S. no longer have the advantages in instrumental power that they once had. Their measures can be considered stymied or defeated. Clearly, in all plurilateral and multilateral forums and societies, where the power differentials are not preponderantly in their favor, particularly in terms of structural power and access to markets, the U.S. and EU are finding it increasingly difficult to impose their disciplinary power and are facing strong, if not successful, resistance from civil society, from other states, and other online industries and companies that are reliant on open source software. Today, it is becoming increasingly clear that multilateralism is on

the wane, and that the United States and the EU find it advantageous to utilize their superior bargaining power through bilateral country-to-country relationships, and bilateral and regional free trade agreements. According to Benvenisti and Downs, the U.S. and the E.U. have used a combination of FTAs and regional trade agreements (RTAs) "to shape the evolution of norms in areas such as intellectual protection and drug pricing" (Benvenisti and Downs, quoted in Gathii, 2011, p. 464). Indeed, starting with Israel in 1985 and Canada in 1989, the U.S. has concluded 16 bilateral FTAs with countries whose economies are disproportionately smaller than that of the United States. It is at the bilateral level where the U.S. and the EU can take advantage of differences in structural power to impose their standards of digital IPR. It should be noted that enhanced IPP is not really about free trade at all, but about protecting the competitive advantage of corporations in intellectual property. As Kimberlee Weatherall (2004) states, "When the US strengthens IP law, and hence increases the rewards reaped by its creators in the US market, it is likely that a significant proportion of the profits will go to American creators" (p. 20).

However, where does this leave the United States and its efforts to impose its norms globally? The United States clearly had not given up forum shifting, once again in 2008, to a plurilateral forum, the Trans-Pacific Partnership (TPP). The TPP is composed of countries that the U.S. can more easily dominate, most of whom already have FTAs with the U.S. Members include Brunei, Chile, Singapore, Malaysia, New Zealand, Peru, Australia, and Vietnam, with Canada and Mexico joining in June 2012 and Japan in April 2013. The TPP is a very complex agreement, with provisions on banking, investment, food, and digital copyright. The negotiations of the TPP parallel the ACTA in terms of strict emphasis on secrecy. Participants, both negotiating countries and select corporations, must sign confidentiality agreements as a condition of entry into the talks.

As of May 2013, there had been 17 rounds of negotiations, but little is known about its contents except for the occasional leaked text. The only leaked text on copyright proposals was made available to the public date at the time of the fifth round of negotiations in February 2011. In the absence of transparency of content and any final draft, the leak has shaped the perceptions among civil society opponents of the copyright provisions by increasing their sense of insecurity and sense of risk to Internet freedoms and openness. For example, Article 16 of the leaked text, entitled "Special Measures Relating to Enforcement in the Digital Environment," reflects parts of the DMCA governing online service providers, including "notice and take-down" provisions (TPP, 2011). Users, moreover, would be prevented from breaking digital locks. In the end, the actual content may belie these fears, but as Public Knowledge (2013) notes, "It's hard to know the full extent of the harms the TPP's copyright provisions may pose to the public interest because the public has been kept in the dark." Ignoring public interest concerns may be counterproductive. As Public Knowledge (2013) notes, "ACTA's secrecy was a big factor in its downfall in Europe."

To date, however, resistance to the TPP has not been particularly strong. A comparison of blog mentions from December 2011 to March 2012 indicates that the TPP received only one-fifth the mentions per day as the ACTA.[15] The greatest resistance appears to center around other aspects of the proposed agreement, in particular restrictions on the use of generic drugs and provisions allowing corporations to sue a government for regulatory actions. One reason that the TPP has received so little attention or resistance to date may be due to the fact that negotiations are very secret with limited leaks. Perhaps spurred by the PIPA–SOPA debacle in June 2012, 132 members of the U.S. House of Representatives signed a letter to USTR Ambassador Ron Kirk demanding a more open process and consultation with Congress (Public Citizen, 2012).

Even if the TPP is eventually approved, what would the U.S. gain? It could, perhaps, induce other smaller countries, particularly those in the Global South, to sign on. However, what about larger countries such as China and India that the U.S. has on its 301 watch list as major violators of copyright? Until China becomes a significant exporter of IPR, why would it sign? In addition,

given that the European Parliament has rejected ACTA, it most likely would never accept the provisions of the TPP. It would thus seem that the U.S. would be a long way from imposing disciplinary power, except on a patchwork basis. The result may be, as Jadish Bhagwati put it, "a spaghetti bowl of rules" in the international trading system (quoted in Rimmer, 2006, p. 28).

CONCLUSION

The outset of this article spoke of two contradictory U.S. perspectives on the Internet. The first addressed the commitment of the U.S. government to Internet freedom. The second addressed the concern of the Internet as a dark, wild, and untamed space full of digital pirates that posed a risk to U.S. intellectual property and therefore was in need of control and discipline. The first view is promoted with vigor by the State Department, but the second is where the United States now places its priorities in terms of economics. The second view has been strongly supported by all administrations since the Clinton administration, along with large pharmaceutical, media, film, recording, and computer industries and Congressmen from both parties. Collectively they have actively promoted a widespread sense of insecurity and risk leading up to a ratcheting up of norms of intellectual property protection. Others have viewed these as limiting freedom and innovation online. As a result, the balance between the owners of copyright and users becomes increasingly upset.

At first, U.S. hegemony seemed insurmountable, with the U.S. framing the debate and determining policy formation through such means of global governance as the WTO and TRIPS. Today, there are clear cracks in U.S. hegemony. According to Immanuel Wallerstein (2007), "By 2007, the United States had lost its credibility not only as the economic and political leader of the world-system but also as the dominant military power" (p. 50). This view, echoed by Yale H. Ferguson (2008), asserts that "any notion of . . . US hegemony in the present day context is profoundly misleading" (p. 277). Michael F. Oppenheimer (2008) puts it this way:

The liberal form of globalization that has shaped the world over the past 60 years is in steep decline. The reason for that decline—principally, the loss of American hegemony—is now coming into focus, but what will replace the liberal form of globalization remains unclear. . . . The new globalization will be—inevitably—more heterogeneous. (p. 1)

Today, the U.S. and the EU can only impose their norms of IPR on much weaker states, increasingly in the form of bilateral agreements. Even here, there are skeptics. Morin (2009), for example, argues concretely that, "Thus far, more than a decade of active bilateralism has not produced preferred results for the United States" and questions "whether the negotiation of these bilateral agreements, at least in the realm of intellectual property law, is a wise investment of US Trade Representative's resources" (pp. 175 and 177).

Moreover, the U.S. is increasingly unable to silence resistance. Insecurity and risk are being redefined by social movement organizations in terms of threats to freedom and openness on the Internet. In fact, a counter-frame of user freedom, openness, privacy, innovation, and a re-appropriation of the term "pirates" has gained credence. In terms of the latter, the Internal Market Directorate General of the European Commission has suggested stepping away from the use of the term "pirate," feeling it "has heroic connotations" (McCreevy, 2008). So far, this suggestion has failed to gain traction. Today, civil society resistance has become much better organized, pronounced, and effective, particularly in Europe and now the United States with politicians paying attention. After the SOPA–PIPA debacle, the White House, a traditional champion of ratcheting up norms of IPR, is trying to have it both ways by reacting to protests in this manner: "We will continue to work with Congress on a bipartisan basis on legislation that provides new tools needed in the global fight against piracy and counterfeiting, while vigorously defending an open Internet based on the values of free expression, privacy, security and innovation" (Espinel, Chopra, & Schmidt, 2012). The emergence of large online industries and companies that are reliant on open source software, including Google, which supported the Obama administration with campaign donations, speaks to the rise of a competing business model that may eventually rival in power the outdated business model of media and other corporations demanding enhanced IP protection. In conclusion, the Internet is probably destined to remain, as it has been since the beginning, a highly contested space of power.

NOTES

1. What are being normalized are the technologies, not the specific political views underlying the use of copyright.

2. This has been done in other areas of norm setting at the global level. See Clapp and Fuchs (2009).

3. More specifically, hackers are participants in the networks of computer programmers who collaborate autonomously online on projects of creative programming, while crackers are those who penetrate someone's computer system to cause havoc. See Castells (2001).

4. For an insightful analysis on how intellectual property protection has become key to the U.S. asserting its economic hegemony, see Ngai-Ling (2003).

5. These figures were calculated from Table 5.2, Exports and imports of services—royalties and license fees. *UNCTAD Handbook of Statistics*, 2012.

6. However, as noted previously, piracy is not a new concept in terms of intellectual property. Antecedents to current battles over intellectual property existed much earlier. See, for example, Johns (2010).

7. The list of U.S. companies, which is dominated by pharmaceutical, computer, and media giants, includes Bristol Meyers, CBS, Du Pont, General Electric, General Motors, IBM, Johnson and Johnson, Merck, Monsanto, Hewlett-Packard, and Pfizer.

8. In 2001, the European Union approved the European Copyright Directive implementing the WCT.

9. For example, P. B. Hugenholtz was very active in trying to prevent the Copyright Directive from taking the form it did, and published regularly on the subject. See Hugenholtz (2000).

10. "Consolidated text: Anti-Counterfeiting Trade Agreement." Office of the United States Trade Representative.

11. The United Arab Emirates appeared to have participated in the 2008 negotiations.

12. The list of corporations with privileged access includes Google, Verizon, eBay, and the Consumer Electronics Association. The only civil society groups

allowed to see any document on a read-only and not-to-divulge basis have been Public Knowledge and the Center for Democracy and Technology (Weatherall, 2009, p. 4).

13. It is important to point out that according to the Canadian Library Association, " . . . in Canada, that ISPs are not just telephone and cable companies. Frequently school boards, colleges and universities, and sometimes public libraries serve as ISPs" (April 30, 2008, http://www.international.gc.ca/trade-agreements-accords-commerciaux/assets/pdfs/CLASubmissionanticounterfeiting080430.pdf).

14. The issue network was produced using "Issue Crawler," which utilizes Web network location and visualization software. A researcher uses a variety of methods including search engines to identify potential organizations in a network, and their URLs are then entered into Issue Crawler to identify the issue network and the links between them.

15. This comparison comes from the use of IceRocket (http://trend.icerocket.com/trend) to analyze trend lines over a three-month period (December 17, 2011 to March 17, 2012) in terms of blog mentions, with TPP receiving only one-fifth the mentions per day as ACTA.

REFERENCES

ACTA New Zealand. (2010). Retrieved from http://acta.net.nz/

Anstead, N., & Chadwick, A. (2009). Parties, election campaigning, and the Internet: Toward a comparative perspective. In A. Chadwick and P. N. Howard (Eds.), *Routledge handbook of Internet politics* (pp. 56–71). New York: Routledge.

Archibugi, D., & Filippetti, A. (2010). The globalisation of intellectual property rights: Four learned lessons and four theses. *Global Policy, 1*(2), 137–149.

Australian Digital Alliance. (2010). *Principles for ACTA negotiations.* Retrieved from http://www.digital.org.au/our-work/publication/principles-acta-negotiations

Béland, D. (2007). Insecurity and politics: A framework. *Canadian Journal of Sociology, 32*(3), 317–340.

Birnhack, M. D., & Elkin-Koren, N. (2003). The invisible handshake: The reemergence of the state in the digital environment. *Virginia Journal of Law and Technology, 8*(6), 1–48.

Brainwrap. (2012). Al Franken issues his PIPA backtrack & explanation. *Daily Kos.* Retrieved from http://www.dailykos.com/story/2012/01/20/1056840/-Al-Franken-issues-his-PIPA-backtrack-explanation#

Castells, M. (2001). *The Internet galaxy: Reflections on the Internet, business, and society.* Oxford, England: Oxford University Press.

Castells, M. (2010). *The power of identity* (2nd ed.). Malden, MA: Blackwell Publishing.

Clapp, J. A., & Fuchs, D. A. (2009). Agrifood corporations, global governance, and sustainability: A framework for analysis. In J. A. Clapp and D. A. Fuchs (Eds.), *Corporate power in global agrifood governance* (pp. 1–25). Cambridge, MA: MIT Press.

Clinton, H. R. (2010, January 21). *Remarks on Internet freedom.* Retrieved from http://www.state.gov/secretary/rm/2010/01/135519.htm

Deibert, R., & Rohozinski, R. (2010a). Beyond denial: Introducing next-generation information access controls. In R. J. Deibert, J. G. Palfrey, R. Rohozinski, & J. Zittrain (Eds.), *Access controlled: The shaping of power, rights, and rule in cyberspace* (pp. 3–15). Cambridge, MA: MIT Press.

Deibert, R., & Rohozinski, R. (2010b). Liberation vs control: The future of cyberspace. *Journal of Democracy, 24*(1), 43–57.

della Porta, D., Andretta, M., Mosca, L., & Reiter, H. (2006). *Globalization from below.* Minneapolis: University of Minnesota Press.

Denegri-Knott, J. (2004). Sinking the Online "Music Pirates:" Foucault, Power and Deviance on the Web. *Journal of Computer-Mediated Communication, 9.* doi: 10.1111/j.1083-6101.2004.tb00293.x

Drahos, P. (2004). Securing the future of intellectual property: Intellectual property owners and their nodally coordinated enforcement pyramid. *Case Western Reserve Journal of International Law, 36*(1), 53–77.

Drahos, P., & Braithwaite, J. (2002). *Information feudalism: Who owns the knowledge economy?* London: Earthscan Publications.

Electronic Frontier Foundation. (2012). A history of protecting freedom where law and technology collide. Retrieved from https://www.eff.org/about/history

Espinel, V., Chopra, A., & Schmidt, H. (2012). *Combating online piracy while protecting an open and innovative Internet.* Retrieved from https://wwws.whitehouse.gov/petition-tool/response/combating-online-piracy-while-protecting-open-and-innovative-internet

European Digital Rights. (2012, February 2). *ACTA fact sheet.* Retrieved from: http://www.edri.org/ACTAfactsheet

European Parliament. (2010). *Resolution of 10 March 2010 on the transparency and state of play of the ACTA negotiations.* Retrieved from http://www.europarl.europa.eu/sides/getDoc.do?pubRef=-//EP//TEXTTAP7-TA-2010-00580DOCXMLV0//EN

Ferguson, Y. H. (2008). Approaches to defining "empire" and characterizing United States influence in the contemporary world. *International Studies Perspectives, 9*(3), 272–280.

Foucault, M. (1990). *The History of Sexuality: An Introduction.* (Robert Hurley, Trans.). New York: Vintage Books.

Foucault, M. (1991). Governmentality. In G. Burchell, C. Gordon, and P. Miller (Eds.), *The Foucault effect* (pp. 87–104). Chicago: University of Chicago Press.

Gagatek, W. (Ed.). (2010). *The 2009 elections to the European Parliament: Country reports*. Florence, Italy: European University Institute.

Gathii, J. T. (2011). The neoliberal turn in regional trade agreements. *Washington Law Review, 86*(42), 421–474.

Geist, M. (2011, October 3). *Canada signs ACTA: What comes next*. Retrieved from http://www.michaelgeist.ca/content/view/6040/408/

Geist, M. (2012, March 2). *Assessing ACTA: Video of my talk at the European Parliament*. Retrieved from http://www.michaelgeist.ca/index.php?option=com_tags&task=view&tag=acta&Itemid=408

Google. (2012). *Google and the Open Source Developer*. Retrieved from http://code.google.com/opensource/

Haufler, V. (2006). Global governance and the private sector. In C. May (Ed.), *Global corporate power* (pp. 85–105). Boulder, CO: Lynne Rienner.

Henry, C., & Stiglitz, J. E. (2010). Intellectual property, dissemination of innovation, and sustainable development. *Global Policy, 1*(3), 237–251.

Hugenholtz, B. (2000). Why the copyright directive is unimportant, and possibly invalid. *European Intellectual Property Review, 11*, 501–502.

Huygen, A., Rutten, P., Huveneers, S., Limonard, S., Poort, J., Leenheer, J., et al. (2009). *Ups and downs: Economic and cultural effects of file sharing on music, film and games*. TNO Report. Retrieved from http://www.ivir.nl/publicaties/vaneijk/Ups_And_Downs_authorised_translation.pdf

Internet Industry Association, Australian Digital Alliance, Choice, & Australian Library and Information Association. (n.d.). *Principles for ACTA negotiations*. Retrieved from http://www.digital.org.au/submission/documents/PrinciplesforACTAnegotiations.pdf

Johns, A. (2010). *Piracy: The intellectual property wars from Gutenberg to Gates*. Chicago: Chicago University Press.

Kaminski, M. (2009). The origins and potential impact of the Anti-Counterfeiting Trade Agreement (ACTA). *Yale Journal of International Law, 34*(247), 247–256.

Kaminski, M. (2010). *The Anti-Counterfeiting Trade Agreement, Part II*. Retrieved from http://balkin.blogspot.com/2010/04/anti-counterfeiting-trade-agreement.html

Kapczynski, A. (2010). Access to knowledge: A conceptual genealogy. In G. Krikorian and A. Kapczynski (Eds.), *Access to knowledge in the age of intellectual property* (pp. 17–57). Cambridge, MA: MIT Press.

Khan, Z. (2008). Copyright piracy and development: United States evidence in the nineteenth century. *Revista de Economia Institucional, 10*(18), 21–54.

Kroes, N. (2012). *Comment: Neelie Kroes*. Retrieved from http://commentneelie.eu/sentence.php?s=2743

La Quadrature du Net. (2012, March 6). *ACTA may already be dead*. Retrieved from http://www.laquadrature.net/en/a-strategy-looking-through-acta-and-beyond

Loughlan, P. (2006). Pirates, parasites, reapers, sowers, fruits, foxes . . . The metaphors of intellectual property. *Sydney Law Review, 28*(2), 211–226.

Magid, L. (2012, January 18). What Are SOPA and PIPA and why all the fuss? *Forbes*. Retrieved from http://www.forbes.com/sites/larrymagid/2012/01/18/what-are-sopa-and-pipa-and-why-all-the-fuss/

Masnick, M. (2012, January 25). What is ACTA and why is it a problem? *techdirt*. Retrieved from http://www.techdirt.com/articles/20120124/11270917527/what-is-acta-why-is-it-problem.shtml

May, C. (2006). Between "commodification and openness": The information society and the ownership of knowledge. *Journal of Information Law and Technology, 2*(3). Retrieved from http://www2.warwick.ac.uk/fac/soc/law/elj/jilt/2005_2–3/may/

May, C. (2007). *Digital rights management: The problem of expanding ownership rights*. Oxford, England: Chandos Publishing.

May, C. (2010). *The global political economy of intellectual property rights* (2nd ed.). New York: Routledge.

May, C., and Sell, S. K. (2006). *Intellectual property rights: A critical history*. Boulder, CO: Lynne Rienner.

McCreevy, Charlie. (2008). Speech to Conference on Counterfeiting and Piracy [Press release]. Retrieved from http://europa.eu/rapid/press-release_SPEECH-08-237_en.htm

Morin, J.-F. (2009). Multilateralizing TRIPs-plus agreements: Is the US strategy a failure? *The Journal of World Intellectual Property, 12*(3), 175–197.

Morozov, E. (2011). *The net delusion*. New York: Public Affairs.

Newman, J. (2012, January 17). SOPA and PIPA: Just the facts. *PCWorld*. Retrieved from http://www.pcworld.com/article/248298/sopa_and_pipa_just_the_facts.html

Ngai-Ling, S. (2003). Informational capitalism and U.S. economic hegemony. *Critical Asian Studies, 3*(3), 373–398.

Office of the United States Trade Representative. (2008). *Special 301 Report*. Retrieved from http://www.ustr.gov/sites/default/files/asset_upload_file553_14869.pdf

Office of the United States Trade Representative. (2010). *Special 301 Report*. Retrieved from http://www.ustr.gov/webfm_send/1906

Oppenheimer, M. (2008). The end of liberal globalization. *World Policy Journal, 24*(4), 1–9.

Pirate Party UK. (2010, May 4). *What's in a name?* Retrieved from http://www.pirateparty.org.uk/blog/2010/may/4/whats-name/

Postigo, H. R. (2006). *The digital rights movement: The role of technology in subverting digital copyright.* (Doctoral dissertation). Rensselaer Polytechnic Institute, Troy, NY.

Postigo, H. R. (2009). Information communication technologies and framing for backfire in the digital rights movement: The case of Dmitry Sklyarov's advanced e-book processor. *Social Science Computer Review, 28*(2), 232–250.

Public Citizen. (2012). *TPP: corporate power tool of the 1%.* Retrieved from http://www.citizen.org/Page.aspx?pid=3129

Public Knowledge. (2012). *About.* Retrieved from http://www.publicknowledge.org/about

Public Knowledge. (2013). *The Trans-Pacific Partnership Agreement.* Retrieved from: http://tppinfo.org/

Rimmer, M. (2006). Robbery under arms: Copyright law and the Australia-United States Free Trade Agreement. *First Monday, 11*(3). Retrieved from http://firstmonday.org/htbin/cgiwrap/bin/ojs/index.php/fm/article/view/1316

RT Question More. (2012, January 28). *ACTA anger: Protesters hopeful as official resigns.* Retrieved from http://rt.com/news/acta-poland-arif-resignation-931/

Samuelson, P. (1997). The U.S. digital agenda at WIPO. *Virginia Journal of International Law, 37,* 369–439.

Sanders, A. K., Shabalala, D. B., Moerland, A., Pugatch, M., & Vergano, P. R. (2011). *European Parliament report prepared by Directorate-General for External Policies of the Union Directorate B, the Anti-Counterfeiting Trade Agreement (ACTA): An assessment.* Retrieved from http://www.erikjosefsson.eu/sites/default/files/DG_EXPO_Policy_Department_Study_ACTA_assessment.pdf

Sell, S. (1999). Multinational corporations as agents of change: The globalization of intellectual property rights. In A. C. Cutler, V. Haufler, & T. Porter (Eds.), *Private authority and international affairs* (pp. 169–199). New York: State University of New York Press.

Sell, S. (2010). A comparison of A2K movements: From medicines to farmers. In G. Krikorian and A. Kapczynski (Eds.), *Access to knowledge in the age of intellectual property access to knowledge in the age of intellectual property* (pp. 391–415). New York: Zone Books.

Sell, S. K. (2013). Revenge of the "nerds": Collective action against intellectual property maximalism in the global information age. *International Studies Review, 15*(1), 6–85.

Shashikant, S. (2005). *Intellectual property and the WIPO "development agenda."* Retrieved from http://www.twnside.org.sg/title2/FTAs/Intellectual_Property/IP_and_Development/IPandtheWIPODevelopmentAgenda-SangeetaShashikantWSIS.pdf

Sherman, C. (2012). *RIAA comment on rogue Websites legislative development.* Retrieved from http://www.riaa.com/newsitem.php?content_selector=newsandviews&news_month_filter=1&news_year_filter=2012&id=14C5BB7A-C902–934F-B5F5–57B8E898E391

Simons, J. J. (1999). Cooperation and coercion: The protection of intellectual property in developing countries. *Bond Law Review, 11*(1), 57–97.

Trans-Pacific Partnership. (2011, February 10). *Trans-Pacific Partnership intellectual property rights chapter.* Retrieved from http://keepthewebopen.com/assets/pdfs/TPP%20IP%20Chapter%20Proposal.pdf

Trudelle, Alice. (2012, February 17). Polish government asks European Parliament not to sign ACTA. *Warsaw Business Journal.* Retrieved from http://www.wbj.pl/article-58076-polish-government-asks-european-parliament-not-to-sign-acta.html

United Nations Conference on Trade and Development. (2012). *UNCTAD Handbook of Statistics.* Retrieved from http://unctad.org/en/PublicationsLibrary/tdstat37_en.pdf

United States Government Accountability Office. (2010). *Intellectual property: Observations on efforts to quantify the economic effects of counterfeit and pirated goods.* Retrieved from http://www.gao.gov/products/GAO-10–423

Wallerstein, I. (2007). Precipitate decline. *Harvard International Review, 29*(1), 50–55.

Weatherall, K. (2004). Locked in: Australia gets a bad intellectual property deal. *Policy Magazine, 20,* 18–24.

Weatherall, K. G. (2009). The Anti-Counterfeiting Trade Agreement: An updated analysis. In *The Selected Works of K. G. Weatherall.* Retrieved from http://works.bepress.com/kimweatherall/19

Weatherall, K. (2011). Politics, compromise, text and the failures of the Anti-Counterfeiting Trade Agreement. *Sydney Law Review, 33*(2), 229–263.

Occupy Wall Street: A New Political Form of Movement and Community?

Michael J. Jensen
Henrik P. Bang

ABSTRACT. This article analyzes the political form of Occupy Wall Street on Twitter. Drawing on evidence contained within the profiles of over 50,000 Twitter users, political identities of participants are characterized using natural language processing. The results find evidence of a traditional oppositional social movement alongside a legitimizing countermovement, but also a new notion of political community as an ensemble of discursive practices that are endogenous to the constitution of political regimes from the "inside out." These new political identities are bound by thin ties of political solidarity linked to the transformative capacities of the movement rather than thick ties of social solidarity.

In the last few years, the world has seen an explosion of social movement activity across both the Arab world and the industrialized West. The Arab Spring has transformed the landscape of the Middle East with the overthrow of governments and the institution of democratic elections in Egypt, Libya, and Tunisia, while the anti-globalization movement, the Spanish *indignados*, and the Occupy movements have carried out large-scale demonstrations in 82 countries (Hogue, 2012). Movements such as the Arab Spring, the Spanish *indignados*, and Occupy Wall Street (OWS) defy conventional categories of movement composition. Social movements have been defined as "collective challenges, based on common purposes and social solidarities, in sustained interaction with elites, opponents, and authorities" (Tarrow, 1998, p. 4). However, recent research suggests that these movements, to varying degrees, belie each of four defining elements of social movements: the collective nature of the challenge, the enactment of social solidarity, the creation of common purposes across movement participants, and sustained interaction. In particular, the organizational capacities enabled by online social media appeared to have played a critical role in the creation of new movement forms (Bennett & Segerberg, 2011, 2012; Gonzalez-Bailon, Borge-Holthoefer, & Moreno, 2012; Jensen, Jorba, & Anduiza, 2012; Segerberg & Bennett, 2011; Theocharis, 2013).

Manuel Castells has brought considerable empirical data and social theory to bear on

Michael J. Jensen is Research Fellow at the ANZSOG Institute for Governance at the University of Canberra. His research interests include political communication and political participation.

Henrik P. Bang is professor in governance and participation at the ANZSOG Institute for Governance at the University of Canberra. His key research interests are citizen involvement online/offline, multi-level governance, political communication, and marketing.

the emergence of new digitally networked movements through his writings on identity in network societies (2010), "communication power" (2009), and his most recent application of the latter work to studies of the Arab Spring, the *indignados*, and OWS (2012).These technologies cannot be conceived as causal explanations for the emergence of OWS and the *indignados*. But the distributed and scalable communications capabilities of new social media provide the communication infrastructure for these movements to develop and expand without reliance on a formal movement organization. In Castells's formulation, power is not only coercion but also the construction of meaning, which depends on processes of socialized communication. To the extent that the prevailing communication environment changes with the diffusion and adoption of Internet devices, the constitution of power and the basis for its resistance—counterpower—changes. In short, digital communication networks can provide movements with critical communication capacities with which to shape the negotiation of meanings, knowledge, and identities within a virtual public sphere.

Defining the ties between participant and movement identities has become a critical task in recent years. Structural dislocations from the positions within civil society (Beck, 1997; Giddens, 1991), widespread value change, and increasing globalization have combined to produce increasing individuation of political life (Bennett, 1998; Dalton, 2008; Inglehart, 1997; Micheletti, Føllesdal, & Stolle, 2004), as well as shifts in participatory repertoires away from the "old," democratic input politics in civil society and the state toward active involvement in various kinds of governance networks at multiple levels from the local to the global (Bang, 2005; Fischer, 2003; Hajer & Wagenaar, 2003). Dalton (2008) traces these turns to a generation gap between the older generations, which behave according to collective duty norms, and the younger generations, which are more prone to act on engagement norms that spring from more individual action frames. Norris (2007) demonstrates how new engagement norms prompt a swing from the old *citizen-oriented* politics

TABLE 1. Contrasting Dimensions of Participation

	Old forms of participation and movement	New forms of participation and movement
Norms	Duty	Engagement
Activism	Citizen-oriented	Cause-oriented
Identity	Oppositional or legitimizing	Project

relating to voting and parties and toward a new more *cause-oriented politics,* which need neither have formal government as its focus nor be a response to formal governmental concerns (an example being the boycotting of certain goods or companies). Finally, Castells (2010) identifies the outgrowth of engagement norms and cause-oriented action with a shift in identity from the old kinds of oppositional and legitimizing identity toward a project identity potentially capable of societal transformation. We outline these contrasts in Table 1.

When we look at how simple and strongly interconnected the two profiles for old and new forms of participation and movement seem to be at the conceptual level, one wonders why we have not yet organized our research in terms of them. A crucial question for research into political participation and social movements today seems exactly to be how these two types of norms—activism and identity—can be combined in and through the application of digital communication oriented toward reforming representative democracy and, at the same time, meeting the rapidly escalating policy risks, problems, and challenges associated with threats of economic meltdowns, global warming, migration, famine, obesity, and so on.

One example is Norris's (2007) study of protest movements.She convincingly shows how cause politics does not only make everything potentially a political target of protest, thus vastly extending old equations of politics with what goes on in nation-state and government.It also dissolves the old distinction between "conventional" and "protest" politics (Barnes & Kasse, 1979). Whereas the old protest politics was prompted by a sense of duty and willingness to combat "the system" and push it back from the "life-world," cause politics is prompted by specific concerns and issues, and it is more a matter of identity creation and of expressing a specific lifestyle in one's engagement than of demonstrating a certain ideological position. This analysis fits very well into the first two rows in Table 1. However, since Norris hangs on to studying protest movements within the old dichotomies in mainstream political science between conflict and consensus and stability and change, she logically enough interprets the fact that the new protest movements cannot be characterized by an oppositional identity as evidence that they must then be having a legitimizing one. As she argues: "Today, collective action through demonstrations has become a generally accepted way to express political grievances, voice opposition, and challenge authorities" (Norris, 2007, p. 640). However, had Norris been into the ongoing discussions of Castells in sociology and elsewhere, this might have made her contemplate whether her survey findings might not better describe the advent of project identity than the legitimizing identity's victory over the oppositional one. Instead, Norris becomes a spokesperson of the view that since "resistance movements" obviously are not as visible in Western democracies, this must mean that they are both stable and rest on an underlying normative consensus.

The problem is that if it is true that engagement norms, cause-oriented action, and project identity are beginning to dominate in Western politics and society, then we can no longer conclude *ipso facto* that because there is not, and has not been, much rebellion in the West after the death of Marxism and communism, representative democracy must also be based on a strong sense of legality and legitimacy, a high degree of compliance, and also on strong justifications of its legality and legitimation (Beetham, 1991). For example, people with a project identity will tend to assess political leaders and institutions not only by their actual performance and ability to deliver on the output side of political processes (specific output support), but in particular by their abilities to do so over a longer span of time (long-term output support). Hence, their

general support of democratic government may result, to a large extent, from general output support, stemming from their experiences over a longer time period with the quality and efficiency of outputs (Lindgren & Persson, 2010). It follows that their legitimation of "the system" may actually have little to do with the kind of support associated with its representative and moral qualities for meeting demands on the input side. A critical question today is precisely whether Western political systems can resist a long-lasting crisis of performance and delivery on the output side, if the old kind of general input legitimacy is rapidly eroding and being replaced by long-term output support. Perhaps Western democracies are much more vulnerable and in transition than they appear to be in the mainstream frame of reference. If we are to assess how the advent of the project identity and the change toward output legitimacy affect the governability and legitimation of the political system, new conceptual distinctions such as those in Table 1 are highly needed.

Multidisciplinary research into political participation and social movement may help to give us new indications of how simultaneously to enhance support and performance instead of standing idly by when the one destroys the other in theory and society. We cannot solve this riddle in this article, of course. Rather, we tentatively sketch an analytical framework within which we study the OWS movement, and then use this framework to assess how the OWS movement operates between the old and the new forms of participation by examining participant profiles rather than movement organization rhetoric. We explore this framework using the Twitter profiles of over 50,000 participants, opponents, and bystanders who tweeted during a global OWS mobilization in the fall of 2011. Our data show how the OWS movement and its effects belie the compartmentalizations characterizing the old and the new modes of social and political conduct. Yet it is also clear that configurations of both the old and the new modes of participation are present among supporters, opponents, and bystanders of the movement. The idealized movement ethos distilled by these actors is at odds with the complexity revealed in the context of a demonstration.

OLD AND NEW PARTICIPATORY FORMS IN CONTEMPORARY MOVEMENTS

Social movements can be regarded as a species of action community engaged in a political division of labor. A political action community is "thinner" than a social community, based on a strong sense of sharing common goals or a common interest. Nor does it reduce to a national community with a "thick" sense of belonging. An action community pursues common projects even though its members may display irreconcilable differences, whether social, cultural, religious, or ethnic. In fact, such differences tend to be regarded as a resource for, more than a barrier to, doing things in common. Identity construction is neither antecedent to movement emergence nor immutable as identities may evolve over time. Movement identities are not properties of individuals. Rather, they enable individual participants to locate themselves in a wider field of political action, indicating the terms on which a collective "we" is functionally established through the delineation of a particular organization of political roles and tasks within a wider field of political contention. The fact that action communities consist of fluid, overlapping, often incompatible or "inconsistent" identities may be the reason why they appear governed by individual action frames more than by collective ones, providing a motivational locus orienting participants and directing activities (Benford & Snow, 2000; Melucci, 1992; Snow & Benford, 1988; Tarrow, 1998). We will argue that an action community is collectively anchored in that which has to be done in—and through—a political division of labor. Furthermore, the "thin" nature of action communities is, in our view, exactly what motivates reflexive individuals to join them and direct their individual action frames toward solving common concerns. Newer movement forms oriented toward the pursuit of common projects will necessarily tend to eschew "thick" originating identities, such as national and social categories, in order to be able to do their job.

The last year has produced a flurry of academic research on OWS, primarily concentrating on the movement organization and treating the movement ethos in singular terms (Caren & Gabby, 2011; Castells, 2012; Sitrin, 2012; Wright, 2012). However, scholars of social movement organizations have long recognized that the aims of movement participants and movement organizations are often unaligned (McCarthy & Zald, 1977; Snow, 2012; Zald & McCarthy, 1987). This caution is likely warranted all the more so in discussing "leaderless" movements like OWS. In analyzing the movement and its opposition, we consider the variety of movement identities articulated by the various participants in OWS and the countermovement on Twitter.

Participant identities may vary in the manner they relate to the political system. In analyzing the composition of the OWS movement and countermovement, we delineate three identity types: legitimizing identities corresponding to identities connected with the dominant institutions in the political system and civil society; oppositional identities that engage in resistance against the legitimized institutions and structures; and project identities that are transformative of both the participants standing in society and also seeks to reshape the organization of society in the process (Castells, 2010). We will elaborate each of these identity types in turn.

Legitimizing and Oppositional Political Identities

We categorize legitimizing and oppositional identities together because they possess the same norms of participation, differentiated by power stratifications rather than beliefs about the organization of the political system. Legitimizing identities operate in relation to political objects as well as objects within civil society secured by the prevailing organization of political structures. Legitimizing political identities refer to the established entities that generally prevail in a society and the ideologies that underwrite their dominance. Within the United States, the epicenter of the OWS movement, these include a number of conservative entities that have defined OWS as a threat to a coherent set of values and organizations that espouse them: conservative groups, negative liberty, patriotism, and an *exclusionary* discourse underlying a conflictual political imaginary. Although there has been some notable crossover in support and collaboration between them, the Tea Party movement generally has been associated with legitimizing political identities and provides a useful contrast with OWS. Whereas the Tea Party has a clearly defined constituency—primarily white upper middle class Americans who see themselves as victims of an overbearing government—OWS lacks a predefined constituency within the cleavages of civil society (Tarrow, 2011).

For this reason, freedom is defined as a freedom from intervention from agents of government that otherwise limit their capacities to act within civil society and the market. For them, these domains are best vouchsafed from intervention from governments. Examples of this included a common meme by Tea Party supporters claiming to represent the 53% of Americans with a non-zero net income tax burden who are therefore producers and deserving members of the society. This figure was a direct response to claims by OWS that they represent the bottom 99% of incomes and therefore demand political standing. The use of the label "Tea Party" emphasizes an identification of a particular version of the country's founding and wraps their positions within claims of patriotism. The Tea Party does not have a monopoly on these themes, as many other conservative groups have made the same discursive connections.

In addition to the political component, there are corresponding legitimizing positions in civil society. Despite the interdependencies that may exist between the civil society and political society, prominent and diverse theories of democratic politics in general and social movements in particular have been predicated on the division between the political system and an autonomous civil society (Cohen & Arato, 1994; Dahlgren, 2005; Habermas, 1996; Melucci & Avritzer, 2000; Putnam, 2001). Although perhaps politically consequential, civil society is necessarily apolitical, a third space, decoupled from the political system. Castells (2010) argues that states integrate the public through civil society; therefore, legitimizing political identities have corresponding positions within civil society. Legitimizing identities are totalizing

and exclusionary as they define persons in their nonpolitical noncontingent natures either within or outside a social order.

Legitimizing community identities, though not isomorphic with legitimizing political identifications, normally do not challenge that order. In Western democracies, and the United States in particular, legitimizing community identities are connected to a secular order that has carved out a space for Judeo-Christian religion to practice relatively unhindered, as well as family life. Citizenship norms such as "duty" do not have a direct correspondence with legitimizing political identifications. Though traditional philosophical accounts fused the duties of citizenship with the political governance of the polity, today politics typically refers to a more limited conventional activity characterized by contestation, and the terms of conflict are normally irreducible to a normatively stabilized ideal (Luhmann, 1982, p. 106). For this reason, duty-based citizenship more precisely refers to a disposition legitimizing the prevailing order (Dalton, 2008). Finally, depending on the political system, membership in the military may fall under either a legitimizing political identification or a legitimizing community identification. On the one hand, the military is always implicated as a part of the political regime. However, it also has a function in the community life that is politically varied. In the American political system, despite popular perceptions, enlisted members of the military are significantly more likely than the general population to identify themselves as political independents rather than in partisan terms and pride themselves on acceptance of the authority of whichever party is in power (Dempsey, 2009). Furthermore, identification with the military has often served as an indicator of one's identification not with a set of political authorities or the political regime, but with the political community (Klingemann, 1999). Legitimizing community identities are not explicitly political identifications, though they are linked with the exercise of authority and the operations of the prevailing political order.

Oppositional movements often emerge against as a countervailing force. Strain and breakdown theories of social movements hold that movements emerge at times when the "social controls and moral imperatives that normally constrain such behavior are weakened or absent" (Buechler, 2004, p. 48). Under such conditions when the constraints of duties associated with formal citizenship practice give way, oppositional movements may emerge demanding acknowledgment from the political system. Given their outsider status, these movements define themselves against the dominant order. In contrast to the claims of organic commonality invoked by legitimizing identities, oppositional identities depend on explicit expressions of solidarity. Solidarity is not just a resource for mobilization, it serves an integrating function for oppositional movements given the limited availability of social institutions in the wider society (Melucci & Avritzer, 2000).

Project Identities

Project identity movements are greatly facilitated by the advent of the network society. These movements form outside the spaces of civil society and therefore lack the communication infrastructure formal organizations have provided to traditional movements. Project identities correspond to movements that form outside the spaces of civil society. Castells (2010) argues that such identities come into being when "social actors, on the basis of whatever cultural materials are available to them build a new identity that redefines their position in society and, by so doing, seek the transformation of overall social structure" (p. 8). These movements are distinguished from legitimizing and oppositional movements along two dimensions: the form of community they enact and the attendant operations of power they exercise and react against.

Action communities vary in terms of the identifications they enact with respect to their functions within a political movement and its larger place within the political system. Norms, identities, and modalities of activism are interrelated elements distinguishing new and old forms of political participation. Duty norms are linked to juridical conceptions of citizenship defined by sets of rights and responsibilities. Social movements have become an extension of repertoires for interest representation aimed at influencing collective decision making. The motivational locus of new movements is neither the legal guarantees and responsibilities of citizenship nor the latent interests of publics waiting to be actualized in binding decisions. Instead, it stems from the acknowledgment of common concerns and the ability to make a difference in a concrete area. These dimensions manifest in variations with respect to the manner in which movements relate to the political system and take shape in the form of identities inaugurated: legitimizing political identities, oppositional political identities, legitimizing community identities, or project identities.

Traditional accounts of state–civil society relations hold the latter as an autonomous sphere that can bring together collective pressure on political authorities and other opponents. By contrast, new social movements have come to politicize the very nature of civil society, market, and state relations. OWS presents a direct challenge to the bracketing of power operations that characterize the liberal organization of society around a state and relatively autonomous entities in civil society and the market. These capacities, Foucault observed, are mutually implicated; political authority is not only wielded over society, it also operates through civil society (Foucault, 1977, p. 20; Foucault, 2001, p. 290). As Foucault (2008) outlines the evolution of civil society in practice and political theory:

These three elements—the opening up of a domain of non-juridical social relations, the articulation of history on the social bond, in a form which is not one of degeneration, and government as an organic components of the social bond and the social bond as an organic feature of the form of authority—are what distinguish the notion of civil society from (1) Hobbes, (2) Rousseau, and (3) Montesquieu. It seems to me that we enter into a completely different system of political thought and I think it is the thought or political reflection internal to a new technology of government, or to a new problem which the emergence of the

93

economic problem raises for techniques and technologies of government. (p. 308)

These new modalities of project politics eschew the legitimizing/oppositional duality in relation to formal political authority. Rather, their credo is to work with, against, or without political authorities and experts depending on how it suits the situation. In the words of Foucault (2000): "we need to escape this dilemma of being either for or against.... Working with a government doesn't imply either a subjection or a blanket acceptance. One can work and be intransigent at the same time" (pp. 455–456).

Our guiding hypothesis is that OWS is a good example of this new, reflexive, and political sociality, or community, blending individuality and commonality in new ways for responding to policy problems and challenges in the political economy. Although OWS lacks the unifying and integrating social and normative structures typically associated with the building of social trust and social solidarity in civil society, its access to new information technologies and its layering into multiple governance networks provide it with an action potential, which can be employed to contribute to the creation of a new social fabric, new social relations, new economic structure, and thus new forms of government. Because OWS supporters need not rely on ties to formal legitimizing or oppositional groups within civil society, participation in the movement can be expected to transcend partisan and ideological divisions. For this reason, to the extent that they adopt project identities rather than legitimizing or oppositional identities, participants in the OWS movement are more open to discussing and reconciling the negotiation of difference. Not bound by the solidarity of shared origins (organic or constructed), project identities organize because of shared destinies, linking individuals to a role in the division of political labor. Of course, this requires that members of OWS as a reflexive form of action community can ground beliefs in a common cause, building a solitary political community in which widespread acceptance and recognition of difference prevails. In any case, OWS demonstrates how new political civil society depends on the organizational capacities and communicative resources contained within the networks that include but extend beyond the immediate scene of humans connected by technologies.

Hence, we suspect OWS imbricates collective and individual motivational loci: the individual desire to make a difference gives rise to loose networks of persons seeking to collectively enact a political transformation of some portion of the world in which they inhabit. Specifically, this suggests our first hypothesis regarding the incidence of project identities among OWS participants.

H1: The belief in one's ability to make a difference and the expression of an openness to difference will be expressed in common.

If legitimizing identities emerge from thick community ties, project identities enact thin sociality. Bennett and Segerberg (2011, 2012) argue that many contemporary movements, highly dependent on networks of digital communications, rely on personalized rather than collective action frames. In contrast to traditional identity frames that include "both a positive identification of those participating in a certain group, and a negative identification of those who are not only excluded but actively opposed," (della Porta & Diani, 1999, p. 87), personalized action frames express individual identities and eschew exclusion in that they are not defined in terms of selected constituencies and their interests. Although overlapping personal networks between elites in many movements have played a critical role in creating organizational linkages, those between laypersons in a political system do not create binding identifications and linkages (Walgrave et al., 2011). Rather, these movements are able to reach a wider network of persons whose participation is ad hoc and belies the temporal connotations and role differentiation implied by formal membership. As these movements do not correlate with a defined social cleavage, a proximate function of movement contention is the construction of public. Hence, the ethos of such movements is not the definition of interests against others as the creation of commonality across difference. The creation of a shared identity is therefore both a necessary consequence and irreducible to a transactional network of resource diffusion.

Regarding the levels of Twitter activity for these identity groups, previous research has indicated the existence of distinct signatures in their profiles. While legitimizing and oppositional identities have been linked to high levels of tweeting, given their ad hoc nature we can expect participants in project-centered politics to be average-level Twitter users (Mustafaraj et al., 2011).

A second contrasting element of project-centered political movements concerns the manner in which they negotiate freedom and power. As noted earlier, Tea Party groups mobilize around a narrative of victimhood in the face of government and collective oppression. Such groups define freedom in negative terms as a "freedom from," inversely related to the exercise of power by governments or other collectivities. Here we differ from Castells's (2009) alembication of power which ultimately reduces to a power over and against, a resistance to overcome. Although he considers power both in terms of control and as capacity creation, he ultimately concludes that "the power of social actors cannot be separated from their empowerment against other social actors" because social actors necessarily intervene in contested spaces (Castells, 2009, p. 13). Without Foucault's complementary position of power as productive, as "power to" act, it is hard to conceptualize how project identities could ever enact a common project without reengaging the conflictual dynamics of legitimizing and oppositional identities. For this reason, we suggest that the emphasis on "freedom from" or the "power to" are critical distinctions between the legitimizing and oppositional identities of traditional social movements and the project politics of new social movements.

Movements, Countermovements, and the Varieties of OWS Identities

The contentious politics of social movements does not exist in a vacuum. As a movement achieves success in terms of growth in adherents and resources, this can sometimes create the conditions that give rise to a countervailing movement rising against the original movement (Meyer & Staggenborg, 1996). Countermovements form part of the political opportunity structure in which movements operate, and they can span the domains of formal political institutions, market actors, and civil society organizations (Tarrow, 2011, pp. 75–77). They form a "symbiotic dependence during the course of mobilization" as two elements "loosely coupled in conflict" (della Porta & Diani, 1999). Countermovements often appropriate thematic elements of their opponents' discourse. For example, in reply to the demands of the "99%" for economic justice, American opponents of the movement rejoined that they are part of the 53% who pay federal income taxes, a theme that endured into the election cycle a year later. Given the reciprocal structuring of the political environment created by movements and their opponents, "one cannot fully understand movement dynamics without accounting for their countermovements" (Lind & Stepan-Norris, 2011, p. 1598). Despite, their locations in legitimized positions, in the same manner that project politics politicizes spaces within civil society, "social countermovements [sic] inside the political system know how to use the spaces of reflexive democracy" (Beck, 1997, p. 42).

The emergence of a movement need not temporally precede the existence of the organized and semi-organized action communities composing countermovements. Movements often come into being against the backdrop of existing organized and semi-organized action publics.[1] In the case of OWS, the movement emerged in the context of a financial crisis producing significant job losses, stagnant or declining incomes, and a collapse in the housing market, producing massive home foreclosures, many illegal, while major financial institutions received a government bailout and corporate profits reached record levels (van Gelder, 2012). Hence OWS came into being by virtue of a critique of existing arrangements in which a number of actors and groups have significant interests in maintaining. This appears to have consequences for the manner in which OWS rhetorically positions itself as an organization. Although OWS is not organized around distinct constituencies or civil society segments, the OWS organization presents itself as an old kind of oppositional movement: "Occupy Wall Street is a leaderless resistance movement with people of many colors, genders and political persuasions. The one thing we all have in common is that We Are The 99% that will no longer tolerate the greed and corruption of the 1%. We are using the revolutionary Arab Spring tactic to achieve our ends and encourage the use of nonviolence to maximize the safety of all participants."[2] Thus, the new thing about the OWS is that it presents itself as being oppositional and, at the same time, as being non-ideological and multicultural. After all, its basic slogan is "Solidarity Forever!," emphasizing the thick ties of social connection rather than the thin ties of political action connected with project identities. Given the hybridity in the movement organization's self-understanding, we anticipate this will have consequences for the types of identities drawn to participate in the movement. We therefore offer two further hypotheses:

H2: The OWS demonstration will attract a countermovement composed of legitimized identities.

H3: OWS will attract a combination of project and oppositional identities.

In this article, we analyze the range of identifications associated with the participants in the OWS movement, its opponents, and other bystanders. By focusing on the overall set of actors, we are able to determine the range of mobilizing identifications that OWS has brought into being rather than exclusively those associated with OWS.

DATA, METHODS, AND OPERATIONALIZATIONS

Analyzing the participants in contentious activity creates significant sampling issues. The main difficulty concerns the identification of participants in movements and countermovements, particularly when the participants are located across different continents. We address this difficulty by studying the online participants in the movement and countermovement on Twitter, thereby enabling their systematic identification. Researchers in the social sciences have begun to study the organization of protest movements within online social networks, taking the digital artifact as the object of inquiry rather than survey research (Bennett & Segerberg, 2011; Caren & Gaby, 2011; DeLuca, Lawson, & Sun, 2012). The data are the profiles of the contributors to commentary regarding the OWS demonstrations on Twitter. Further details on the search terms are contained in the Appendix. Twitter profiles contain the user's self-description, indicating the essential aspects of their identities that they wish to communicate to persons in this medium. Mining the Twitter profile description lines provides unique insight into participant identities. In contrast to the tweets themselves, these provide insight into fundamental elements out of which they construct their identities behind the tweets they send.

The profiles were compiled from the set of tweets collected during the course of the October 15, 2011 global demonstrations using the Twitter search application programming interface (API).[3] The screen names were extracted and the profile downloaded by a program accessing the Twitter API. From each of these profiles, the 160-character description was extracted for analysis. This approach captures the identities that protest participants communicate in the precise manner they present themselves. This has an advantage over survey research in that it captures not fragments of citizen's identities but those which are exteriorized in the manner in which they organize and relate the elements of their identities. The constitution of identities is an important consideration in its own right as it renders visible configurations of norms and civil society ties, which are less epiphenomenal than tweets, that move persons to discuss OWS—an aspect of mobilization that has not been addressed in previous work on the involvement of social media in new forms of political protest (e.g., Bennett & Segerberg, 2012). Hence, the relatively static nature of the profiles are more likely to indicate significant and underlying elements of identity construction than would be revealed in other contexts than the tweets themselves. This approach also has an advantage over survey research in that it enables us to see the manner in which citizens understand their identities, thereby avoiding the "Humpty Dumpty" problem entailed by the fragmentation of belief systems via discrete survey questions and their subsequent analytical reconstruction (de Certeau, 1984, p. xvii; Rosenberg, Ward, & Chilton, p. 1988). Some accounts may be linked to organizations rather than individuals. This distinction is not important for us as there is communicative parity between accounts; that is, whether or not the holder of an account is an individual or organization does not change the range of communicative operations that may be engaged, adding to the flows of communications in the same manner. Furthermore, as the flows of communications that constitute the demonstration include both organizations and individuals—both enacting relationships to the political system, the profiles provide a fuller picture of participants than survey research.

The descriptions from each profile were extracted. Twitter profile descriptions, although far from an exhaustive account of each Twitter user, signals the manner in they present themselves to others, particularly those they encounter only via Twitter. Twitter user descriptions are constrained by a 160-character limit, thereby forcing users to be highly selective in the terms with which they describe themselves. The text of each tweet was cleaned to remove extraneous .html formatting, spaces, and line breaks. The text was normalized, removing capitalization, and tokenized to separate words from punctuation. The description coding was automated using a natural language processing (NLP) routine scripted in the Python language (Bird, Klein, & Loper, 2009). NLP has been used primarily by computer scientists and linguists (Mueller, 2008; Ramsay, 2003); however, it is beginning to make inroads in political science and other disciplines (McKelvey et al., 2012; Sweetnam & Fennell, 2012). Because these data draw on the population of all those commenting on the OWS demonstrations, they include movement supporters, critics, and bystanders—all with varying levels of organizational integration and affiliations. The profile descriptions were coded according to 12 separate identifications. These categories were arrived at based on a cataloging a random sample of 2000 profiles to select coding terms.

Legitimizing political identities are not necessarily linked to conservative ideologies. However, we treat conservative ideologies as associated with legitimizing identities since OWS is primarily a movement that has emerged in societies with capitalist economies, and our text mining is confined to English-speaking tweets, which are predominantly from countries where legitimizing identities are linked with conservative identities (particularly, the United States, the United Kingdom, and Australia). Historically, conservative politics have protected the self-organization of the market to a greater extent than leftist politics. We operationalize the political dimension of this identity in terms of the following four items.

- *Legitimizing political ideology*: names of conservative political parties, movement organizations such as the Tea Party, or Twitter hashtags signaling that the author has a conservative ideology.
- *Exclusionary discourse*: terms of negation, opposition, or dismissal.
- *Freedom from*: the exercise of a private sphere of rights.
- *Patriotism*: symbols of national identity conferred upon persons as well as objects.

Legitimizing community identities denote one's relationship to historically privileged segments within civil society. As the bulk of the tweets refer to an American context, we select four institutions and norms that have historically played a significant role in organizing American cultural life.

- *Religion*: references to religious organizations or the contents of religious belief systems.
- *Military service*: veteran, reserve, or active duty membership in the armed forces.

- *Duty*: the integration of a set of activities within a horizon of moral obligation.
- *Family*: descriptions and self-references in terms of family roles.

Oppositional identities are "stigmatized by a logic of domination" (Castells, 2010, p. 8) against which they engage in conflict. Like legitimizing identities, oppositional identities are exclusionary and conflictual.

- *Justice*: identification of oneself in relation to a call for justice or a more equitable organization of society and the economy. In relation to the issues of contention raised by OWS, these identities oppose the prevailing organization of the market.
- *Solidarity*: identification with others involved in the OWS movement creating thick affective ties stressing commonality in condition.

Project-centered identities revolve around a political rather than social relationship. Project identities seek to transform their position in society and, in the process, effect wider structural changes. We identify terms relating to the ethos of project identities and the form of power stemming a collective capacity to enact change.

- *Empathy*: communicating an openness to difference rather than a profession of sameness.
- *Power to*: identification with collective capacities for acting together.

Principal components analysis is used to determine the extent to which these terminological categories cluster around the identity categories anticipated and to what extent these categories are representative of the overall distribution identifications among OWS supporters, opponents, and bystanders.

RESULTS

The participants in the OWS movement and counter-mobilization on Twitter are, on average, heavy users of Twitter. Table 2 details the level

TABLE 2. Descriptive Statistics

	Median	Mean	Std. Dev.
Friends	324	935.09	4059.17
Followers	283	2654.96	51456.30
Favorites	10	368.80	4022.74
Statuses	4,066	11477.86	23346.06

of account activity in terms of the friends, followers, status updates, and the number of statuses that have been designated a "favorite" by other users. Friends and followers are distinct entities because, unlike Facebook, these relations need not be reciprocal. The number of "friends" refers to the number of accounts that a user follows, and the number of followers designates the number of accounts that have opted to follow a user. The median friends (324) is higher than the median number of followers (283). However, the ratio between the mean number of friends (935.09) and mean number of followers (2654.96) reverses and dramatically widens. This indicates a large number of accounts are high-profile actors with more out-links than in-links, contrasting greatly with the average Twitter user: 93.6% of users have 100 or fewer followers, and 92.4% have 100 or fewer friends. Additional data, not reported here, reveals that many of these accounts belong to media outlets reporting on the OWS demonstrations. Furthermore, these tend to be fairly active accounts. The median number of posts (4,066) and the mean (11477.86) indicate OWS participants and bystanders are significantly more active than typical users of Twitter (Cheng, Evans, & Singh, 2009).

Each profile was coded with respect to the frequency of terms corresponding to each of the 12 identifications operationalized. The majority of the profile descriptions contained unique and meaningful content. Of the 50,397, only 6,934 (13.76%) were either blank, denoted as "null" or "none," or contained grammatical marks such as a single period or ellipses such that no substantive meaning could be inferred about their political identities. However, the bulk of the profile descriptions were nonpolitical; that is, they do not reference political objects or themes in their descriptions.[4] There are 10,710 (21.25%)

FIGURE 1. Participant identifications.

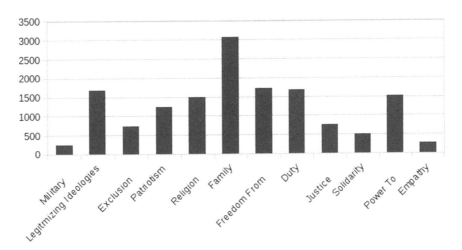

profile descriptions that define users in reference to entities in civil society, the political system, or other norms. Although the majority of cases are undefined, this represents a sizeable number of participants, and there is no evidence they constitute an unusual sample of OWS participants. Although individual users may hold beliefs corresponding to classificatory categories, these data reflect the categories individuals chose to identify, positioning themselves in relation to other Twitter users. The majority of those participating in the OWS demonstration and counterdemonstration do not identify themselves according to locations in civil society or the general profession of political norms.

Figure 1 indicates the overall presence of each of these identifications across the profiles. The instances of each of the coding terms for each category were summed across each of the profiles. Descriptions of family relationships are the most common, present in over 3,000 of the profiles. Identifications with politically conservative causes as well as the ideological conception of freedom articulated by these causes are the second and third most common identifications. References to religious affiliation, expressions of civic duty, and identifications with power as the creation of productive capacities come across in roughly 1,500 of these profiles. Although terms identifying an exclusion are less common, Table 3 shows this identification has the highest

TABLE 3. Descriptive Statistics Profile Attributes

Item	Mean	Std. Deviation	Range
Duty	0.035	0.200	0–4
Empathy	0.007	0.088	0–5
Exclusion	0.016	0.146	0–8
Family	0.086	0.365	0–7
Freedom from	0.040	0.229	0–5
Justice	0.018	0.150	0–3
Military	0.006	0.079	0–3
Partisan ideology	0.042	0.250	0–6
Patriotism	0.026	0.182	0–6
Power to	0.033	0.194	0–4
Religion	0.034	0.205	0–4
Solidarity	0.010	0.107	0–4

variance, suggesting that a small but not insignificant segment of profiles define themselves in terms of exclusions.

The 12 profile attributes were analyzed using a principal components analysis with a varimax rotation. A four-component solution was selected as additional factors failed to contribute one or more eigenvalues. The four-component solution accounts for 40.6% of the variance in the data. The component loadings are presented in Table 4.

Each attribute loads on a separate component, and they cluster in terms of legitimizing political identities, legitimizing community identities, oppositional political identities, and project political identities. The legitimizing

TABLE 4. Item Component Loadings

Item	Legitimizing Political Ideology	Legitimizing Community ID	Oppositional ID	Project ID
Partisan ID	0.728			
Exclusion	0.303			
Patriotism	0.434			
Freedom From	0.748			
Family		0.678		
Military	0.120	0.321		−0.189
Religion	0.179	0.608		
Duty		0.515	0.158	0.152
Solidarity			0.717	0.127
Justice			0.673	0.131
Empathy toward Difference			−0.101	0.731
Power To	0.101			0.611
Eigenvalues	1.443	1.332	1.053	1.038
Proportion of Variance	0.120	0.111	0.088	0.086

Note: Results based on a varimax rotation.

political identification component accounts for the largest amount of variance in the data (12%). This component includes identifications with conservative political ideologies and organizations and the contents of associated ideological positions relating to sentiments about patriotism, a defense of negative liberty, and exclusion is weakly but most closely associated with this component. The second component corresponds to identifications with organic ties to an entity such as family or religious ties. Connected to this component are expressions of motives concerning moral duty or obligation as well as identification as a past or present member of the military. This component accounts for 11.1% of the variance

The third and fourth components account for 8.8% and 8.6%, respectively. The third component consists of items identifying individuals with the OWS movement. These include claims of solidarity with other OWS groups and the demands for justice that were common refrains of OWS organizing agents. Finally, the last component is composed of two items: terms relating to empathy for others and an openness to difference, and terms associated with a conceptualization of freedom as the power to act and a belief in the collective capacities of groups of persons. Although notably lower, both military identification and religion load on the legitimizing political identity component, suggesting that in some cases there is some

overlap between legitimizing political and civil society identifications. This result is consistent with an interpretation that those classified on one component or the other are not all that different from one another, though they tend to emphasize a coherent set of descriptions about themselves rather than the other. Components three and four more likely designate distinct categories of persons given the inverse loadings of solidarity on each component.

Table 5 contains the frequency data for each of the four components. These data reflect the number of profiles that contained at least one element of each the components. These figures are not summable as up to 3.1% of the profiles contain attributes from more than one component. Attributes of a legitimizing community identity are the most common, followed by expressions of a legitimizing political identity, project identities, and oppositional identities. The two categories of legitimizing identities reflect, likely to a large degree, the presence of a countermovement as many with politically conservative and religious backgrounds strongly

TABLE 5. Participant Profile Frequencies

Legitimizing Political ID	Legitimizing Community ID	Oppositional ID	Project ID
4145	5529	1280	1305

opposed the OWS movement. However, that is not the whole story, as it is also the case that one of the Tea Party co-founders came out in support of the OWS the day before these demonstrations were held. Similarly, a number of religious leaders have had high profiles among demonstrators as many of them have detected affinities between religious social doctrines and the critique of economic inequality central to the arguments of OWS. Finally, the large remainder indicates that the majority of those participating do so without defining their identities in political terms. This is consistent with an actor whose relation to politics is ad hoc and periodic, not connected to a political program organizing other domains of life.

DISCUSSION AND CONCLUSIONS

These data provide broad support for our four-part typology of movement participants among those involved in the online OWS movement and counter-mobilization. Though Twitter descriptions are hardly a comprehensive accounting of each participant's identity, they do provide an insight into the terminological associations with which participants understand and identify themselves, particularly those that they choose to emphasize. However, they also show that varieties of identities mobilized online during the course of a demonstration are not much like their own. OWS positions itself as a hybrid, combining a non-ideological movement with the tactics of a traditional oppositional identity emphasizing the theme of solidarity. However, the Twitter profiles show that the demonstrations gave rise to tweets by legitimizing, oppositional, and project identities, providing empirical support for these identity categories demarcating differences between old and new orientations to political participation. We will elaborate the results in relation to each of our hypotheses.

The first hypothesis concerned the presence of project identities. This hypothesis concerned two essential elements of project identities. It posited that the ability to make a difference and an openness to difference are identity traits that would occur in common. The data from the principal components analysis

confirms this, as both items load on the same component. These identity traits indicate a person oriented toward taking political action, aware of both one's individual capacity to effect change as well as one's collective capacity working with others. Whereas oppositional and legitimizing identities emphasize common origins, project identities stem from a mutual recognition of one's place within a division of political labor. Hence, openness to difference trumps exclusionary identifications as persons are related in functional divisions of labor.

The second hypothesis concerns the presence of legitimizing identities. The evidence shows clearly the presence of legitimizing identities connected to both political and civil society entities. These were the most common identities encountered in our data. The additional assumption that legitimizing identities necessarily are related to the countermovement goes one step beyond the data we currently have. Indeed, anecdotally, there is some evidence indicating an overlap between supporters of OWS and the Tea Party, targeting linkages between political authorities and economic organizations deemed corrupt as well as some religious figures linking the OWS critique of economic inequalities with their own social justice agendas. However, it is also possible that an online environment facilitates the countermovement, which can tweet safely—away from a scene of direct confrontation where they would be likely a minority.[5]

This leads us to our third hypothesis concerning the presence of oppositional and project identities. We anticipated the OWS demonstrations would mobilize a combination of oppositional and project identities. Our data supports this contention. The principal components analysis revealed that the extension of solidarity and demands for justice appear jointly in user profile descriptions, linking individuals in a fight against the prevailing distribution of resources and organization of the economic system. At the same time, not everyone participating in OWS appears to define themselves in relation to a fight against the market or capitalism more generally. Our research detected a slightly larger segment of project identities founded on political rather than communal or social relationships. Although project politics is often ad hoc, unlike oppositional politics, we cannot assume that those profiles we were unable to classify are all cases of project identities. Nevertheless, the fact that they neither indicate legitimizing nor oppositional identities confirms that the old categories of oppositional movements and legitimizing countermovements are insufficient.

As our data show, the OWS faces significant problems in living up to this slogan. In fact, oppositional identities were the least common of the identity categories detected in these data while legitimizing ideological identities were the most common, followed closely by those with legitimizing community identities. Though the articulation of such identities may not have been the goal of the organizers of these demonstrations, it appears to be the result. Many of these individuals opposed OWS and formed part of the countermovement. The remaining participants were more loosely defined given the lower levels of coherence in oppositional and project identities as well as the fact that the majority of the participants eschewed any political identification. Moving from level of individuals to characterizations of action communities, these data point to three wider conclusions.

First, those mobilized online during the course of the OWS demonstrations were not a community or communities of average members of the political community. To begin with, Twitter users are a limited segment of the population, and they tend to be more politically active. Additionally, based on the data analysis, those participating in the OWS mobilizations and counter-mobilizations in various capacities are among the most active users on Twitter. These participants therefore represent not a more generalized cross-section of the population but a highly selective set of individuals who play a specialized role in the production and circulation of information regarding the demonstrations.

Second, few participants fit the identity of the action community invoked by the OWS movement itself. Although the majority of participants do not explicitly identify in ideological terms, which is consistent with the OWS ethos, they are not aligned with the oppositional identity reflected in movement documents. The

majority of profiles involved in the Twitter flow of OWS communications during this series of demonstrations were bereft of any political identifications whatsoever. These data suggest that the topography of action communities brought into being by the OWS movement are quite varied rather than a mirror image of that depicted by movement organizers.

Third, the persons mobilized online during the global OWS demonstrations appear to communicate a variety of collective identifications. OWS is a particularly interesting movement because it indicates how individual and community, at least with regard to new forms of participation, placing concerns for freedom and power to make a difference on concrete policy articulation and delivery above fighting for freedom from those who attempt to wield power over them, today is merging in what appears to be, first of all, action- or project-driven communities. Usually, cause-oriented action and the project identity are associated with reflexive individuals more than reflexive communities. As Bennett and Sergerberg (2011) argue:

> (a) the presence of cues and opportunities for customization of engagement with issues and actions; and (b) the relative absence of cues (including action frames) that signal ideological and definitional unanimity. The problem is that public communication of this kind would seem to be at odds with the emphasis on unity and alignment conventionally associated with the communication processes of effective collective action. (p. 772)

However, in place of a common interest, or good, or identity, these new reflexive action communities indicate that a collective action frame can be driven simply by the fact of sharing in a political division of labor. Hence, from the fact that new forms of cause-oriented activity are connected by different individual action frames, which are neither oppositional nor legitimizing in their project modus vivendi, it does not automatically follow that they lack collective foundations. In their articulation of common concerns, they can develop into a belief in sharing a common destiny and perhaps even into a sense of belonging across all established boundaries in self-reflexive political communities inside multilevel systems of governance and meta-governance. Therefore, when the OWS slogan is "solidarity forever," what is meant by it need not be "solidarity" in its old class-based or communitarian sense. It may not be a cry for social solidarity at all. Rather, it seems to demonstrate that in a political community characterized by people doing things together in virtue, rather than despite of, their multiple social, cultural, moral, religious, and political positions and identities, solidarity can only mean the mutual acceptance and recognition of difference. In fact, the pursuit of common concerns in and through political action capacities necessarily and chronically seems to call for just this: political solidarity.

NOTES

1. Many movements emerge in response to policy concerns (Meyer, 2004), placing them in direct confrontation with networks of actors composing the attendant policy subsystems.

2. http://occupywallst.org/

3. The search API retrieves 1,500 tweets at a time, filtered by relevance. Consequently, these are not a comprehensive set of those communicating about OWS but the most germane to this topic. Furthermore, this constitutes the stream of tweets that most Twitter users would have access to if they chose to follow the OWS demonstrations via the platform.

4. Many accounts included media outlets and many other description lines referenced hobbies or varied professional identities.

5. This is not to say that a countermovement is always a minority. However, there is no evidence that opponents of OWS were mobilizing widespread counter-demonstrations on this date.

6. An account may be irretrievable due to a change in the screen name or its closure.

REFERENCES

Bang, H. (2005). Among everyday makers and expert citizens. In J. Newman (Ed.), *Remaking governance: Peoples, politics and the public sphere* (pp. 159–178). Bristol, England: The Policy Press.

Barnes, S. H., & Kaase, M. (1979). *Political action mass participation in five western democracies.* Beverly Hills, CA: Sage Publications.

Beck, U. (1997). *The reinvention of politics: Rethinking modernity in the global social order.* Oxford, England: Wiley-Blackwell.

Beetham, D. (1991). *The legitimation of power.* Hounsmill, Basingstoke, England: Macmillan.

Benford, R. D., & Snow, D. A. (2000). Framing processes and social movements: An overview and assessment. *Annual Review of Sociology, 26,* 611–639.

Bennett, W. L. (1998). The uncivic culture: Communication, identity, and the rise of lifestyle politics. *Political Science, 31*(4), 740–761.

Bennett, W. L. (2012). The personalization of politics political identity, social media, and changing patterns of participation. *The Annals of the American Academy of Political and Social Science, 644*(1), 20–39.

Bennett, W. L., & Segerberg, A. (2011). Digital media and the personalization of collective action. *Information, Communication & Society, 14*(6), 770–799.

Bennett, W. L., & Segerberg, A. (2012). The logic of connective action. *Information, Communication & Society, 15*(5), 1–30.

Bird, S., Klein, E., & Loper, E. (2009). *Natural language processing with Python.* Sebastopol, CA: O'Reilly Media.

Buechler, S. M. (2004). The strange career of strain and breakdown theories. In D. A. Snow, S. A. Soule, & H. Kriesi (Eds.), *The Blackwell companion to social movements* (pp. 47–66). Malden, MA: John Wiley & Sons.

Caren, N., & Gaby, S. (2011). Occupy online: Facebook and the spread of Occupy Wall Street. *SSRN eLibrary.* Retrieved from http://papers.ssrn.com/sol3/papers.cfm?abstract_id=1943168

Castells, M. (2009). *Communication power.* Oxford, England: Oxford University Press.

Castells, M. (2010). *The power of identity: The Information Age: Economy, society, and culture.* New York: John Wiley & Sons.

Castells, M. (2012). *Networks of outrage and hope. Social movements in the Internet age.* Malden, MA: Polity Press.

Cheng, A., Evans, M., & Singh, H. (2009). *Inside Twitter: An in-depth look inside the Twitter world.* Retrieved from http://www.sysomos.com/insidetwitter/

Cohen, J. L., & Arato, A. (1994). *Civil society and political theory.* Cambridge, MA: MIT Press.

Dahlgren, P. (2005). The Internet, public spheres, and political communication: Dispersion and deliberation. *Political Communication, 22*(2), 147–162.

De Certeau, M. (1984). *The practice of everyday life.* Berkeley: University of California Press.

della Porta, D., & Diani, M. (1999). *Social movements: An introduction.* Oxford, England: Blackwell.

DeLuca, K. M., Lawson, S., & Sun, Y. (2012). Occupy Wall Street on the public screens of social media: The many framings of the birth of a protest movement. *Communication, Culture & Critique, 5*(4), 483–509.

Dempsey, J. K. (2009). *Our army: Soldiers, politics, and American civil–military relations.* Princeton, NJ: Princeton University Press.

Fischer, F. (2003). *Reframing public policy: Discursive politics and deliberative practices.* New York: Oxford University Press.

Foucault, M. (1977). *Discipline and punish* (A. Sheridan, Trans.). New York: Pantheon.

Foucault, M. (2001). *Power* (J. D. Faubion, Ed.). New York: New Press.

Foucault, M. (2008). *The birth of biopolitics.* Basingstoke, England: Palgrave MacMillan.

Giddens, A. (1991). *Modernity and self-identity: Self and society in the late modern age.* Stanford, CA: Stanford University Press.

Gonzalez-Bailon, S., Borge-Holthoefer, J., & Moreno, Y. (2012). Broadcasters and hidden influentials in online protest diffusion. *SSRN eLibrary.* Retrieved from http://papers.ssrn.com/sol3/papers.cfm?abstract_id=2017808

Habermas, J. (1996). *Between facts and norms: Contributions to a discourse theory of law and democracy.* Cambridge, MA: MIT Press.

Hajer, M. A., & Wagenaar, H. (2003). *Deliberative policy analysis: Understanding governance in the network society.* New York: Cambridge University Press.

Hogue, I. (2012). Occupy is Dead! Long live Occupy! *The Nation.* Retrieved from http://www.thenation.com/article/166826/occupy-dead-long-live-occupy

Inglehart, R. (1997). *Modernization and postmodernization: Cultural, economic, and political change in 43 societies.* Princeton, NJ: Princeton University Press.

Jensen, M. J., Jorba, L., & Anduiza, E. (2012). Introduction. In E. Anduiza, M. J. Jensen, & L. Jorba (Eds.), *Digital media and political engagement worldwide: A comparative study* (pp. 1–15). New York: Cambridge University Press.

Klingemann, H. D. (1999). Political support in advanced industrial democracies. In P. Norris (Ed.), *Critical citizens: Global support for democratic government* (pp. 57–77). New York: Oxford University Press.

Lind, B., & Stepan-Norris, J. (2011). The relationality of movements: Movement and counter movement resources, infrastructure, and leadership in the Los Angeles Tenants' Rights Mobilization, 1976–1979. *The American Journal of Sociology, 116*(5), 1564–1609.

Lindgren, K. O., & Persson, T. (2010): Input and output legitimacy: Synergy or trade-off? Empirical evidence from an EU survey. *Journal of European Public Policy, 17*(4), 449–467.

Luhmann, N. (1982). *The differentiation of society.* New York: Columbia University Press.

McCarthy, J. D., & Zald, M. N. (1977). Resource mobilization and social movements: A partial theory. *American Journal of Sociology, 82*(6), 1212–1241.

McKelvey, K., Rudnick, A., Conover, M. D., & Menczer, F. (2012). *Visualizing communication on social media: Making big data accessible.* Retrieved from http://arxiv.org/abs/1202.1367

Melucci, A. (1992). Liberation or meaning? Social movements, culture and democracy. *Development and Change, 23*(3), 43–77.

Melucci, A., & Avritzer, L. (2000). Complexity, cultural pluralism and democracy: Collective action in the public space. *Social Science Information, 39*(4), 507–527.

Meyer, D. S. (2004). Protest and political opportunities. *Annual Review of Sociology, 30,* 125–145.

Meyer, D. S., & Staggenborg, S. (1996). Movements, countermovements, and the structure of political opportunity. *American Journal of Sociology, 101*(6), 1628–1660.

Micheletti, M., Føllesdal, A., & Stolle, D. (2004). *Politics, products, and markets: Exploring political consumerism past and present.* Piscataway, NJ: Transaction Publishers.

Mueller, M. (2008). Digital Shakespeare, or towards a literary informatics. *Shakespeare, 4*(3), 284–301.

Mustafaraj, E., Finn, S., Whitlock, C., & Metaxas, P. T. (2011). Vocal minority versus silent majority: Discovering the opinions of the long tail. In *Privacy, security, risk and trust* (passat), 2011 IEEE Third International Conference and 2011 IEEE Third International Conference on Social Computing (socialcom), pp. 103–110.

Noris, P. (2007). Political activism: New challenges, new opportunities. In R. J. Dalton & H.-D. Klingemann (Eds.), *The Oxford handbook of political behavior* (pp. 724–743). New York: Oxford University Press.

Putnam, R. D. (2001). *Bowling alone: The collapse and revival of American community.* New York: Simon and Schuster.

Ramsay, S. (2003). Reconceiving text analysis: Toward an algorithmic criticism. *Literary and Linguistic Computing, 18*(2), 167–174.

Rosenberg, S., Ward, D., & Chilton, S. (1989). *Political reasoning and cognition: A Piagetian view.* Durham, NC: Duke University Press.

Segerberg, A., & Bennett, W. L. (2011). Social media and the organization of collective action: Using Twitter to explore the ecologies of two climate change protests. *The Communication Review, 14*(3), 197–215.

Sitrin, M. (2012). Horizontalism and the Occupy movements. *Dissent, 59*(2), 74–75.

Snow, D. A., & Benford, R. D. (1988). Ideology, frame resonance, and participant mobilization. *International Social Movement Research, 1*(1), 197–217.

Sweetnam, M. S., & Fennell, B. A. (2012). Natural language processing and early-modern dirty data: Applying IBM Languageware to the 1641 depositions. *Literary and Linguistic Computing, 27*(1), 39–54.

Tarrow, S. (1998). *Power in movement: Social movements and contentious politics.* New York: Cambridge University Press.

Tarrow, S. (2011). Why Occupy Wall Street is not the Tea Party of the Left. *Foreign Affairs.* Retrieved from http://www.foreignaffairs.com/articles/136401/sidney-tarrow/why-occupy-wall-street-is-not-the-tea-party-of-the-left

Theocharis, Y. (2013). The wealth of (Occupation) networks? Communication patterns and information distribution in a Twitter protest network. *Journal of Information Technology & Politics, 10*(1), 35–56.

Van Gelder, S. (2012). *This changes everything: Occupy Wall Street and the 99% movement.* San Francisco: Barrett-Koehler.

Walgrave, S., Bennett, W. L., Van Laer, J., & Breunig, C. (2011). Multiple engagements and network bridging in contentious politics: Digital media use of protest participants. *Mobilization: An International Quarterly, 16*(3), 325–349.

Wright, A. L. (2012). Counterpublic protest and the purpose of Occupy: Reframing the discourse of Occupy Wall Street. *Plaza: Dialogues in Language and Literature, 2*(2), 138–146.

Zald, M. N., & McCarthy, J. D. (1987). *Social movements in an organizational society.* Piscataway, NJ: Transaction Publishers.

APPENDIX: COLLECTION OF TWEET DATA AND RETRIEVAL OF USER PROFILES

The tweet search terms included *OWS* and *occupy*. Human inspection of a sample of 5,000 tweets encountered only two tweets unrelated to the demonstrations. Although the search API are not a census of the global production of tweets over this interval, the dataset approximates the entire field of tweets produced during this time as well as the field of tweets that are normally available to most users. The data collection began approximately four hours before the simultaneous demonstrations began in multiple cities around the world, including Barcelona, Madrid, London, and New York. The data collection concluded 24 hours later in order to capture the tweets related to demonstrations in more distant time zones over the same cycle of activity. The total corpus of OWS tweets totals 97,583, produced by 54,963 different accounts. The profiles of 50,397 of these accounts were retrievable.[6]

A Policymaking Process "Tug-of-War": National Information Security Policies in Comparative Perspective

Kenneth Rogerson
Daniel Milton

ABSTRACT. There is tension between the ideal of government transparency and the need to protect vital information. What types of information do governments protect on national security grounds? What arguments do governments use to justify the protection of this information? What will influence an open government information policy as opposed to a closed information policy? Through an examination of more than 250 information security–related policies from around the world, it is clear that (a) all governments limit the flows of information, (b) there are different reasons for this, and (c) the reasons are not always correlated to government type. In other words, sometimes democracies and authoritarian countries limit the same types of information issues. The policies and policy discussions are dependent on a variety of actors and which actor(s) wield the strongest influence at the time, which makes them often get caught up in a policy "tug-of-war" that most often results in incremental policy change and implementation.

In a networked and information-saturated world, information security is critical to states and policymakers. A confluence of factors and actors, including divergent political and economic interests, policy-making processes, government types, and technical expertise at the policy-making level, all combine to produce disparate information security polices among states. Scant attention has been paid in the information security literature to the important issue of differences in information security polices among states, especially to the differences between the information security polices of authoritarian and democratic states and how disparate policy-making processes contribute to those differences. Do authoritarian and democratic governments address information security policy similarly or differently, and, through the lens of the tension between the variety of actors and stakeholders in the different types

Kenneth Rogerson is a lecturer and Director of Undergraduate Studies at Duke University's Sanford School of Public Policy.

Daniel Milton is an assistant professor at the United States Military Academy and an associate at the Academy's Combating Terrorism Center.

The authors express gratitude to the anonymous reviewers for their extremely helpful comments and guidance.

of governments, what might best explain those similarities or differences?

Policies, in general, come in two broad categories: (a) specific policies that governments enact and (b) policies that are proposed, but may not be enacted, and the discussions surrounding these proposals. Both types of policy are relevant to this project. Within the context of information security, we ask the following: What classes of information do governments protect? What arguments do governments use to justify the protection of this information? Note that the answer to the second question is *not* simply that governments can do what they want to do as long as they relate it to national security. This is particularly true where more actors and interests are involved and more coordination is required to shift the status-quo policy.

There are two challenges in understanding how states address information security policy. The first is that there are a variety of actors, both public and private, interested in how information security policy functions. However, these actors do not operate in a vacuum. They are constrained by political, ideological, and institutional factors. This leads to the second challenge, which is that the institutional nature of the government (whether democratic or authoritarian) also affects how the government addresses these issues. While policy-makers and private actors in both democracies and authoritarian countries interact to address the securing of what they consider vital information, these interactions may differ across government types. Consequently, the policy-making process may resemble a "tug-of-war" in countries in which policy-making authority is diffuse. In these countries, interactions between policy-makers and private actors "tug" policies in one direction or another, depending on the political and ideological climate. In such an environment, it is rare to find that information security policies, as very broadly defined above, find themselves completely dominated by one way of thinking. However, this is less the case when policy-making power is concentrated, as it is in authoritarian governments. Even though multiple actors are interested, they are less capable of influencing policy, which looks less like a

tug-of-war and is more focused on the state's own interests.

Governments deal with policy-making in different ways when it comes to securing information. In particular, the broad range of actors and interests involved in policy-making in democracies create unique tensions that are not found in authoritarian countries, where access can be more restricted and the policy-making process more centralized. Notwithstanding these ideals, there is literature that suggests that democracies may not always measure up to their own stated ideals, particularly those concerning information transparency and when facing threats (see, for example, the literature on information privacy: Klosek, 2007; Rosenzweig, 2013). To evaluate these ideas in the context of information security policy, this study examines a dataset of 250 actual and proposed information security policies from around the world in which governments have addressed information security policy. The findings suggest that information security policy-making in democracies resembles a multiple-actor tug-of-war, in which information security policy-making seldom results in large changes or policy adaptations (Anderson, 2011). This differs from the policy-making process in autocratic countries, which is still a tug-of-war, but involves fewer actors and a less diverse set of interests. These findings are consistent with general beliefs about democracies and autocracies. There are, however, exceptions to these general findings, particularly when democracies experience serious national security threats.

INFORMATION SECURITY POLICY-MAKING AND GOVERNMENT TYPE

Much of government intervention in information security has been in two large categories: (a) military and defense and (b) consumer protection/identity, though there are others as well. For example, in *Conquest in Cyberspace: National Security and Information Warfare* (2007), Libicki laid out the structure of how the U.S. Department of Defense understands information security, providing some important broad concepts that could be applied in a variety of cases and possibly even countries. These categories help the reader understand what is happening, but not how they might change over time.

On the consumer side, Bob Sullivan provides an overview of the policy that protects (and often does not protect) a consumer's identity. In *Your Evil Twin: Behind the Identity Theft Epidemic* (2004), Sullivan presents what he calls the "Kafkaesque trials" that people face when their identity is stolen and, instead of helpful policy for some redress of grievances, they find "government ineffectiveness and law enforcement indifference" (p. xvi). Again, Sullivan provides a rich arena for understanding what is happening, and also proposes some policy changes to help. But, which actors and interests need to come together to nudge policy in a direction that will work? And what are the strategies and rationale they might use to do it?

With both democratic and authoritarian governments, there is a wide variety of factors that play a role in how the state makes information security policy. Such factors include those found in written documents, such as constitutions, as well as those cultural, political, and economic rules of engagement that are simply part of how the country functions. The fact that there are so many factors in so many different countries may lead some to conclude that an analysis of the way in which democracies and autocracies generally deal with information security policy is not useful. However, domestic intricacies notwithstanding, analyzing these general government types can serve meaningful academic and public policy purposes. Understanding how democracies and autocracies generally deal with information security policy provides a better context for understanding how country-specific differences play out. It also provides policymakers with a better understanding of the limits and constraints faced in these different types of governance structures.

When it comes to democracies and information, there is a general belief that democracies should seek transparency in their policies and actions to citizens and to other nations (Florini, 1998, 2004). Acting on these ideals, policymakers should build their information-security policies on the goal of an open-access society in which information is abundant and government processes are transparent. While advocating the benefits of this open-access approach to information security, such as the accountability of political agents to an electorate, some proponents of this view acknowledge that, even in democratic societies, a more stringent form of information security may be necessary in some circumstances to protect vital state interests, but that such control should be as limited as possible (Florini, 2004; Thompson, 1999, pp. 192–193).

One limitation of this argument is that it does not address the transitory period between norms and policy. Even if the assumption is made that democratic norms support complete—or nearly complete—transparency and stand in contrast to government secrecy, the question still remains: How do the norms find their way through the policy process and into enforceable laws? Even more, how do normative arguments account for the fact that governments still classify information at relatively high rates? It is not enough to wave the wand of national security at these questions. After all, the decision to classify information is made by actors with interests, whether for country or self.

Another limitation in some of the arguments regarding information security deals with the institutional origins of secretive government policy. There is an assumption that the executive branch of government, especially in the United States, is responsible for the increase or continued presence of government secrecy (Florini, 2004, pp. 20–21). While the executive branch may have an interest in maintaining secrecy, the argument misses the fact that, in a democracy, there are multiple actors that participate in the policy-making process. Making recommendations for policy based on an understanding of only one actor, instead of a more broad understanding of the policy-making process as it relates to information security, is incomplete. In general, the amount of research that directly addresses information security in its policy-making context is limited.

In contrast to the democratic ideal of transparency, authoritarian governments rely on the principle of self-preservation (see O'Donnell,

Schmitter, & Whitehead, 1986). Resultant information security policies normally reflect this principle, focusing on governmental access to the nodes of information flow and providing legal power for government representatives to request information with minimal recourse. One strength of this position is that government structures are set up to approve and implement information security policies without formal questioning. If there is an opposition, it is in a position of relative weakness.

Of course, authoritarian governments are not immune from debate and dissent about policies. In particular, authoritarian governments may face the threat of protest because of their policies. The institutional differences between democracy and authoritarian governments allow the latter to deal with the problem more directly. In other words, while this threat may be consistently real, some governments have found ways to prevent it. Peter Jones (2012) writes that while there is a trend in the recent "revolutions" in the Middle East, fewer have happened in monarchies. He reasons that this may be because of the societal control that the regimes have through a paternalistic "social contract" that the majority of citizens accept, or even that they "buy off" their citizens through financial incentives (Jones, 2012).

Comparing information security policy over the two types of governments, Helen Milner (2006) applied the idea of democratic exceptionalism to the spread of different means of technology, claiming that the factions in power in authoritarian governments can see and prevent the spread of technology that might undermine their power, while factions within democratic governments have many more institutional hurdles to overcome (pp. 178, 184, and 195).

It is not inconceivable to view authoritarian governments as desiring to limit the release of sensitive information, while viewing democratic institutions as encouraging openness. Both of these arguments appear in the preceding paragraphs. However, one of Milner's key points is the groups that desire to block technological diffusion within a democracy often do not have the support of political institutions (2006, 195). This may (or may not) be the case

when dealing with information security. There are a number of actors—both institutional and individual—who wield great amounts of power and who might oppose policies designed to increase transparency.

Early research on information flows, especially concerning the World Wide Web, assumed a democratic imperative. That is, greater flows of information will lead to more openness. But scholars immediately began to test this proposition. From Robert McChesney's (1996) early work criticizing corporate control of the internet to Stephen Lax's (2001) edited volume exploring similar issues, academics have studied whether theories such as Milner's can be empirically supported. McChesney finds that democratic governments have more autocratic tendencies when it comes to information restriction, and Lax's contributors find that most governments at the time of the study seemed to be erring on the side of security rather than dissemination.

Other more recent scholarship by Ronald Diebert, John Palfrey, Rafal Rohozinski, and Jonathan Zittrain has provided a wealth of information about the ways that different countries control the flow of information. In *Access Denied* (2008) and *Access Controlled* (2010), this group of researchers catalogs the information-controlling activities of several countries. Similarly, Giacomello (2005) examines the different way in which democratic countries deal with control of the Internet. In particular, his analysis of democracies showed that while they often dealt with similar internet challenges, their methods of dealing with these challenges differed according to dialogue and culture.

Building on these conceptual and empirical works, a next research step would be to find some trends and patterns in this cataloguing, and to address how the ideals of a particular government type are represented in its policy-making. What types of information do governments protect? What arguments do governments use to justify the protection of this information? And what best explains the give-and-take, or the tug-of-war, in the formulation of these information security policies?

METHODOLOGY

To understand these competing policy-making interests, we surveyed examples of policies around the world that address the issue of information security. The data set contains approximately 250 policies (both proposed policies and those passed into law) that resulted in either changes to laws, new laws, or the creation of new governmental agencies addressing the issue of information security. The examples represent all regions of the world: Africa, the Americas, Asia, Europe, and the South Pacific. It covers the time period from 1998 to the present. While some of the laws and examples may seem outdated, the importance of this project is in the policy analysis over time, not only in its relevance to current events.

These policies do not represent randomly distributed events. Countries that have information security policies have them because circumstances are such that the policy has enough support that it can be adopted through the existing institutional process. However, the goal is not to look at the effect of information security policy on other variables. Rather, it is to explore the non-randomness itself. What variables, or factors, influence the type or focus of the information security policies that a given country will adopt?

The dataset is not exhaustive; certain countries are not represented. The primary sources for gathering the information were news and political databases, such as LEXIS/NEXIS, and country parliamentary document repositories. The policies were analyzed based on three questions. First, what type of information is secured or limited? The answers were meant to represent the policy issue area. Some laws overlap among categories. Second, what is the rationale that governments use for securing or limiting the information? This includes the goals of the policy, though these are not always explicitly stated. Third, what are the circumstances around which the policy is formulated? This is the most difficult question to answer, since the situations are not always specifically stated in the news articles or legislative archives. But, where possible, this context can provide a wealth of understanding about the extent to which governments go to secure information. The second and third questions speak specifically to the tug-of-war.

NATIONAL INFORMATION POLICIES FROM AROUND THE WORLD

While some information policies are designed to free the flow of information—such as sunshine laws or freedom of information acts—other policies are targeted at limiting, securing, or controlling the flow of information. The types of controlled information fall into the following categories: external threats (national security issues), internal threats (antigovernment or antistability information), infrastructure information, personal or individual information, commercial information, and news media information.

External Threats (National Security Issues)

Issues of national security policy have always been targets of policy-limiting information flows. In *Empire and Communications* (2007), Harold Innis makes the argument that the control of information (what he referred to as "monopolies of knowledge") was indispensable in the making of empires from the Egyptians to the British. Defense of national priorities against external threats is the most obvious—and often the most accepted—reason to limit the flows of information within a country. However, external threats, such as war and some forms of terrorism, differ from internal threats, such as antigovernment protests and seditious acts (which may include terrorist acts but are distinguished from others such as the U.S. "War on Terror"). While internal threats matter (addressed in the subsequent section), external threats and the policies designed to address them take on a different tenor that makes them an analytically separate category.

For example, the Patriot Act gave the U.S. government access to some information it had not had before. While the U.S. military uses the Internet and other mass media to communicate with the Iraqis and Americans (Bernard, 2005) about the war (some have called this propaganda; see Sandoval, 2006), it also limits the use of specific types of media by soldiers, who may want to blog about or comment on the war, justified by the argument that such communication may potentially empower enemies or create disunity.

In addition to allowing governments to broaden the scope of information they monitor and regulate, external threats could reveal new vulnerabilities. War between nations also provides a powerful motivation for developing information security policies that can protect against foreign intrusion. Smith (2012) argues that this is the most enduring lesson of the Russian cyber efforts against Estonia in 2007 and Georgia in 2008. In particular, the tension between Russia and Georgia demonstrated the need to protect computer networks (civilian and military alike) in the case of armed conflict.

Such lessons are not unique to interactions among state actors. There has been an increased focus since 9/11 on the role of nonstate actors. The external threat of terrorism has figured prominently in shaping the types of information security policies that have emerged over the past decade or so. The 2001 attacks in New York City and Washington, DC, by al Qaeda, have spurred other countries to enact information controlling policies. Senator Chris Ellison of the Australian Parliament referenced the September 2001 events as being influential in the country's need to have modern laws and policing powers to investigate cybercrimes, and to prevent incidents of cyber-terrorism: "Previously if a terrorist attack had been carried out on Australia's national information infrastructure police did not have the power to compel suspects to assist in an investigation of complex computer systems protected by passwords or encryption, or to conduct searches on-line across different locations" (Australia's Attorney General's Department, 2001). The new policies gave Australian law enforcement broader authority to access and subsequently limit information flows if necessary.

Internal Threats (Antigovernment and Antistability Information)

Limiting information has been relatively common when dealing with threats to a country's internal stability. The Sedition Acts of 1798 in the United States criminalized treasonous language. More recently, changes in Russian media law during the 2000s made discussions that opposed the sitting administration more liable for prosecution.

Singapore, for example, has been recognized for programs that electronically connect its citizens and government. The government has claimed it wants to be a "paperless" society. However, in 2003, the parliament passed the Computer Misuse Act, which interpreters have called a response to the Internet as a "weapon of mass disruption." The government states it will judiciously use the power bestowed by the law, but "It could be misused to invade into the privacy of citizens to gather information,' said Sinapan Samydorai, president of Think Centre, a Singaporean civil liberties group. He said the new laws could be used as an "'instrument of oppression' by the government" (Singapore Cyberterrorism, 2003).

For China, combating threatening information flows is an implicit policy:

> For companies and individuals alike, understanding Chinese online political censorship is made more difficult by the secrecy in which it is shrouded. Officials routinely deny that it happens at all. "As I understand it, the censorship of web sites or online content is completely impossible," says Wang Guoqing, vice-minister of the State Council Information Office, the government body responsible for media monitoring. But top leaders have left no doubt that controlling the web is a political priority. "Whether or not we can actively use and effectively manage the internet . . . will affect national cultural information security and the long-term stability of the state," Hu Jintao, China's president, told a meeting of the Communist party's governing Politburo in January. It was necessary to

"purify the internet environment." (Dickie, 2007)

Infrastructure Information

Information infrastructure development around the world has traditionally been a mixture of public and private initiatives, with some countries leaning toward one or the other. Those that tend to implement publicly funded programs might do so with the intent to control the information that goes through those networks.

For example, in 2006, Kenya, Uganda, and Tanzania began the process of adopting harmonized cyber laws to enable the establishment of e-government and e-commerce programs. The respective governments recognized the trans-border flows of information that were already taking place, and wanted to assure that they had some type of control (and possibly income) from these existing connections (Ruiz, 2006). This type of control is not necessarily negative. Those in authority simply want to know what is happening.

Another example of infrastructure control is the debate over the liability of privately run Internet service providers (ISPs) in the flow of information over their networks. ISPs, organizations or companies providing the channels through which most Internet information flows, can be publicly or privately run. The truth is that, while the technology exists to monitor the information that flows through their networks, many ISPs, especially privately owned ones, do not. Governments have been engaged in policy debates about this issue of infrastructure control.

According to India's Information Technology Act of 2000, ISPs are not liable for criminal activity on their networks:

> For the removal of doubts, it is hereby declared that no person providing any service as a network service provider shall be liable under this Act, rules or regulations made thereunder for any third party information or data made available by him if he proves that the offence or contravention was committed without his knowledge or that he had exercised all due diligence to

prevent the commission of such offence or contravention. (India IT Act, 2000, p. 21)

But, complete autonomy is usually not possible. Subsequently, the law states that the police shall have authority to enter any establishment and search its electronic records (p. 22) if the situation merits.

The United States is addressing this same issue through proposed legislation to update the Foreign Surveillance Act of 1978. U.S. lawmakers have hesitated to protect ISPs in the name of civil liberties.

> The companies are hamstrung from defending themselves in court, however. The Bush administration is invoking the 'state secrets' privilege to block the companies from revealing secret documents that might bolster their argument that the eavesdropping program was legal. The House compromise bill would encourage the federal district judge hearing the telecommunications lawsuits to review those classified documents in secret to determine whether the companies acted legally. (Hess, 2008)

Personal/Individual Information

The privacy of personal information has long been a topic of discussion in national parliaments, especially in more democratic societies. Some have passed laws and others have not. Because cultures understand privacy from differing perspectives, it can be difficult to pass laws on this topic. The difference in the culture of privacy is readily apparent in information-related discussions between the United States and the European Union (see Rogerson & Strauss, 2002). In order to formulate and implement a privacy policy or program, governments must control information somehow, usually limiting the information that can be collected or stored by governments or private industries. For example, the European Union Convention on Cybercrime recognizes a right to privacy: "Mindful also of the right to the protection of personal data, as conferred, for example, by the 1981 Council of Europe Convention for the Protection of Individuals with regard to Automatic Processing of Personal Data" (EU Convention on Cybercrime, 2001, Preamble, paragraphs 10 and 11).

This is not always the case, and in other countries, information on individuals does not receive the same type of protection. For example, Kazakhstan has passed the "On Protection of State Secrets of the Republic of Kazakhstan," which de-emphasizes individual privacy in favor of more official information.

Commercial Information

Countries may also have policies pertaining to commercial information, that is, financial transactions, e-commerce, online taxation, etc. In some cases, these policies may be deregulatory in nature and designed to stimulate growth according to free market principles. In other cases, they may be regulatory in order to provide stimulus or monetary infusions into a region. The East African Community has started a program called The E-Legislation Policy Development Initiative:

> The primary objective of the project is to create model electronic transactions laws piloted in Kenya that can be customized for the East African Community partner states of Uganda, Tanzania, Rwanda and Burundi. The initiative is in recognition of the fact that eTransactions laws have the potential to generate significant economic and political development for Kenya and East Africa as a whole. (Ouma, 2007)

This program recognizes both the nature of information to cross borders and the desire of governments to be involved in the development of the project, and thus have some control of the information that flows through the newly created networks.

News and Media Coverage

Information policies may also be initiatives to limit media coverage. For example, the Russian government attempted to control coverage of its conflict with the breakaway province of Chechnya, some of which was based on its existing media laws:

> On 4 November [1999], the Russian Information Centre and the military General Staff summoned executives of Russia's leading TV and radio companies to draw up plans for broadcasts to Chechnya and adjacent regions. All the reports, both from Moscow and locally, will be prepared under the aegis of the Russian Information Centre and will be transmitted in Russian and possibly, in time, also in Arabic, Russia TV reported. (Feuilherade, 1999)

Some countries have media laws that delineate the types of information that are or are not appropriate to publish or broadcast. Few countries have freedom of speech and press laws similar to those found in the U.S. Constitution.

Worms and Viruses

Finally, there is a category of laws that targets hackers and those who maliciously send worms, viruses, and Trojan horses across information networks. Japanese law enforcement reported that, in December 2002 alone, there were 58,000 hacker attacks against Japanese police computers. More than 40% of the attacks came from Israel, 20% from the United States, 9% from Japan, and 7% from South Korea. More than 90% of the attacks were simple preparatory attacks to see what programs were on the police computers, but the remaining attacks were serious attempts to close down the computers. So, in 2003, Japan passed a law that would criminalize these activities, even those that were simply preparatory in nature. In addition, it created a monitoring center to track down the offenders (Seeman, 2003).

RATIONALE FOR SECURING THE INFORMATION

The second research question is identifying the rationale—stated or inferred—for passing the law or implementing the policy. These fall into three categories: (a) defending national interests, (b) protecting the citizens, and (c) facilitating cross-border information-sharing.

Defending national interests is the largest category and has a number of components. There is always an interest in using military and defense as a rationale for limiting the flow of information. Countries want to protect intelligence in times of conflict so that the "enemy" will not discover sensitive information and to protect—as much as possible—those who are on the ground fighting. In 2006, Chinese government officials published a report entitled "China's National Defense in 2006" that states that China is pursuing a three-step development strategy to modernize its national defense and armed forces that includes building "informationized armed forces" capable of winning "informationized wars" by 2050 (Greenemeier, 2007, p. 2).

Also in the arena of security issues is maintaining control within borders. Again, China provides the example. The Chinese government has a reputation for censoring speech that comes through the Internet, though it is not the only country to do so (see Kalathil & Boas, 2003).

> While the GFW [Great Firewall] protects the government from information assault from without, internally another system applies [also known as the Golden Shield]. Vaguely worded laws against any speech judged seditious, superstitious or merely "harmful to social order" give officials wide discretion to punish those who post or host sensitive content. But the main burden of routine censorship is left to internet service providers and suppliers of content. (Dickie, 2007)

And, since the latter groups can be targets of government crackdowns as easily as individuals, they are often willing participants. While not suppressing opposition completely, China has succeeded in limiting the impact of some societal groups through this censorship and monitoring, resulting in a tilt toward the ruling party's desired policy.

A second rationale is protecting citizens. This could be protection from worms and viruses, as in the Japanese example cited above. It can be in the form of regulating annoyances like spam (unsolicited commercial e-mail), as with the CanSpam Act of 2003 in the United States. But the language of protection has also been utilized more broadly. In South Africa, parliament passed the Electronic Communications and Transactions Bill, which was designed to protect citizens from cyber-terrorism. Given the broad language of the bill, there were bound to be critics: "The new law was strongly criticized, especially by the Democratic Alliance party, which voted against it, and by internet freedom organizations and private firms. The law allows telecommunications minister Ivy Matsepe-Casaburri to appoint inspectors to monitor telecommunications networks and their content, which they are authorised to seize" (Reporters Without Borders, 2003, p. 103).

In one case, a policy strongly reflected damage that was inflicted on citizens. In April and May 2007, the Estonian government was subjected to a number of denial-of-service attacks on the country's Internet infrastructure. The event incapacitated banks and government institutions (Finn, 2007, A1). The Estonian parliament responded later that fall, voting for a change to the country's penal code. "A computer attack would become an act of terrorism when committed with the same aims as a conventional act of terrorism. Under existing law, crimes of terror are crimes whose goal is to seriously upset or destroy the country's political, constitutional, economic or social order" (Estonia Gets Tough, 2007). The reaction of Estonians, and of the tech-savvy ones in particular, provided a pull toward citizen protection in subsequent policies.

In early 2012, negative citizen reaction to the Stop Online Piracy Act (SOPA) and the Protect IP Act (PIPA) resulted in a number of policy-makers changing their minds about how they perceived the legislation. At least some of the credit for this change has been attributed to the citizen outcry (Schmitz, 2013, p. 213), which pulled the policy-makers away from what initially seemed to be easy passage of the legislation. This, in particular, provides a salient example of the role that citizens play in the tug-of-war, not just political figures.

A third category of explanations for information-securing policies is that they facilitate cross-border information sharing. As seen in the Kenyan and East African Community (EAC) examples, there is a desire to take advantage of already existing networks and connections for the benefit of the state. One reason is to exchange information about criminal activity. The EAC "began harmonizing its laws to prosecute cyber criminals operating across national boundaries" (Ouma, 2007). It is not always easy to get information about hackers or other cybercriminals who do not live within national boundaries. The EU Convention on Crime, for example, is particularly focused on tracking down those who distribute child pornography, the only content-related offense in the convention. Chapter III of the convention is entirely devoted to international cooperation and sharing of information. At the same time, the convention allows for countries to make individual decisions on bilateral arrangements with each other.

CIRCUMSTANCES AROUND WHICH INFORMATION IS SECURED

The rationale is the stated reason for which a policy has been proposed or adopted. The circumstances are the unique situations that might have led to the policy's proposal or adoption. While each circumstance or situation can be distinctive, there are some trends. At this point, most information policy adoption or change seems to be in response to some type of threat.

The most visible and most cited threat is terrorism, both online and offline. The Australian Cybercrime Act and the policy changes in Estonia, while not defining terrorism as others might, were proposed, adopted, and implemented because of what each interpreted as terrorist acts. The Australian parliamentarian explicitly stated that he proposed the bill because of the events of September 2001, and the Estonians were responding to what they felt was a terrorist attack from the Russians.

The expansion of cyber-related research funding is another type of policy reaction. Since September 2001, the United States and Israel have been working together on information security and monitoring programs, which, according to Mark Last of Ben-Gurion University of the Negev, are designed to predict future terrorist activities and targets by searching Web pages, e-mails, and other online data: "It may be nerdy mathematicians and computer scientists who have as much to do with victory in the War on Terror as conventional warriors. Perhaps in response to the shutdown of Terror Information Awareness, the US is quietly funding research in Israel designed to detect terrorist use of the Internet" (Abbey, 2004). Other programs include developing mathematical models to locate specific terrorists and their activities. The National Institute for Systems Test and Productivity, a U.S. government-funded research institute operated by the University of South Florida, is financing the research.

Some refer to these threats in a less provocative way, calling them antigovernment hackers. In 2000, the government in Azerbaijan claimed that Armenian hackers attacked the country's ISPs. During the Armenian–Azerbaijani "electronic war," the Web sites of all large Internet users, including humanitarian organizations, in Azerbaijan were hacked into and vandalized. The e-mail connections of all major Azerbaijani newspapers were severed. A site posting incorrect information about Azerbaijani President Heydar Aliyev appeared. Armenian State Television and Armenian Assembly in America sites were attacked in retaliation. In response to some pressure from these organizations, the government created a new technical council to deal with the matter. Members included experts from the National Security Ministry and owners and operators of ISPs (Azerbaijan to Secure, 2000). While the government itself was not attacked, policy-makers were persuaded that an attack on the institutions of Armenian civil society were a threat to the country and thus were pulled toward acting in the interests of those institutions. It might be argued that the creation of a council is not a very effective response, simply contributing to an increased bureaucracy. But, the council would not have been established without the pressure from the groups that were attacked.

Another threat is that to personal information. Some believe that governments can use legislation and programs to gather personal information about their citizens and use it against them. In Pakistan, the parliament passed a bill to "Make Provision for Prevention of Electronic Crimes." While much of the legislation mirrors other cybercrime laws from around the world, it also includes the creation of a new government agency: "The Federal Government shall establish a specialized investigation and prosecution cell within Federal Investigation Agency [FIA] to investigate and prosecute the offences under this Act" (Pakistan, 2007). An anonymous Pakistani blogger known as Teeth Maestro responded in this way:

> The FIA has been given complete and unrestricted control to arrest and confiscate material as they feel necessary, without forcing them to present a credible case before an arrest warrant is issued, if the FIA follows the law by the book they can pick up any person or property, hold them in custody for up to one year (extensions allowed) before even presenting the case in court. A very dangerous supposition as it opens the door for the rouge FIA agency to do as they please *without any safeguards and protection for the innocent.* (Maestro, 2007, emphasis in original)

While the blogger's commentary did not seem to result in any policy change in the end, the very existence of it exemplifies the attempt.

A final threat is not being at the cutting edge of economic competitiveness in an age of global information flows. A number of policies were aimed at opening up borders and sharing information, under very specific conditions. The interests involved were represented by the private sector. In these cases, governments seem to see the value of more open information flows with the goal of economic development. They are open to partnerships with business to encourage and facilitate this. While there was no immediate evidence of private sector pull on policy change, research has provided some empirical and theoretical support that this could be the case (see Browne, 1998).

THE INFORMATION POLICY TUG-OF-WAR

What, then, best explains the processes that result in the formation of information security policy? Information security policy is the result of the choices of a conglomeration of independent political actors, having their own set of interests and goals. By understanding how these forces act and counteract each other, the end result is clearer, i.e., the actual information security policy adopted by a particular county. There may be a wide variety of actors in play, but the policy results differ depending on the institutions that empower those actors.

Imagine a game of tug-of-war between two actors. There is usually a flag somewhere in the middle of the rope, which helps signal when one player wins. To determine the actual location of the policy, in our case the information security policy, we should look at the location of the flag in the game. Once the tugging begins, how is the location of the policy determined? It could be a result of the relative strengths of the actors or the geography of the terrain upon which they stand. Indeed, there is a variety of factors that would determine how the policy will fluctuate as the competition continues.

Now imagine that more actors are added to both sides. The location of the flag shows where the policy stands. Figuring out what influences the location of the flag entails analysis similar to the discussion above, but more detailed. The actors pull from different directions because, presumably, not all actors share the same point of view. Instead of a straight line of competing actors, there is now a web of forces that compete to move the policy closer to their preferred point. The more the policy-making process resembles a web, the more subtle changes in the location of the flag might not be noticeable in such an atmosphere. This is interesting, because when there are noticeable changes in the location of a policy, it is a signal that a number of actors were able to move their ideal points close enough to each other such that they had enough political strength to move the location of the policy. To understand what has affected the location of policy, multiple factors come into play, not just the number of voters for or against the policy proposal.

This model posits that the location of actors and information security policy in a policy space is not directly contingent on the type of government. If this were the case, democracies should have information policies similar to other democracies and autocracies to other autocracies. While the type of government does influence the ability of actors to shift the local of information security policy, both have a variety of types of policies, even though democracies have many actors and factors that can affect the process, as opposed to the relatively fewer actors that may exist in an authoritarian government. The type of policy in a democracy might, therefore, also be the result of international and domestic factors that result in the "lining up" of actors on either side of the tug-of-war policy game. The lax or strict nature of information security policy in a given country seems to reflect more the relative strength of one policy position versus another.

Who are these actors? A principal actor is the executive of a government. The theoretical assumption is that the executive in a democracy has an interest in promoting and adopting a policy that results in flexible regulations regarding information security. Flexible regulation gives the executive more discretion on whether to release sensitive information. This does not mean tht the executive will always choose to be secretive rather than to be open, but merely reflects the fact that the executive would prefer to have the choice rather than having the limit defined by the legislature. Executives have the desire to retain their office and to work effectively within it. To do so, they must maintain public support, which may be damaged by a more complete disclosure of his policy actions. The executive in an autocracy is worried about long-term self-preservation, so policy decisions made at the top level could be described in a similar way: wanting the choice to reside there, regardless of the substance of the choice.

Other branches of government are also participating in the tug-of-war. Each separate actor represents a separate point in the policy contest. The role of the legislature is paramount, as it passes the laws that define the rules regarding information security. Within the legislature, ideological and social factions exist that have important functions. Some may agree with the executive and not want to place limits on the office itself, while others may want to offer a more concrete check on executive power. In this case, less flexible standards regarding information security may assist them in exercising an oversight role more effectively. When the standards are less flexible, or more defined, then it is easier to detect violations of the standard. While the legislative branch in an autocracy may fill the role of a "rubber stamp," its existence still provides a visible and publicized action to which the autocrat can refer to for legitimacy.

Interest groups may also play a role in the policy-making process regarding information security policy. These groups can be represented by media organizations that exist in single or multiple markets. International organizations such as Amnesty International and Human Rights Watch also have desires for favorable information security policies. The role of these groups is twofold. First, they desire and press for laws that allow for access to information. Second, they act as watchdogs that call attention to excessive government secrecy or lack of information on important issues. Other institutions that take part in this tug-of-war include the media and other representatives of civil society, such as religions or ethnic groups or ad hoc citizens groups.

CONCLUSION

This article illustrates a paradox: The countries that should be the most interested in protecting information are those who (under certain conditions) will abuse information just like every other nation. While this analysis has illustrated some of these conditions, these findings certainly do not represent the final word. Rather, they provide concepts that can illuminate some of the nuances of the tug of war.

Understanding policy give and take, or tug-of-war, has vexed scholars for some time. The results have begun to converge onto processes that fold back on themselves, responding to feedback and playing off other actors' actions, such as James Anderson's (2011) policy cycles or John Kingdon's *Policy Primeval Soup* (2011, Chap. 6). While the "tug-of-war" we propose does not encompass every part of the policy process, it sheds some light on the actors' actions, especially in the context of information and technology.

First, even though the multiple-actor tug-of-war is an appropriate visualization, outcomes differ depending on the types of information that governments are trying to control. The Singaporean case illustrates the fact that even though there is sufficient political will to extend information access to all citizens, there is still little expectation that the desire for openness in this area will lead to less security in terms of how the government chooses to monitor this extended information access. Labeling countries as "open" or "secretive" must be done very cautiously, as this designation might be more fitting in some circumstances as opposed to others.

Also, this tug-of-war usually means that incrementalist policy-making is the norm (Birkland, 2005, p. 216): small changes and adjustments in existing policy or new policy that does not create a lot that is new. For example, the U.S. anti-spamming policy only criminalizes misleading subject lines (Can Spam Act of 2003) and the 2006 amendments to the India IT Bill that limit its impact. But, there are exceptions when one group in the tug-of-war is stronger, such as with China's censorship policies or when multiple groups come together, such as with post–September 2001 U.S. policy.

A second related point addresses the impact of democratic principles and ideals and addresses the normative question brought up earlier. The results are definitely mixed. Democracies, when faced with threats from others, limit their openness in favor of greater protection. This conclusion is not robust and may depend on other factors, as demonstrated by the debate of updating the Foreign Intelligence Surveillance Act (FISA) statutes. There is a clear opposition in the U.S. Congress toward limiting civil liberties, although it is hard to say whether or not this opposition

represents a normative distinction between actors trying to influence the location of the policy or whether it represents a simple political fight. Generally it seems that even democracies exhibit closed-society tendencies from time to time, despite the continual debate over openness vs. secrecy.

Third, there appears to be a clear connection between the ability to effect change in information security policy and the threat of terrorism or war. Issues of national security have a strong influence. There is a tendency by governments and other interest groups to believe that information security policies can be instrumental in securing whatever stability or victory is sought in a conflict. This connection begs the questions of how and why this is the case, and would require greater study into the implementation phase of the information-related policies and programs.

Finally, there are some countries that place more of a cultural value on individual privacy than others, sometimes to the detriment of other global or national issues—and vice versa. These types of policies tend to ask implicitly that citizens give up some of their information control for the interests of the state. For example, the Electronic Crimes Act in Pakistan is designed to protect citizens from the consequences of online crime, but it also gives law enforcement greater latitude to intrude into citizen activities. The EU Convention on Cybercrime is an exception to this, but the European cultural commitment to privacy also seems to be different from the rest of the world.

Conceptually, then, a model of information policy-making along these lines would need to take into account the actors who have an interest in the formulation of the policy, the arguments that the actors are using to support their positions, and the circumstances under which the policy formulation is happening. First, as defined here, the actors include a broad range of political, economic, and societal groups, not all of which will be interested in every piece of information security–related policy. But, it is not too difficult to identify interested parties through a study of legislative hearings and media coverage. Second, the rationale or arguments in policy positioning can be identified through similar sources: cataloguing statements and utilizing content analysis to uncover and understand them. Third, the circumstances require some historical and contextual research through archives and media coverage.

Throughout the policy-making process, there can be tension between actors and stakeholders: the policy-makers, interest groups, those in the private sector, citizens, and what Hsu, Liang, and Chen (2007) refer to as "technical elites," those practitioners who understand how the technology works. Some of these actors—especially the policy-makers—may have difficulty grasping the nuances of information security policy or even information policy more broadly defined. In 2012, Rose Gottemoeller, U.S. Acting Undersecretary for Arms Control and International Security, said that cyber-defense policy has been "slow moving due to the current generation of policy-maker's lack of technological understanding" (Kaiser, 2012). At a broader level, information security policies are also an example of the tension between decisions that are made in response very specific situations but whose consequences might be unforeseen. These two tensions inspire a potentially rich research agenda about the dynamic nature of information technology and its resultant security and/or transparency requirements.

REFERENCES

Abbey, A. (2004, May 6). Virtual Jihad. *Jerusalem Post*. Retrieved from http://www.globalsecurity.org/org/news/2004/040506-virtual-jihad.htm

Anderson, J. (2011). *Public policymaking*. Boston: Wadsworth Publishing.

Australia's Attorney General's Department. (2001, September 27). *New laws combat cyber terrorism* [Press Release]. Retrieved from http://www.crimeprevention.gov.au/Pages/default.aspx

Azerbaijan to secure Internet sites from Armenian Hackers. (2000, February 15). *Armenian Daily Digest*. Retrieved from http://www.eurasianet.org/resource/armenia/hypermail/200002/0021.html

Bernard, R. L. (2005, January 9). *IO Marines fight insurgency through interaction* [U.S. Military Press Release]. Retrieved from http://www.iwar.org.uk/news-archive/2005/01-09.htm

Birkland, T. A. (2005). *Theories, concepts, and models of public policy making*. Armonk, NY: M.E. Sharpe.

Browne, W. P. (1998). *Groups, interests and U.S. public policy*. Washington, DC: Georgetown University Press.

Controlling the Assault of Non-Solicited Pornography and Marketing Act of 2003 (Can Spam Act). (2003). Pub. L. 108–187, §1, 117, Stat. 2699.

Deibert, R., Palfrey, J., Rohozinski, R., & Zittrain, J. (2008). *Access denied: The practice and policy of global Internet filtering*. Cambridge, MA: MIT Press.

Deibert, R., Palfrey, J., Rohozinski, R., & Zittrain, J. (2010). *Access controlled: The shaping of power, rights and rule in cyberspace*. Cambridge, MA: MIT Press.

Dickie, M. (2007, November 12). China traps online dissent. *The Financial Times*. Retrieved from http://www.ft.com/cms/s/0/ef0e7d64-9138-11dc-9590-0000779fd2ac.html#axzz28598ORX8

Estonia gets tough on cybercrime. (2007, September 17). *The Baltic Times*. Retrieved from http://www.baltictimes.com/news/articles/18815/

European Union Convention on Cybercrime. (2001, November 23). Retrieved from http://conventions.coe.int/Treaty/en/Treaties/Html/185.htm

Feuilherade, P. (1999, November 19). Russia's media war over Chechnya. *BBC News*. Retrieved from http://news.bbc.co.uk/2/hi/world/monitoring/528620.stm

Finn, P. (2007, May 19). Cyber assaults on Estonia typify a new battle tactic. *Washington Post*, p. A01. Retrieved from http://www.washingtonpost.com/wp-dyn/content/article/2007/05/18/AR2007051802122.html

Florini, A. (1998). The end of secrecy. *Foreign Policy, 111*, 50–63.

Florini, A. (2004). Behind closed doors: Governmental transparency gives way to secrecy. *Harvard International Review, 26*, 18–21.

Giacomello, G. (2005). *National governments and the control of the Internet: A digital challenge*. New York: Routledge.

Greenemeier, L. (2007, September 18). China's cyber attacks signal new battlefield is online. *Scientific American*. Retrieved from http://www.sciam.com/article.cfm?id=1A9C210F-E7F2-99DF-3C85F17B1680980D&page=2

Hess, P. (2008, March 11). House Democrats refuse to give telecoms immunity. *Associated Press*. Retrieved from http://www.law.com/jsp/article.jsp?id=900005560729&House_Democrats_Refuse_to_Give_Telecoms_Immunity

Hsu, N., Liang, J., & Chen, Y. (2007). Taiwan's information security policy enhancement: n analysis of patent indicators and patent documents. In T. E. Simos & G. Maroulis (eds.), *Computation in modern science and engineering: Proceedings of the International Conference in Science and Engineering* (Vol. 2, Part B; pp. 1228–1231). College Park, MD: American Institute of Physics.

India Information Technology Act of 2000. (2000). Retrieved from http://www.cyberlawsindia.net/itbill2000.pdf

Innis, H. (2007). *Empire and communications.* Lanham, MD: Rowman and Littlefield.

Jones, P. (2012). The Arab Spring. *International Journal, 67,* 447–463.

Kaiser, T. (2012, April 4). U.S. gov official: Current generation of policymakers lack understanding of technology. *Dailytech.* Retrieved from http://www.freerepublic.com/focus/f-news/2868152/posts

Kalathil, S., & Boas, T. C. (2003). *Open networks, closed regimes: The impact of the Internet on authoritarian rule.* Washington, DC: Carnegie Endowment for International Peace.

Kingdon, J. (2011). *Agendas, alternatives and public policies.* Boston: Longman.

Klosek, J. (2007). *The war on privacy.* Westport, CT: Praeger Publishers.

Lax, S. (2001). *Access denied in the Information Age.* New York: Palgrave.

Libicki, M. C. (2007). *Conquest in cyberspace: National security and information warfare.* Cambridge, MA: Cambridge University Press.

Maestro, T. (2007, September 8). *Draconian cyber crime law in Pakistan.* Retrieved from http://www.teeth.com.pk/blog/2007/09/08/draconian-cyber-crime-law-in-pakistan/

McChesney, R. W. (1996). The Internet and U.S. communication policy-making in historical and critical perspective. *Journal of Communication, 46,* 98–124.

Milner, H. V. (2006). The digital divide: The role of political institutions in technology diffusion. *Comparative Political Studies, 39,* 176–199.

O'Donnell, G., Schmitter, P. C., & Whitehead, L. (1986). *Transitions from authoritarian rule: Southern Europe.* Baltimore, MD: The Johns Hopkins University Press.

Ouma, M. (2007, August 5). Kenya's cyber law being developed. *East Africa Standard.* Retrieved from http://www.ifg.cc/index.php?option=com_content&task=view&id=23641

Pakistan: Bill to make provision for prevention of the electronic crimes. (2007). Retrieved from http://www.t2f.biz/events/wp-content/prevention-of-electronic-crimes-act.pdf

Reporters Without Borders. (2003). *The Internet under surveillance.* Paris: Author. Retrieved from http://en.rsf.org/IMG/pdf/doc-2236.pdf

Rogerson, K., & Strauss, J. (2002). Policies for online privacy in the United States and the European Union. *Telematics and Informatics, 19,* 175–209.

Rosenzweig, P. (2013). *Cyber warfare: How conflicts in cyberspace are challenging America and changing the world.* Westport, CT: Praeger Publishers.

Ruiz, M. (2006, July 12). Internet law—Kenya, Uganda and Tanzania adopt cyber laws. *Internet Business Law Services.* Retrieved from http://www.ibls.com/internet_law_news_portal_view.aspx?s=latestnews&id=1539

Sandoval, G. (2006, August 22). Now playing on the Net: War propaganda. *CNET News.com.* Retrieved from http://www.news.com/Now-playing-on-the-Net-War propaganda/2100-1038_3-6108004.html

Schmitz, S. (2013). The US SOPA and PIPA—a European Perspective. *International Review of Law, Computers & Technology, 27,* 213–229.

Seeman, R. H. (2003). *2003 Japan law: Cybercrime cyberterrorism.* Retrieved from http://www.japanlaw.info/law2003/2003_CYBERCRIME_CYBERTERRORISM.html

Singapore cyberterrorism law raises fears of abuse. (2003, November). *The Hindustan Times.* Retrieved from http://www.crime-research.org/news/2003/11/Mess2401.html

Smith, D. (2012). *Russia cyber operations.* Washington, DC: Potomac Institute for Policy Studies.

Sullivan, B. (2004). *Your evil twin: Behind the identity theft epidemic.* New York: John Wiley and Sons, Inc.

Thompson, D. F. (1999). Democratic secrecy. *Political Science Quarterly, 114,* 181–193.

Index

References to figures are shown in *italics*. References to tables are shown in **bold**. References to notes consist of the page number followed by the letter 'n' followed by the number of the note, e.g. 29n13 refers to note no. 13 on page 29.

9/11 terrorist attacks, and information security policy-making 111

A2K (Access to Knowledge) movement 74, 77
Abbey, A. 115
Access Impediment Act (Zugangserschwerungsgesetz/ ZugErschwG, Germany 2009) 25–6
Access to Knowledge (A2K) movement 74, 77
access-to-medicines campaign, and IPR 74
ACI (actor-centered institutionalism) 14–15, 26
ACLU (American Civil Liberties Union) 36; and Communications Decency Act 1996 (CDA, U.S.) 36
ACTA *see* Anti-Counterfeit Trade Agreement (ACTA)
action communities 91, 93, 94, 95, 102
actor-centered institutionalism (ACI) 14–15, 26
Aliyev, Heydar 115
Allen, Ernest E. 39
al Qaeda, 2001 attacks on New York/Washington (U.S.) 111, 115, 118
Amazon, and WikiLeaks 59
American Civil Liberties Union (ACLU), and Communications Decency Act 1996 (CDA, U.S.) 36
American Library Association 36
America Online *see* AOL (America Online)
Amnesty International, and information security policy-making 117
Anderson, James 118
Anonymous, and ACTA 81
Anstead, N. 69
Anti-Counterfeit Trade Agreement (ACTA): agreement 67, 68, 72, 75–7; backlash 73; backlash-stage one 77–9; backlash-stage two 79–82; blog mentions statistics 83; Internet and ACTA protests 6; issue network *78*; STOP ACTA day 80, *81*; U.S. IPR arsenal after ACTA 82–3
anti-globalization movement 88
anti-Semitism, French legislation against (1990 Gayssot law) 18
AOL (America Online): and Communications Decency Act 1996 (CDA, U.S.) 36; self-regulatory model 39, 41, 42
AOL Germany 24
API (application programming interface) 96, 105

Arab Spring 2, 6, 88, 89, 96
Arbeitskreis gegen Internet-Sperren und Zensur, AK Zensur 25, 26
Arbeitskreis gegen Vorratsdatenspeicherung, AK Vorrat 25
ARCEP (Autorité de régulation des communications électroniques et des postes, France) 19
Archibugi, D. 72
Argentina, and Access to Knowledge (A2K) movement 74
Arif, Kader 81
ARJEL (Autorité de Régulation des Jeux en Ligne, France) 22
Armenia: "electronic war" with Azerbaijan 115; genocide denial, French legislation against 17, 19
Association des Fournisseurs d'Accès et de Services Internet (AFA, France) 19–20
audiovisual transmissions, and state regulation 15
Australia: and ACTA 75, 77–8, 79; and cyber-terrorism 111, 115; and legitimizing/conservative identities 97
Australian Digital Alliance 77–8
Australian Library and Information Association 77
autocracies/authoritarian regimes: and censorship 49, 68; and information security policy-making 106–7, 108–9, 117; and Internet content regulation 16; and Internet filtering/blocking mechanisms 13–14
Autorité de régulation des communications électroniques et des postes (ARCEP, France) 19
Autorité de Régulation des Jeux en Ligne (ARJEL, France) 22
Azerbaijan, "electronic war" with Armenia 115

"balkanization" of opinion, and "cyber-pessimist/ dystopian" perspective 5
Balkin, J. M. 34
Bambauer, D. E. 16
Bang, Henrik P. 10, 88
Barlow, John Perry 75, 77; Declaration of the Independence of Cyberspace (1996) 3
Bebo 40
Beck, U. 95
Béland, D. 69
Bendrath, R. 14

Bennett, B. 44
Bennett, W. L. 94, 102
Benvenisti, E. 82
Berkman Center for Internet & Society (Harvard University) 77
Beschizza, R. 59
Bevir, M. 52
Bhagwati, Jadish 83
bilateralism vs. multilateralism, and IPR 75–6, 82, 84
Birnhack, M. D. 54, 55, 56, 62, 69
BITKOM 24
blocking *see* filtering/blocking mechanisms; "over-blocking"
boycotting, and cause-oriented politics 89
Boyd, D. M. 40
BPjM (Bundesprüfstelle für jugendgefährdende Medien, Germany) 24, 26
BPjS (Bundesprüfstelle für jugendgefährdende Schriften, Germany) 23, 24, 26
Braithwaite, J. 51, 52
Brazil: and Access to Knowledge (A2K) movement 74; and ACTA 76
Breindl, Yana 8, 13, 21
Briatte, F. 21
broadcasting: and "self-regulated regulators" concept 4; and U.S. content regulation 35
Brown, I. 7, 26
Buechler, S. M. 93
Bundesprüfstelle für jugendgefährdende Medien (BPjM, Germany) 24, 26
Bundesprüfstelle für jugendgefährdende Schriften (BPjS, Germany) 23, 24, 26
Burundi, E-Legislation Policy Development Initiative 113
Bush, George W. 112
Business Software alliance, and ACTA 76
Buskirk, M. 63
Büssow, Jörgen 25

Cahill, C. 51, 52, 53
Canada, and ACTA 75, 77, 78, 79
CanSpam Act (2003 U.S.) 114, 118
capacity/expertise, of private regulators 5
capitalism *see* laissez-faire capitalism; markets; regulatory capitalism, copyright law and online freedom of speech
Castells, Manuel: civil society and the state 92; communication power 88–9; hackers and freedom 69; network and governance 3, 52, 71; oppositional identities 98; vs. P. Norris 90; power 95; project identities 93
cause-oriented politics 89–90, 102–3
CBS, and SOPA/PIPA 79
CBS v. Democratic National Committee (1973) 57, 58
censorship: and authoritarian vs. democratic regimes 49, 68; Chinese online political censorship 111–12, 114, 118; and copyright 48, 49, 54–6, 57–63; copyright as (England until 18th century) 55; Renaissance/early Modern period 33
Center for Democracy and Technology, and ACTA 84n12
CEOP (Child Exploitation & Online Protection Centre, UK), and Facebook 42–3
Chadwick, A. 69

Chaos Computer Club (CCC) 25
Chechnya, and Russian control of media coverage 113
Chen, Y. 119
child abuse online materials: and Facebook 41, 42–3; and information security policy-making 115; and Internet content regulation 16; and Internet content regulation in France 19, 20, 22–3; and Internet content regulation in Germany 23, 24, 25, 27; and Internet content regulation in the U.S. 36–8, 39, 40; prevention of access to 6; and TOR onion browser 8
Child Exploitation & Online Protection Centre (CEOP, UK), and Facebook 42–3
child pornography *see* child abuse online materials
Children's Internet Protection Act 1999 (CIPA, U.S.) 36
Children's Online Privacy Protection Act (COPPA, U.S.) 41, 42, 45
China: and ACTA 76; censorship 49, 68; expression governance and Chinese Empire 33; firewall systems 6; Great Firewall (GFW) 16, 114; information security policies and national defense 114; online political censorship 111–12, 114, 118; online restricted content, nature of 6–7; and Trans-Pacific Partnership (TPP) 83
Chirac, Jacques 18
Choice (Australian consumer organization) 77
Chun, W. 34, 37
CIPA (Children's Internet Protection Act 1999, U.S.) 36
Citigroup 59–61, 62, 63
citizen-oriented politics 89–90
citizens, protection of and information security policies 114
citizenship: and legitimizing community identities 92; and oppositional identities 93; and project identities 93
civil society: and ACTA 76, 77; Foucault on 93–4; and German content regulation legislation 25–6, 28; and German corporatist system 24; increased effectiveness of resistance by 84; and information security policy-making 117; and legitimizing/oppositional political identities 92; and mobilization via the Internet 6; and project identities 93–4
classical liberalism 51
Clinton, Bill 45, 83
Clinton, Hillary 49, 67
code, and Internet regulation/copyright 5, 6, 16, 40, 49, 61
collective insecurity: politics of 69, 71, 75; *see also* national information security policy-making
commercial information, and information security policy-making 113
commercial speech, and First Amendment (U.S. Constitution) 35
communication power 89
Communications Decency Act 1996 (CDA, U.S.) 17, 36, 38, 39, 44
communications technology, and governance of expression 33–4
CompuServe, child pornography case (Germany, 1995) 23, 27
computer code *see* code
Computer Misuse Act (2003, Singapore) 111, 118
Conseil national du numérique (France) 20
Conseil supérieur de la Télématique (CST, France) 19
Conseil supérieur de l'audiovisuel (CSA, France) 19

consensual model (of democracy) 18, 27
conservatives identities, and legitimizing identities 97–8, 100
Consumer Electronics Association, and ACTA 84n12
consumer protection, and information security 107–8
content-hosting platforms: and copyright 57; *see also* Internet content providers
Convention on Cybercrime (EU, 2001) 112–13, 115, 118
COPPA, U.S. (Children's Online Privacy Protection Act) 41, 42, 45
copyright: and censorship 48, 49, 54–6, 57–63; and computer technologies/piracy 70; copyright infringement online notices 6; copyright infringement vs. false endorsement 63; Digital Millennium Copyright Act (DMCA, U.S.) 3, 39, 57, 61, 64, 67, 73–6; European Copyright Directive 20, 73, 84n8; and fair use 54, 56–7, 60–2, 63; and First Amendment (U.S. Constitution) 50, 54–7, 60–1; and freedom of expression 48–9, 54–6; and French Internet content regulation legislation 20–1; and "intermediarization" process of regulation 49; and ISPs/content-hosting platforms 57–8; and ISPs, voluntary agreements with 4; and neoliberalism 62–3; and "notice and takedown" procedures 7; and piracy 48; as property 55, 62–3, 64; and self-regulation 57–8, 59, 64; and suppression of speech/information 48–9; *see also* Intellectual Property Rights (IPR); Internet freedoms and IPR legislation; regulatory capitalism, copyright law and online freedom of speech
Copyright Act 1976 (U.S.) 56
Copyright Term Extension Act (CTEA, U.S.) 54
corporate actors: and actor-centered institutionalism (ACI) 14–15; and "cyber-pessimist/dystopian" perspective 5–6; and expertise/capacity for regulation 5; and governance networks 3; and Internet content control 16–17; and self-regulating regulation 4
corporatist system, German 24, 27
Cotter, T. F. 55
counterfeit: lumping of with IPR laws 75; and SOPA/PIPA 79; *see also* Anti-Counterfeit Trade Agreement (ACTA)
countermovements 95–6, 100–1, 102
crackers, definition 84n3
Craigslist, and SOPA/PIPA 80
Creative Commons license 75
Creative Freedom Foundation NZ 78
criminal activity, and cross-border information sharing 115
criminal prosecution, and Internet content regulation 16
cross-border information sharing, and information security policy-making 115, 116
CSA (Conseil supérieur de l'audiovisuel, France) 19
CST (Conseil supérieur de la Télématique, France) 19
CTEA, U.S. (Copyright Term Extension Act) 54
Culpepper, P. 54
Cuomo, Andrew M. 39
cyber-attacks 111, 114, 115
cybercrime 111, 115, 116
cyberlibertarians 3, 13–14, 15
cyberporn 36–7; *see also* child abuse online materials; pornography
cyber-related research funding 115

cybersecurity risks 34
Cyberspace, Declaration of the Independence of by J P Barlow (1996) 3
cyber-technologies, freedom vs. control 68–9
cyber-terrorism 111, 114, 115
CyberTipline 38, 40
"cyber-utopian (optimists)/dystopian(pessimists)" perspectives on 2, 5–6, 67
Cyworld 40

DADVSI bill (France, 2006) 20–1
Dalton, R. J. 89
"decentralized" regulation, and neoliberalism/regulatory capitalism 50–4
Declaration of the Independence of Cyberspace (J P Barlow, 1996) 3
Declaration of the Rights of Man and of the Citizen (France, 1789) 18
Dedman, B. 39
deep-packet inspection 14
defamation, French legislation against 18, 19
defense/military, and information security 107, 110–11, 114
Deibert, R. 62, 69
della Porta, D. 94, 95
democracies: and censorship 49, 68; and freedom vs. Internet content regulation 16; and governance of expression 33, 34; and information security policy-making 106–7, 108, 109, 117, 118; and Internet filtering/blocking mechanisms 13–14; and legitimizing community identities 92; and privacy of personal information 112–13; and specific vs. long-term output support 90; and suppression of information 49
democracy: majoritarian vs. consensual model 18, 27; and private actors' expression governance 43, 45
democratic exceptionalism, and information security policy-making 109
deregulation, and neoliberalism 51, 63–4
developing countries: and Access to Knowledge (A2K) movement 74; and ACTA 76, 79; and TRIPS 72
Diani, M. 94, 95
Dickie, M. 111–12, 114
Diebert, Ronald 109
Digital Millennium Copyright Act (DMCA, U.S.) 3, 39, 57, 61, 64, 67, 73–6
digital rights: digital rights management (DRM) 72–3; digital rights movement 74–5, 77; *see also* Intellectual Property Rights (IPR)
disciplinary power 72
discursive power 68, 71, 77, 80, 81, 82
DMCA. (Digital Millennium Copyright Act, U.S) 3, 39, 57, 61, 64, 67, 73–6
DNS tampering 22, 25
Downs, G. W. 82
Drahos, P. 71
DRM (digital rights management) 72–3; *see also* digital rights; Intellectual Property Rights (IPR)
droit d'auteur 29n10
due process, and filtering/blocking of online content 17
Dutton, W. H. 3
duty: and legitimizing community identities 98; and OWS/Twitter study 99, **99**, *99*, 100, **100**

INDEX

East African Community, E-Legislation Policy
  Development Initiative 113, 115
eBay: and ACTA 84n12; and SOPA/PIPA 80
ECHR (European Convention on Human Rights) 16
Eckert, S. 4
eco (German interest group) 24
E-Commerce Directive (2000/31/EC) 3, 4–5, 17, 19, 24,
  57–8, 61, 64
economic interests, and Internet content regulation 16
eG8 Summit (Deauville, France) 20
Egypt, Arab Spring 2, 6, 88
Eisgruber, C. L. 55, 56–7, 59
Eldred v. Ashcroft (2003) 54–5, 56, 61, 62
Eldred v. Reno 62
Eldritch Press 54
Electronic Frontier Foundation 75, 77
Electronic Privacy Information Center 77
E-Legislation Policy Development Initiative (East African
  Community) 113, 115
Elkin-Koren, N. 69
Ellison, Chris 111
Ellison, N. B. 40
empathy: and OWS/Twitter study **99**, *99*, 100, **100**; and
  project identities 98
England: copyright as censorship until 18th century 55;
  see also United Kingdom (UK)
entertainment industry, and French copyright laws 20–1,
  28
environmental regulation, and "self-regulated regulators"
  concept 4
Estonia: 2007 cyber-attacks and citizen protection 114;
  Russia's cyber-attacks against 111, 115
European Convention on Human Rights (ECHR) 16
European Copyright Directive 20, 73, 84n8
European Digital Rights, on ACTA 80
European Union: and ACTA 75, 77, 78–9, 80–2;
  Convention on Cybercrime (2001) 112–13, 115, 118;
  Copyright Directive 20, 73, 84n8; E-Commerce
  Directive (2000/31/EC) 3, 4–5, 17, 19, 24, 57–8, 61,
  64; European Convention on Human Rights (ECHR)
  16; France/Germany's influences on EU legislation 17;
  Information Society Directives (2001/29/EC) 3;
  INHOPE network 38; Internet-related directives and
  national states 16; and Internet Service Providers
  (ISPs) 4, 17; IPRs 70, 82, 84; patent protection and
  WIPO 74; privacy, culture of and information security
  112, 118; Telecommunications Rules (2002) 21; and
  Trans-Pacific Partnership (TPP) 83; and TRIPS 72
exclusionary discourse: and legitimizing identities 92, 97;
  and OWS/Twitter study 99, **99**, *99*, 100, **100**, 101
expertise/capacity, of private regulators 5
expression governance and public vs. private regulation:
  chapter abstract and introduction 33–5; chapter
  overview 8–9; expression governance, historical
  perspective 33–4; private sector regulation and
  Facebook 34–5, 40–3; public sector regulation in the
  U.S. 34–40; summary and conclusion 43–5
external threats: and information security policy-making
  110–11; *see also* defense/military

Facebook: and child protection 41, 42–3; and expression
  governance 34–5, 40–3, 44–5; and First Amendment

(U.S. Constitution) 42, 43; Hate and Harassment team
  40; STOP ACTA day 80, *81*
fair dealing, and digital rights management (DRM) 73
"Fairness Doctrine" 35
fair use doctrine 54, 56–7, 60–2, 63
family: and legitimizing community identities 98; and
  OWS/Twitter study 99, **99**, *99*, 100, **100**
Farrand, Benjamin 9, 48
FBI, investigation into child abuse images and TOR
  browser 8
Federal Communications Commission (FCC, U.S.) 35
Ferguson, Yale H. 83
Feuilherade, P. 113
FIfF (Forum InformatikerInnen für Frieden und
  gesellschaftliche Verantwortung, Germany) 25
Filippetti, A. 72
filtering/blocking mechanisms 6, 13–14, 16, 17, 20
finance, and "self-regulated regulators" concept 4
Finland, broadband access as legal right 29n1
firewalls 6; Great Firewall (GFW, China) 16, 114
First Amendment (U.S. Constitution): and commercial
  speech 35; and copyright 50, 54–7, 60–1; and
  Facebook 42, 43; freedom of expression amendment
  16; and NCMEC 40; and speech self-regulation 38, 44;
  and Wikileaks 34; *see also* fair use doctrine
FISA (Foreign Intelligence Surveillance) Act (U.S.) 112,
  118
FITUG (Förderverein Informationstechnik und
  Gesellschaft, Germany) 25
Föbud (Verein zur Förderung des öffentlichen bewegten
  und unbewegten Datenverkehrs, Germany) 25
FOD (Friends of Development) 74
Fogel, Jeremy (Judge) 61–2
Förderverein Informationstechnik und Gesellschaft
  (FITUG, Germany) 25
Ford, Gerald 56
Foreign Intelligence Surveillance (FISA) Act (U.S.) 112,
  118
Forum des droits sur l'Internet (France) 20
Forum InformatikerInnen für Frieden und
  gesellschaftliche Verantwortung (FIfF, Germany) 25
forum shifting: and IPR advocacy 68, 70–1, 82; and
  WIPO 72
Foucault, Michel 2, 68, 69, 71, 93–4, 95
framing: and digital rights movement 77; and IPR
  advocacy 70, 71; and opposition to ACTA 81, 82; and
  opposition to SOPA/PIPA 80; and politics of collective
  insecurity 69; and re-appropriation of "pirates" term
  71, 78, 84; and risk 79
France: anti-racism legislation 18, 20; anti-xenophobia
  legislation 18; Armenian genocide denial, legislation
  against 17, 19; Association des Fournisseurs d'Accès et
  de Services Internet (AFA) 19–20; Autorité de
  régulation des communications électroniques et des
  postes (ARCEP) 19; Autorité de Régulation des Jeux
  en Ligne (ARJEL) 22; Conseil national du numérique
  20; Conseil supérieur de la Télématique (CST) 19;
  Conseil supérieur de l'audiovisuel (CSA) 19;
  constitution and freedom of expression 16, 17;
  DADVSI bill (2006) 20–1; Declaration of the Rights of
  Man and of the Citizen (1789) 18; defamation
  legislation 18, 19; Forum des droits sur l'Internet 20;

124

Freedom of Communication Law (2000–79) 20; Gayssot law (1990) 18; gender-based hate speech legislation 19; HADOPI bill (2009) 21, 22, 23, 28; hate speech legislation 17, 18–19; Holocaust denial legislation 17, 19; interest groups 18; Internet content regulation (comparison with Germany 26–8; content regulation 18–20; copyright 20–1; cyber child pornography 22–3; democratic model 17–18, 27; online gambling 22); *Licra v. Yahoo!* (2000) 3, 5, 27, 29n25; Loi dans la confiance dans l'économie numérique (LCEN 2004-575) 19; LOPPSI 1 (Loi d'orientation et de programmation pour la performance de la sécurité intérieure) 20; LOPPSI 2 (Loi d'orientation et de programmation pour la performance de la sécurité intérieure) 22–3, 27, 28; Minitel 19, 27; Online Gambling Law (2010) 22; parental control filters 20; Union pour un Mouvement Populaire (UMP) 18; and UN Report on Freedom of Expression 29n13

France Télécom 19

Franken, Al 79

freedom: 'freedom from' and OWS/Twitter study 99, **99**, *99*, 100, **100**, 102; 'freedom from' and political identities 92, 95, 97; *see also* freedom of expression

Freedom Hosting 8

Freedom of Communication Law (2000–79, France) 20

freedom of expression: and authoritarian vs. democratic regimes 16; and copyright 48–9, 54–6; and cyber-technologies 68–9; and Facebook 42, 43; and Internet content control 7, 17, 28–9; restrictions to in France 17, 18–19, 27; restrictions to in Germany 17, 23, 27; and U.S. vs. French/German judiciaries 27; *see also* First Amendment (U.S. Constitution); Internet freedoms and IPR legislation

freedom of speech *see* First Amendment (U.S. Constitution); freedom of expression; regulatory capitalism, copyright law and online freedom of speech

Free Software Foundation 75, 77

free trade agreements (FTAs) 75–6, 82

Freiwillige Selbstkontrolle Multimedia-Dienstanbieter (FSM, Germany) 7, 24, 26

Friedman, Milton, *Capitalism and Freedom* 51

Friends of Development (FOD) 74

FSM (Freiwillige Selbstkontrolle Multimedia-Dienstanbieter, Germany) 7, 24, 26

FTAs (free trade agreements) 75–6, 82

fundamental rights *see* human rights

gambling (online), and French content regulation legislation 22

Gathii, J. T. 75–6

GATT (General Agreements on Tariffs and Trade) 71, 72

Geist, Michael 78, 79, 80

gender-based hate speech, French legislation against 19

Georgia, Russia's cyber-attacks against 111

Germany: Access Impediment Act (Zugangserschwerungsgesetz/ZugErschwG, 2009) 25–6; and ACTA 80; anti-Nazi propaganda legislation 23; Arbeitskreis gegen Internet-Sperren und Zensur, AK Zensur 25, 26; Arbeitskreis gegen Vorratsdatenspeicherung, AK Vorrat 25; Bundesprüfstelle für jugendgefährdende Medien (BPjM) 24, 26; Bundesprüfstelle für jugendgefährdende Schriften (BPjS) 23, 24, 26; Chaos Computer Club (CCC) 25; CompuServe and 1995 child pornography case 23, 27; constitution and freedom of expression 16; corporatist system 24, 27; Förderverein Informationstechnik und Gesellschaft (FITUG) 25; Forum InformatikerInnen für Frieden und gesellschaftliche Verantwortung (FIfF) 25; Freiwillige Selbstkontrolle Multimedia-Dienstanbieter (FSM) 7, 24, 26; hate speech legislation 23, 24; Holocaust denial legislation 23; interest groups 24, 25; Internet content regulation (comparison with France 26–8; competency for online content 23–4; content regulation 23; democratic model 17–18, 27–8; interest groups, civil society and political parties 24–5; regulated self-regulation 26, 27); Internet content regulation legislation and child abuse materials 23, 24, 25, 27; Jugendmedienschutz-Staatsvertrag (JMStV, 2003) 24; Jugendschutzgesetz (JuSchG, 2002) 24; jugendschutz. net 24, 26; Kommission für Jugendmedienschutz der Landesmedienanstalten (KJM) 24; Landesmedienanstalten 23; Mediendienste-Staatsvertrag (MDStV) 24; national census (1987) 25; Online-Demonstations-Plattform für Menschen-und Bürgerrechte im digitalen Zeitalter (ODEM) 25; Pirate Party 26; Telemediengesetz (TMG, 2007) 24; Verein zur Förderung des öffentlichen bewegten und unbewegten Datenverkehrs (Föbud) 25

Giacomello, G. 109

Ginsburg, Ruth Bader (Justice) 55

global governance: and intellectual property rights (IPR) 71–3; and rise of resistance against IPR legislation 73–5

globalization *see* anti-globalization movement

going "black" 7–8

Golan v. Holder (2012) 55, 56

Goldsmith, J. L. 5, 53

Google: and ACTA 76; and expression governance 35, 41, 44–5; and IP protection 84; Open Source Programs Office 74; and SOPA/PIPA 80

Google Germany 24

Gordon, W. J. 61

Gottemoeller, Rose 119

governance: and network society 2, 3, 52, 71; *see also* expression governance and public vs. private regulation; global governance; networked Internet governance (editorial)

"graduated response" mechanism, and online piracy 21

Great Firewall (GFW, China) 16, 114

Greenemeier, L. 114

Grossman, E. 18

The Guardian, and WikiLeaks 58

hackers: and Chaos Computer Club (CCC) 25; and concept of Internet freedom 69; definition 84n3; and digital rights movement 75; viruses/worms and information security policies 113, 114, 115

HADOPI bill (France, 2009) 21, 22, 23, 28

Harper & Row v. Nation Enterprises (1985) 55, 56, 60

Harvard University, Berkman Center for Internet & Society 77

Harvey, D. 50–1, 53

hate speech: and Internet content regulation 16; legislation against in France 17, 18–19; legislation against in Germany 23, 24

Hayek, Friedrich von, *The Road to Serfdom* 51

Hazlett, T. 36

Held, T. 26

Helft, M. 41

Henry, C. 72

Héretier, A. 4

Hess, P. 112

HIV/AIDS drugs, and TRIPS 72

Hobbes, Thomas 93

Hollande, François 21, 23

Holocaust denial, legislation against: in France 17, 19; in Germany 23

Hsu, N. 119

Hugenholtz, P. B. 84n9

Hughes, Howard 56, 60

Hu, Jintao 111–12

human rights: and content filtering/blocking 17; in France 17; in Germany 17, 23; and Internet access 16; and Internet content regulation 7; *see also* freedom of expression

Human Rights Watch, and information security policy-making 117

Hurley v. Irish-American Gay, Lesbian and Bisexual Group of Boston Inc. (1995) 63

ICANN 3

identity/ies: identity construction on Twitter 96–7; identity theft 108; legitimizing identities 91–2; legitimizing identities and conservative identities 97–8, 100; legitimizing identities and OWS/Twitter study *99*, 100, **100**, 101, 102; oppositional identities 91, 92–3, 98; oppositional identities and OWS/Twitter study 100, **100**, 101–2; participant/movement identities 89–90, 91; project identities 93–5, 98; project identities and OWS/Twitter study 100, **100**, 101–2

ideology *see* partisan ideology

IMF (International Monetary Fund), and neoliberalism 51

India: and Access to Knowledge (A2K) movement 74; and ACTA 76; Information Technology Act (2000) and ISPs 112, 118; and Trans-Pacific Partnership (TPP) 83

indignados (Spain) 88, 89

individual/personal information: of children and parental consent 41; and information security policy-making 112–13, 116, 118

informational technologies, normalization of 67

information security *see* national information security policy-making

information sharing *see* cross-border information sharing

Information Society Directives (2001/29/EC) 3

infrastructure control, and information security policy-making 112

INHOPE network 38

Innis, Harold 110

insecurity: politics of collective insecurity 69, 71, 75; *see also* national information security policy-making

instrumental power 68, 77, 80; *see also* forum shifting

Intellectual Property Rights (IPR): and access-to-medicines campaign 74; and ACTA 67, 82–3; essential purpose of 70; Protect Intellectual Property Act (PIPA,

U.S.) 77, 79–80, 83, 114; and U.S. economic hegemony 69–70; *see also* copyright; digital rights; Internet freedoms and IPR legislation; regulatory capitalism, copyright law and online freedom of speech; Trade Related Aspects of Intellectual Property Rights (TRIPS)

interest groups: in France 18; in Germany 24, 25; and information security policy-making 117

"intermediarization" process of regulation 49

intermediary-based regulation 17, 49, 54, 57–8, 64

internal threats, and information security policy-making 111–12

International Covenant on Civil and Political Rights 16

International Monetary Fund (IMF), and neoliberalism 51

International Studies Association (ISA), International Convention (San Diego, 2012) 2

Internet: conceptualization of as borderless 5; "dual-use" function of 2; and governance of expression 33–4; government control of 109; Hillary Clinton on 49, 67; infrastructure control and information security policies 112; Internet users statistics (U.S.) 36, *37*; and near anonymous access to restricted content 8; "network of networks" and regulatory capitalism 52; normalization of 67; *see also* filtering/blocking mechanisms; hackers; Internet content regulation in France and Germany; Internet freedoms and IPR legislation; Internet Service Providers (ISPs); networked Internet governance (editorial); notice-and-takedown procedures; social media; spam; *terms beginning with cyber*; Web sites

Internet content providers, and outsourcing of content filtering/blocking 14

Internet content regulation in France and Germany: chapter abstract and introduction 13–14; chapter overview 8; defining the issues 15–17; French case (content regulation 18–20; copyright 20–1; cyber child pornography 22–3; democratic model 17–18; Internet content regulation 26–8; online gambling 18–20); German case (comparison with France 26–8; competency for online content 23–4; content regulation 23; democratic model 17–18; interest groups, civil society and political parties 24–5; regulated self-regulation 26, 27); summary and conclusions 28–9; theoretical framework 14–15; *see also* networked Internet governance (editorial)

Internet freedoms and IPR legislation: ACTA (Anti-Counterfeit Trade Agreement) 75–7; ACTA backlash - stage one 77–9; ACTA backlash - stage two 79–82, *81*; ACTA issue network *78*; chapter abstract and introduction 67–8; chapter overview 9–10; cyber-technologies and freedom vs. control 68–9; global governance and intellectual property 71–3; global governance and rise of resistance 73–5; IP protection and discourse of risk/piracy 69–70; IPR advocates' strategies (forum shifting and framing) 70–1; IPR and Trans-Pacific Partnership 82–3; summary and conclusion 83–4; *see also* regulatory capitalism, copyright law and online freedom of speech

Internet Industry Association (Australia) 77

Internet misogyny 34

Internet Service Providers (ISPs): and ACTA 76, 77–8, 80; and Armenian–Azerbaijani "electronic war" 115; and copyright 57–8; and copyright holders, voluntary agreements with 4; and Digital Millennium Copyright Act (DMCA, U.S.) 57, 61, 64, 73; and E-Commerce Directive (2000/31/EC) 24; expertise/capacity of and regulation 5; and filtering/blocking, outsourcing of 14, 17; and French content regulation legislation 19, 20, 22; and German content regulation legislation 24–5; liability of 17, 112; and network governance 3; and notice-and-takedown procedures 57–8; and "opt-in" system for pornographic/extreme content 7; and PROTECT Our Children Act 2008 (U.S.) 39; regulating role of 69; and self-regulating regulation 4; and SOPA/PIPA 79

Internet Watch Foundation (IWF, UK) 7, 37
"invisible handshake" (public-private nexus of power): and ACTA 76; and regulation 69, 71, 73
IPR *see* Intellectual Property Rights (IPR); Internet freedoms and IPR legislation; Trade Related Aspects of Intellectual Property Rights (TRIPS)
Iran: censorship 49, 68; pervasive surveillance/censorship systems 16
ISA (International Studies Association), International Convention (San Diego, 2012) 2
ISPs *see* Internet Service Providers (ISPs)
Israel, cyber-related research funding 115
issue network, and ACTA 77, *78*
IWF (Internet Watch Foundation, UK) 7, 37

Japan: and ACTA 75, 79; anti-hacking laws 113; and IPRs 70; patent protection and WIPO 74; and TRIPS 72; and WTO and WIPO 73
Jensen, Michael J. 10, 88
Jones, Peter 109
Jordana, J. 51
Journal of Information Technology & Politics 2, 8, 10
Jugendmedienschutz-Staatsvertrag (JMStV, Germany, 2003) 24
Jugendschutzgesetz (JuSchG, Germany, 2002) 24
jugendschutz.net 24, 26
justice: and oppositional identities 98; and OWS/Twitter study **99**, *99*, 100, **100**, 101

Kaminski, M. 76–7
Kapczynski, A. 74
Kapur, A. 59–60
Kazakhstan, privacy vs. protection of state secrets 113
Keats, John 56
Kenya: cyber laws and infrastructure control 112; E-Legislation Policy Development Initiative 113, 115
Kingdon, John 118
Kirk, Ron 83
Kommission für Jugendmedienschutz der Landesmedienanstalten (KJM, Germany) 24
Kroes, N. 82
Kuellmer, Bjoern 8, 13

laissez-faire capitalism 51, 53
Landesmedienanstalten (Germany) 23
Lapousterle, J. 20, 21
La Quadrature du Net: and ACTA 77, 82; and "graduated response" mechanism 21; and John Perry Barlow 75
Last, Mark 115

law: scholarship and Internet regulation 2; *see also* due process; rule of law
Law on Guidelines and Programming for the Performance of Internal Security (LOPPSI 2, France) 22–3, 27, 28
Lax, Stephen 109
Lazer, D. 52
LCEN 2004-575 (Loi dans la confiance dans l'économie numérique, France) 19
leaderless movements 91, 96
legitimizing identities 91–2; and conservative identities 97–8, 100; and OWS/Twitter study *99*, 100, **100**, 101, 102
Lessig, L. 6, 16, 49, 61, 75
Levi-Faur, D. 51
Levin, J. 40
Leyen, Ursula von der 25
Liang, J. 119
liberal democracies *see* democracies
liberalism *see* classical liberalism; neoliberalism
Libicki, M. C. 107–8
Libya, Arab Spring 88
Licra v. Yahoo! (2000) 3, 5, 27, 29n5
Lieberman, Joe 59
Lijphart, A. 18
Lind, B. 95
Lindberg, S. W. 55
Locke, John 56
Loi dans la confiance dans l'économie numérique (LCEN 2004-575, France) 19
Loi d'orientation et de programmation pour la performance de la sécurité intérieure (LOPPSI, France) 20
LOPPSI 2 (Law on Guidelines and Programming for the Performance of Internal Security, France) 22–3, 27, 28
Loughlan, Patricia 71
"lowest common dominator" entertainment and politics, and "cyber-pessimist/dystopian" perspective 5
Lumbard, J. Edward (Chief Judge) 60
Lycos Europe 24

McCain, John 62
McChesney, Robert 109
McCreevy, Charlie 84
McGreal, C. 58
McIntyre, T. 26, 39
MacKinnon, R. 54
Magid, L. 79
Mailland, J. 18
majoritarian model (of democracy) 18, 27
Manning, Chelsea (born Bradley) 6, 58
markets: and neoliberal theory 53; and OWS/Twitter study 98, 101; as regulatory mechanisms 51
Marsden, C. T. 17
Masnick, M. 75
MasterCard, and WikiLeaks 58
Matsepe-Casaburri, Ivy 114
May, C. 70, 72
Mayer, F. 36
Mayer, Martin 25
media coverage, and information security policy-making 113
media organizations, and information security policy-making 117

INDEX

media technologies, and governance of expression 33–4
Mediendienste-Staatsvertrag (MDStV, Germany) 24
Miard, F. 52
Middle East: Arab Spring 88; monarchies and paternalistic social contract 109
military, the: and legitimizing community identities 92, 97; and OWS/Twitter study **99**, *99*, 100, **100**; *see also* defense/military
Milner, Helen 109
Milton, Daniel 10, 106
Minitel 19, 27
misogyny, and the Internet 34
Modine, A. 62
Moerland, A. (Sanders *et al.*) 74, 75, 79
Montesquieu 93
moral panics, and restriction of online material 7, 39, 44
Morin, J.-F. 84
Morozov, E. 67
Motion Picture Association, and ACTA 76
movie studios, and SOPA/PIPA 79
Mozilla, and SOPA/PIPA 80
MSN Germany 24
Mueller, M. L. 3, 5, 14, 15, 40, 52, 58
multilateralism vs. bilateralism, and IPR 75–6, 82, 84
multi-stakeholder processes 3, 8
MySpace 40

National Center for Missing and Exploited Children (NCMEC, U.S.) 37–8, 39, 40, 41–2
National Child Pornography Tipline (U.S.) 37
national information security policy-making: chapter abstract 106–7; chapter overview 10; democratic vs. authoritarian regime 106–9; methodology 110; national information policies (commercial information 113; external threats 110–11; infrastructure information 112; internal threats 111–12; news and media coverage 113; personal/individual information 112–13; worms, viruses and hackers 113); rationale for securing the information 113–14 (cross-border information sharing 115; defense of national interests 114; protecting citizens 114); situations/circumstances leading to policies 115–16; tug-of-war process and conclusion 116–19
National Security Agency (NSA, U.S.) 6
national states *see* State, the
natural language processing (NLP) 97
Nazi propaganda, legislation against, in Germany 23
NCMEC. (National Center for Missing and Exploited Children, U.S) 37–8, 39, 40, 41–2
neoliberalism: and copyright as property 62–3; and deregulation 51, 63–4; discrepancies between theory and practice 52–3; and regulatory capitalism/"decentralized" regulation 50–4; and self-regulating regulation 53–4; and self-regulation 64; and state vs. network governance 3; and suppression of speech 49; theory of 50–1; *see also* privatization
Netanel, N. W. 55, 56, 63
Net freedoms *see* Internet freedoms and IPR legislation
networked Internet governance (editorial): chapter abstract 1; ISA International Convention (San Diego, 2012) and issues 2; online content regulation, networked nature of 2–5; online content regulation, social/cultural impacts on 5–8; overview of book's

articles 8–10; suggestions for further research 10–11; *see also* global governance
network society: and governance 2, 3, 52, 71; and project identities 93
news coverage, and information security policy-making 113
The New York Times, and WikiLeaks 58
New Zealand, and ACTA 75, 77, 78, 79
Nimmer. M. B. 55
NLP (natural language processing) 97
Norris, P. 89–90
notice-and-takedown procedures 7, 19, 50, 57–8, 60–4, 73, 76, 83
NSA (National Security Agency, U.S.) 6
NZ Open Source Society 78

Obama, Barack 62, 84
Occupy movements 6, 88
Occupy Wall Street (OWS) and Twitter: chapter abstract 88; chapter introduction (new social media and social movements 88–9; participant/movement identities issue 89–90; participation, new/old forms of 89, **89**); chapter overview 10; participatory forms (academic research on OWS 91; action communities and participant identities 91; legitimizing and oppositional political identities 91–3; project identities 93–5; project identities and OWS 94; "Solidarity Forever!" OWS slogan 96, 103; varieties of OWS identities and countermovements 95–6); Twitter study methodology 90, 96–8, 105; Twitter study results (account activity 98, **98**; item component loadings 99–100, **100**; participant identifications 98–9, **99**, *99*; participant profile frequencies 100–1, **100**); Twitter study results analysis 101–3
ODEM (Online-Demonstations-Plattform für Menschen- und Bürgerrechte im digitalen Zeitalter, Germany) 25
Office of Communications (OFCOM, UK) 35
Ogus, A. 53–4
Olivennes, Denis 21
online content regulation *see* Internet content regulation in France and Germany; networked Internet governance (editorial)
Online-Demonstations-Plattform für Menschen-und Bürgerrechte im digitalen Zeitalter (ODEM, Germany) 25
Online Gambling Law (France, 2010) 22
online service providers (OSPs) *see* Internet Service Providers (ISPs)
Open Policy Group v. Diebold (2004) 61–2
open source software movement 69, 77; and Access to Knowledge (A2K) movement 74; and digital rights movement 74–5
Oppenheimer, Michael F. 83–4
oppositional identities 91, 92–3, 98; and OWS/Twitter study 100, **100**, 101–2
"opt-in" system (for pornographic/extreme content) 7
Ouma, M. 113, 115
"over-blocking" 17
OWS *see* Occupy Wall Street (OWS) and Twitter

"page not found" message, and filtering mechanisms 6
Pakistan, cybercrime law and threat to personal information 116, 118

Palfrey, J. 62, 109
parental consent, for Web sites' collecting of children's personal information 41
parental control filters, in France 20
participation: new/old forms of 89, **89**; *see also* identity/ies; Occupy Wall Street (OWS) and Twitter
partisan ideology, and OWS/Twitter study **99**, **100**
patents: and Access to Knowledge (A2K) movement 74; and WIPO 74
Patriot Act (U.S.) 36, 110–11
patriotism: and legitimizing identities 97; and OWS/Twitter study **99**, *99*, 100, **100**
Patterson, L. R. 55, 59, 61, 63
PayPal: and SOPA/PIPA 79; and WikiLeaks 59
Peltu, M. 3
personal/individual information: of children and parental consent 41; and information security policy-making 112–13, 116, 118
perversity, "technology-inducing" 34
Pfizer, and SOPA/PIPA 79
Pharmaceutical Research and Manufacturers of America, and ACTA 76
pharmaceuticals, access-to-medicines campaign and IPR 74
PIPA, U.S. (Protect Intellectual Property Act) 77, 79–80, 83, 114
piracy: and copyright 48; and framing 71, 78, 84; and "graduated response" mechanism 21; Stop Online Piracy Act (SOPA, U.S.) 7–8, 77, 79–80, 82, 83; and TRIPS 72; and the U.S. 69–70
Pirate Parties: and ACTA 78; German party 26; Swedish party 78; UK party 78
Poland, and ACTA 80
Polanyi, Karl 53
policy networks, and public vs. private actors 3
Political Gates, and Citigroup 60
political philosophy, on power 2
politics: cause-oriented politics 89–90, 102–3; citizen-oriented politics 89–90; and Internet mobilization 6; political videos and YouTube 62, 63; protest vs. conventional politics 89–90; *see also* identity/ies; Occupy Wall Street (OWS) and Twitter
Pollack, M. 54, 55
pornography: and online restriction of online material 7; *Time* magazine 1995 Internet pornography story 36; and U.S. public regulation of Internet 36–7; *see also* child abuse online materials
Postigo, H. R. 74–5
power: communication power 88–9; disciplinary power 72; discursive power 68, 71, 77, 80, 81, 82; Foucault on 2, 68, 95; instrumental power 68, 77, 80; and political philosophy 2; 'power to act' and OWS/Twitter study 99, **99**, *99*, **100**, 102; "power to act" and project identities 95, 98; structural power 68, 72
principal components analysis 98, 99
print media: and copyright/censorship 48; and governance of expression 33; and state regulation 15; and U.S. content regulation 35
PRISM project 6
privacy: and information security policy-making 112–13, 118; and Internet content control 7, 17, 28–9
Privacy International 77

private regulators: and concept of network 2; expertise/capacity of 5; expression governance by and democracy 43, 45; Facebook 34–5, 40–3, 44–5; and Internet regulation 3–4; and policy networks 3; *see also* expression governance and public vs. private regulation; self-regulated regulation
privatization: concept 51; and regulation (UK) 51; of social services and neoliberalism 53; *see also* neoliberalism
project identities 93–5, 98; and OWS/Twitter study 100, **100**, 101–2
Protect Intellectual Property Act (PIPA, U.S.) 77, 79–80, 83, 114
PROTECT Our Children Act 2008 (U.S.) 39
protest politics, vs. conventional politics 89–90
Public Knowledge 77; and ACTA 83, 84n12; and Trans-Pacific Partnership (TPP) 83
public-private partnerships 3
public regulators: and concept of network 2; and expertise/capacity of private regulators 5; and Internet regulation 3–4; and policy networks 3; public sector regulation in the U.S. 34–40; *see also* expression governance and public vs. private regulation
publishers, and SOPA/PIPA 79
Pugatch, M. (Sanders *et al.*) 74, 75, 79
Python language 97

Quadrature du Net, La *see* La Quadrature du Net

racism, French legislation against 18, 20
radio: and governance of expression 33; and U.S. content regulation 35
Reagan, Ronald 51
Recording Industry Association of America (RIAA): and ACTA 76; and SOPA/PIPA 79, 80
Reddit, and SOPA/PIPA 80
regional trade agreements (RTAs) 82
The Register (WEb site) 62
regulation: "intermediarization"/decentralization of 49; intermediary-based regulation 17, 49, 54, 57–8, 64; ISPs' role 69; and laissez-faire capitalism 53; and neoliberalism 51, 63–4; and public-private nexus of power ("invisible handshake") 69, 71, 73; and the State 2–3, 15–17, 53; *see also* deregulation; expression governance and public vs. private regulation; Internet content regulation in France and Germany; private regulators; public regulators; regulatory capitalism, copyright law and online freedom of speech; self-regulated regulation; self-regulation
regulatory bodies: non-state bodies 52; proliferation of and neoliberalism 51
regulatory capitalism, copyright law and online freedom of speech: chapter abstract and introduction 48–50; chapter overview 9; concept of "regulatory capitalism" 49, 51–2; copyright and First Amendment 50, 54–7; neoliberalism, regulatory capitalism and "decentralized' regulation 50–4; regulatory capitalism and private enforcement of copyright 50, 57–63; summary and conclusions 63–4; *see also* Internet freedoms and IPR legislation
Reichman, J. 73

religion: and legitimizing community identities 97; and OWS/Twitter study 99, **99**, *99*, 100, **100**, 101

Renaissance: censorship regimes 33; and copyright/censorship 48

Reno v. American Civil Liberties Union (1997) 30n27

Reporters Without Borders 20, 114

representative democracy: and specific vs. long-term output support 90; *see also* democracies; democracy

repression, and "cyber-pessimist/dystopian" perspective 5–6

reputation management, and Facebook's content regulation 41

Rhodes, R. A. 52

rights *see* digital rights; human rights; International Covenant on Civil and Political Rights

risk: Foucault on 69; and framing 79; intellectual-property protection at risk 69–70

Robertson, M. 51, 62

Rogerson, Kenneth 10, 106

Rohozinski, R. 62, 69, 109

Romania, and ACTA 81

Rosemont Enterprises, Inc. v. Random House, Inc. (1966) 56, 60–1

Rousseau, Jean-Jacques 93

RTAs (regional trade agreements) 82

rule of law, and filtering/blocking of online content 17

Russia: cyber-attacks against Estonia/Georgia 111, 115; media coverage control and Chechnya conflict 113; media law and antigovernment criticism 111

Rwanda, E-Legislation Policy Development Initiative 113

SABAM v. Netlog (2012) 4

Samuelson, P. 73

Samydorai, Sinapan 111

Sanders, A. K. 74, 75, 79

Sarkozy, Nicolas 18, 20, 21, 22, 27, 28

Saudi Arabia: censorship 49, 68; centralized firewall systems 6

Saurugger, S. 18

Scarlet Extended v. SABAM (2011) 4, 29n1, 29n2

Schulz, W. 26

Scribd, and Citigroup 60, 63

security *see* collective insecurity; national information security policy-making

Sedition Acts (1798, U.S.) 111

Segerberg, A. 94, 102

self-preservation principle, and information security policy-making 108–9

self-regulated regulation 4, 7; in France 19–20, 27; in Germany 24–5, 26, 27–8; in the UK 53–4; *see also* self-regulation

self-regulation: and copyright 57–8, 59, 64; and neoliberalism/regulatory capitalism 53–4, 57, 64; and regulation of speech 49; speech self-regulation and First Amendment (U.S. Constitution) 38; and U.S. Internet 38, 39–40, 44, 45; *see also* regulatory capitalism, copyright law and online freedom of speech; self-regulated regulation

Sell, S. 69, 72, 75

Seltzer, W. 58, 64

service providers *see* Internet Service Providers (ISPs)

Shabalata, D. B. (Sanders *et al.*) 74, 75, 79

Sherman, C. 80

Simons, J. J. 70

Singapore, Computer Misuse Act (2003) 111, 118

Slovenia, and ACTA 81

Smith, Adam 56

Smith. D. 111

Smith, Peter Jay 9–10, 67

SMOs (social movement organizations) 74, 75, 77

social media: and new social movements 88–9; *see also* social networking sites

social movement organizations (SMOs) 74, 75, 77

social movements: countermovements 95–6, 100–1, 102; definition/concept 88, 91; leaderless movements 91, 96; and new social media 88–9; strain and breakdown theories of 92–3; *see also* identity/ies

social networking sites 40; *see also* Facebook; social media

social services, privatization of 53

solidarity: and oppositional identities 93, 98; and OWS/Twitter study **99**, *99*, 100, **100**, 101; social vs. political solidarity 103; "Solidarity Forever!" OWS slogan 96, 103

Sony Pictures, and ACTA 76

SOPA. (Stop Online Piracy Act, U.S) 7–8, 77, 79–80, 82, 83, 114

Sosa, D. W. 36

South Africa, Electronic Communications and Transactions Bill 114

Spain, *indignados* 88, 89

spam, and information security policy-making 114, 118

speaking for freedom *see* Internet freedoms and IPR legislation

speech self-regulation, and First Amendment (U.S. Constitution) 38

Stallman, Richard 75

state repression, and "cyber-pessimist/dystopian" perspective 5–6

State, the: and civil society 92; and Internet regulation 2–3, 15–17, 53; and network governance 71; and regulatory capitalism 51–3

Stepan-Norris, J. 95

Stiglitz, J. E. 72

STOP ACTA day 80, *81*

Stop Online Piracy Act (SOPA, U.S.) 7–8, 77, 79–80, 82, 83, 114

strain and breakdown theories (of social movements) 92–3

structural power 68, 72

Sullivan, B. 39, 108

Swedish Pirate Party 78

Switzerland, and ACTA 75

Tanzania: cyber laws and infrastructure control 112; E-Legislation Policy Development Initiative 113

Tarrow, S. 88

Tauss, Jörg 25

Tea Party movement (U.S.): and 'freedom from' stance 92, 95; and OWS movement 92, 97, 101

technological elites 119

technology *see* cyber-technologies; informational technologies; media technologies

technology-aware policy research 14, 26

"technology-inducing perversity" 34

Teeth Maestro (blogger) 116

telecommunications: and "self-regulated regulators" concept 4; and U.S. content regulation 35

Telemediengesetz (TMG, Germany, 2007) 24

television: and governance of expression 33; TV networks and SOPA/PIPA 79; and U.S. content regulation 35

Terror Information Awareness 115

terrorism: cyber-terrorism 111, 114, 115; and French content regulation legislation 20; and information security policy-making 110, 111, 115, 118; and online content regulation 16

Thatcher, Margaret 51

Think Centre (Singapore) 111

threats *see* external threats; internal threats

Time magazine, 1995 Internet pornography story 36

Time Warner, and ACTA 76

TMG (Telemediengesetz, Germany, 2007) 24

T-Online 24

TOR onion browser 8

Townshend, Pete 63

Trade Related Aspects of Intellectual Property Rights (TRIPS) 68, 72, 73, 76, 77

Trans-Pacific Partnership (TPP), and IPR 82–3

transparency, and information security policy-making 108, 109, 119

TRIPS (Trade Related Aspects of Intellectual Property Rights) 68, 72, 73, 76, 77

tug-of-war, and information security policy-making 107, 109, 110, 114, 116–18

Tunisia, Arab Spring 2, 88

Tusk, Donald 80

TV networks: and SOPA/PIPA 79; *see also* television

Twitter: API (application programming interface) 96, 105; and expression governance 35; identity construction on 96–7; and legitimizing/oppositional/project identities 95; and SOPA/PIPA 80; STOP ACTA day 80, *81*; *see also* Occupy Wall Street (OWS) and Twitter

Tyfield, D. 63

Uganda: cyber laws and infrastructure control 112; E-Legislation Policy Development Initiative 113

Uhlir, P. 73

Union pour un Mouvement Populaire (UMP, France) 18

United Kingdom (UK): 2011 London riots and Internet mobilization 6; Child Exploitation & Online Protection Centre (CEOP) and Facebook 42–3; Internet Watch Foundation (IWF) 7, 37; laissez-faire capitalism (19th-century) and regulation 53; legitimizing and conservative identities 97; Office of Communications (OFCOM) 35; Pirate Party 78; privatization and proliferation of regulators 51; restricted online content, nature of 7; "section 63" of the Criminal Justice and Immigration Act (2008) 7; self-regulated regulation 53–4

United Nations, Report on Freedom of Expression 29n13

United States Trade Representative (USTR) 67, 71, 72, 75–6, 83

United States (U.S.): al Qaeda's 2001 attacks on New York/Washington 111, 115, 118; American hegemony, waning of 83–4; CanSpam Act (2003) 114, 118; *CBS v. Democratic National Committee* (1973) 57, 58;

Children's Internet Protection Act 1999 (CIPA) 36; Children's Online Privacy Protection Act (COPPA) 41, 42, 45; Citigroup bailout 60; Communications Decency Act 1996 (CDA) 17, 36, 38, 39, 44; content regulation, historical perspective 35; Copyright Act (1976) 56; Copyright Term Extension Act (CTEA) 54; cyber-related research funding 115; CyberTipline 38, 40; Digital Millennium Copyright Act 1998 (DMCA) 3, 39, 57, 61, 64, 67, 73–6; *Eldred v. Ashcroft (2003)* 54–5, 56, 61, 62; "Fairness Doctrine" 35; fair use doctrine 54, 56–7, 60–2, 63; FBI investigation into child abuse images and TOR browser 8; Federal Communications Commission (FCC) 35; filtering systems vs. free speech protection 16; freedom of speech and press laws 113; *Golan v. Holder* (2012) 55, 56; *Harper & Row v. Nation Enterprises* (1985) 55, 56, 60; *Hurley v. Irish-American Gay, Lesbian and Bisexual Group of Boston Inc.* (1995) 63; information security policy-making 107, 108, 110–11; Internet freedoms, curtailing of 67–8; Internet regulation and child abuse materials 36–8, 39, 40; Internet users statistics 36, *37*; IP protection and economic hegemony 69–70; IPR and bilateralism vs. multilateralism 75–6, 82, 84; ISPs and Foreign Intelligence Surveillance (FISA) Act 112, 118; ISPs' liability 17; legitimizing and conservative identities 92, 97–8; National Center for Missing and Exploited Children (NCMEC) 37–8, 39, 40, 41–2; National Child Pornography Tipline 37; National Security Agency (NSA) surveillance 6; *Open Policy Group v. Diebold* (2004) 61–2; patent protection and WIPO 74; piracy issue 69–70; privacy, culture of and information security 112; Protect Intellectual Property Act (PIPA) 77, 79–80, 83, 114; PROTECT Our Children Act 2008 39; public sector regulation 34–40; *Reno v. American Civil Liberties Union* (1997) 30n27; restricted online content, nature of 7; *Rosemont Enterprises v. Random House Inc.* (1966) 56, 60–1; Sedition Acts (1798) 111; Stop Online Piracy Act (SOPA) 7–8, 77, 79–80, 82, 83, 114; Tea Party and 'freedom from' stance 92, 95; Tea Party and OWS movement 92, 97, 101; USA-PATRIOT Act 36, 110–11; USTR (United States Trade Representative) 67, 71, 72, 75–6, 83; and WTO and WIPO 73; *see also* First Amendment (U.S. Constitution); Internet freedoms and IPR legislation; Occupy Wall Street (OWS) and Twitter; WikiLeaks

Universal Declaration of Human Rights 16

UN Report on Freedom of Expression 29n13

USA-PATRIOT Act 36, 110–11

USTR (United States Trade Representative) 67, 71, 72, 75–6, 83

Verein zur Förderung des öffentlichen bewegten und unbewegten Datenverkehrs (Föbud, Germany) 25

Vergano, P. (Sanders *et al.*) 74, 75, 79

Verizon, and ACTA 84n12

Veyne, P. 2

viruses/worms: and information security policy-making 113, 114; *see also* hackers

Visa: and SOPA/PIPA 79; and WikiLeaks 58

voluntary agreements, between ISPs and copyright holders 4

Wagner, Ben 8–9, 33
"walled gardens" 16
Wallerstein, Immanuel 83
Wang, Guoqing 111
war, threat of, and information security policy-making 110, 118
WCT (WIPO Copyright Treaties) 72–3, 79; *see also* World Intellectual Property Organization (WIPO)
Weatherall, Kimberlee 79, 82
Web 2.0 40
Web sites: and Children's Online Privacy Protection Act (COPPA, U.S.) 41; and French content regulation legislation 19, 22; going "black" 7–8
Western political systems *see* democracies
White Pride (band) 63
WikiLeaks 6, 34, 49, 58–9, 62
Wikipedia: and going "black" 7–8; and SOPA/PIPA 80
World Intellectual Property Organization (WIPO) 71, 72, 74; WIPO Copyright Treaties (WCT) 72–3, 79
World Trade Organization (WTO): and Access to Knowledge (A2K) movement 74; and forum shifting 71; and neoliberalism 51; Trade Related Aspects of

Intellectual Property Rights (TRIPS) 68, 72, 73, 76, 77; and U.S./Japan 73
WorldWideWeb *see* Internet
worms/virus: and information security policy-making 113, 114; *see also* hackers
Wright, J. S. 4, 52
WTO *see* World Trade Organization (WTO)
Wu, T. 5, 52, 53

xenophobia, French legislation against 18

Yahoo!: and Freiwillige Selbstkontrolle Multimedia-Dienstanbieter (FSM) 24; *Licra v. Yahoo!* (France, 2000) 3, 5, 27, 29n5
YouTube: and copyright 57; and political campaign videos 62, 63

Zittrain, J. 49, 62, 109
Zuckerman, E. 39
Zugangserschwerungsgesetz/ZugErschwG (Access Impediment Act 2009, Germany) 25–6

T - #0020 - 311024 - C0 - 276/219/8 [10] - CB - 9781138927070 - Gloss Lamination